EAST TEXAS LUMBER WORKERS

EAST TEXAS LUMBER WORKERS

An Economic and Social Picture, 1870–1950

by RUTH A. ALLEN

AUSTIN 1961
UNIVERSITY OF TEXAS PRESS

Library of Congress Catalog Card No. 59–10165

Manufactured in the United States of America by the
Printing Division of the University of Texas

ACKNOWLEDGMENTS

The author is indebted to the University of Texas for financial assistance which has enabled her to have time and aid for examining and selecting from the tremendous amounts of material contained in the records of the Gilmer Lumber Company in the archives of the University. William Wagoner, Lawrence Rogers, and numerous other graduate students in economics have helped in finding and checking sources. The staff of the University of Texas Library have been most helpful in making materials available, especially the unpublished records of the United States Commission of Industrial Relations, known at the time as the Walsh Commission. Many thanks go to Bonnie Whittier, whose willingness to render aid and assistance was unfailing.

RUTH A. ALLEN

The University of Texas

CONTENTS

TABLES

MAPS

EAST TEXAS LUMBER WORKERS

CHAPTER ONE

A study of the Poverty of nations has even more urgency than a study of the Wealth of nations.—GERALD M. MEIER and ROBERT E. BALDWIN

LAND OF DEEP POVERTY

IN THE STATE OF TEXAS in 1950 approximately one million people—more than one-tenth of its total population—lived in a region in which one family out of every two had incomes less than $2,000 a year. The Joint Committee of Congress which studied the Economic Report of the President in that year took note of the situation by spotting the area as one of "deep poverty." The Committee defined as "low-income families" those living in cities whose yearly incomes were less than $2,000 and those living on farms with incomes less than $1,000. Falling in the group so defined were one-fourth of the families of the nation. One region dominated by such families, the Committee found, was the northeastern section of Texas. At the same time it stated that the minimum budget necessary to maintain "an adequate scale of living" was $3,000 for a family of four in New Orleans and $1,365 for an elderly couple in Houston.[1]

[1] Joint Committee Print, *Low-Income Families and Economic Stability: Materials on the Problem of Low-Income Families*, 81st Cong., 1st Sess., 1949, pp. 2, 4, cited hereinafter as JCP, *Low-Income Families*, 1949.

The reports of the United States Bureau of the Census list more reliably and more fully than any other source the broad outlines of national life. But the over-all picture that they represent is a composite built from information regarding smaller units. The major component is, of course, the political state, but the political state is not necessarily—nor indeed even commonly—a closely-knit, homogeneous economic unit. Within a state there may exist strongly-marked regions where the inhabitants, because of available resources, carry on the same type of activity and receive most incomes, if not all, from the same source. Furthermore, the different types of economic life, namely, the industrial, the nonindustrial, and the industrializing, may exist at the same time not only within the nation but within a state, and the divergence there may be as great as that in the nation. The macrocosm by its nature submerges the microcosm, and although generalization takes place at the level of the macrocosmic, the knowledge and understanding basic to the making of policies and programs are rooted in the microcosmic. Characterizing regions by terms such as "backward," "industrial," or "depressed" certainly sets the dominant note. But variant groups, wherever found, are sources of tension. To search them out, to examine the sources of the existing and potential results of their divergence, is part of a rational approach to securing the highest development of both the individual and the state.

For the past half-century, the national pattern has been one of increasing total income, increasing per-capita incomes, and increasing productivity, in short, a rising scale of living. The same pattern is true for the state of Texas; the picture is one of expansion, a boom economy. But, because chronic unemployment and low incomes, with their resulting scale of life, are symptoms of significant weakness in an otherwise prosperous and expanding nation, they have been, and are being, given increased attention.

The present study concerns itself with a subdivision of Texas classified as one of the areas of deep poverty. While the region cannot be rigidly demarcated by survey lines, it can be satisfactorily delimited within statistical information published in reports of the decennial census for 1950. To anyone studying scales of living, figures relating to income are of paramount importance. But often the "average" or "median" size of incomes for the political state—the unit most often noted—reveals little and conceals much about the economic and social conditions of life within its boundaries. The most casual survey of the findings of census enumerators for Texas impresses the reader with the wide disparity of income between geographical divisions and economic groups within the state. A closer inspection reveals an area where incomes are far below the level of those in many other sections and below that of the state as a whole. As shown on Map 1, the area includes roughly 32 counties lying north of Houston and east of Dallas. The county is the unit of statistical description. Median yearly income of families and unrelated individuals in the 254 counties of the state was $2,273, ranging from $4,100 in Crane County to $810 in Zapata; 13 counties had median incomes between $3,500 and $4,000, and 3 had less than $1,000. A glance at the map shows that the 10 highest-income counties are in the western section of the state. Of the lowest-income counties, 2 are in the northeastern part and one in the southwestern.

But the *proportion* of families and unrelated persons in each county who received less than $2,000 median income is a much more revealing figure in relation to the population and its scale of living. Counties in which 50 per cent or more of income-receiving units had less than $2,000 are markedly concentrated: 14 along the lower Rio Grande River and all the others in northeastern Texas. But there is a still more marked concentration. In the state, 45 per cent of incomes are below $2,000, but in 22 counties, 70 per cent of incomes are below that amount. Of these, 6 are near the Rio Grande border, 5 are in the center of the state, and 11 are in the northeastern area. For the well-being of all the citizens of the state, the situation in the last-named region is of great significance, for there 200,000 persons live. In the same area 6 counties, with from 65 per cent to 70 per cent of incomes below $2,000, have a population of 133,000; 9 others, with from 60 per cent to 65 per cent below $2,000, have 176,000 people; and 10 counties, with from 50 per cent to 60 per cent with less than that amount, have a population of 360,000.

The area is undoubtedly one of comparative poverty in relation to

20% or more

1–Moore, 2–Hutchinson, 3–Tarrant, 4–Marion, 5–Sabine, 6–Newton, 7–Jasper, 8–Tyler, 9–Polk, 10–Trinity, 11–San Jacinto, 12–Montgomery, 13–Harris, 14–Hardin, 15–Jefferson, 16–Orange, 17–Brazoria, 18–Comal

15%—20%

19–Grayson, 20–Palo Pinto, 21–Parker, 22–Dallas, 23–Morris, 24–Cass, 25–Harrison, 26–Cherokee, 27–Nacogdoches, 28–Liberty, 29–Galveston, 30–Calhoun

12%—15%

31–Garza, 32–Hood, 33–Ellis, 34–Camp, 35–Upshur, 36–Smith, 37–Gregg, 38–McLennan, 39–Shelby, 40–San Augustine, 41–Walker

70% or more

1–Red River, 2–Franklin, 3–Camp, 4–Rains, 5–Marion, 6–Shelby, 7–San Augustine, 8–Sabine, 9–Leon, 10–Houston, 11–Trinity, 12–San Jacinto, 13–Milam, 14–Burleson, 15–Washington, 16–Grimes, 17–Hudspeth, 18–Edwards, 19–Maverick, 20–Dimmit, 21–Zapata, 22–Starr

65%—70%

23–Cass, 24–Upshur, 25–Erath, 26–Henderson, 27–Nacogdoches, 28–Freestone, 29–Limestone, 30–Falls, 31–Robertson, 32–Madison, 33–Walker, 34–Newton, 35–Waller, 36–Lee, 37–Fayette, 38–Gonzales, 39–Hays, 40–Zavalla, 41–Frio, 42–Lasalle, 43–Hidalgo

60%—65%

44–Lamar, 45–Delta, 46–Hopkins, 47–Wood, 48–Morris, 49–Denton, 50–Rockwall, 51–Kaufman, 52–Cherokee, 53–Mills, 54–Hamilton, 55–Bosque, 56–Brazos, 57–Tyler, 58–Jasper, 59–Bastrop, 60–Presidio, 61–Kinney, 62–Real, 63–Bandera, 64–Medina, 65–Goliad, 66–Webb

50%—60%

67–Montague, 68–Cooke, 69–Grayson, 70–Wise, 71–Collin, 72–Titus, 73–Bowie, 74–Harrison, 75–Panola, 76–Rusk, 77–Anderson, 78–Ellis, 79–Hill, 80–Somervell, 81–Comanche, 82–Brown, 83–Coleman, 84–Concho, 85–McCulloch, 86–San Saba, 87–Lampasas, 88–Coryell, 89–Menard, 90–Kimble, 91–Gillespie, 92–Blanco, 93–Burnet, 94–Bell, 95–Williamson, 96–Kendall, 97–Guadalupe, 98–Caldwell, 99–Colorado, 100–Austin, 101–Fort Bend, 102–Montgomery, 103–Liberty, 104–Hardin, 105–Polk, 106–Dewitt, 107–Karnes, 108–Atascosa, 109–Live Oak, 110–Bee, 111–Calhoun, 112–Duval, 113–Jim Hogg, 114–Cameron, 115–Uvalde, 116–Valverde, 117–Brewster, 118–Jeff Davis, 119–Hutchinson

the state, and since the per-capita income of the state is below that of the United States, the poverty of this region in relation to the nation is notable. Furthermore, the immediate past has shown not only no improvement but a positive deterioration in the standard of living of the people of the section. Using the level of living of farm families in the United States in 1945 as 100, the level of Texas was 101, a gain of 20 points over that of 1940. Though in all the 32 counties included in this study the level of family living has risen between 1940 and 1945, in only 8 did it reach one-half that of the state and in only one—Gregg, with 84 per cent—did it reach more than 60 per cent of state level.[2]

What are the general characteristics of the economic life of these 32 counties? The situation in all of them is suggested and oriented by the broad statistical outline of Sabine County, one of the 11 with 70 per cent of yearly median incomes less than $2,000 at the time of the 1950 census. Of the total of 8,600 persons in the county, not one lives in a community of as many as 2,500 people.[3] The median age of the population is 28.9, one year higher than that of the state. Households are somewhat larger than average, having 3.64 persons, compared with 3.4 for the state. The inhabitants of the county were notably stable: 85 per cent of those one year of age and over were living in the same house which they had lived in the preceding year, compared with 73 per cent for the state. Educationally, the county was well below the state level of 9.3 years. Median school years completed by persons twenty-five years of age and over was 7.2 for males, 7.8 for females. Of the 8,600 persons in Sabine County, 140 had never completed a year of school, 870 had completed no more than four years, and 230 had completed four years of high school; 185 had attended college, and 95 had completed four years or more.

Of persons over fourteen years of age, 2,275 were in the labor force: 640 in agriculture and 1,035 (39.2 per cent) in manufacturing. Of the latter, 996 were employed in the processing of lumber and wood products.

[2] *Ibid.*, pp. 133–135.

[3] Preliminary report, *U.S. Census, 1950; Texas, General Characteristics.*

If, as commonly held, industrialization means the introduction of secondary industries (in mining and manufacturing, the percentage of a population engaged in manufacturing is a significant index of considerable scale), then Sabine County is one of the most highly industrialized counties in the state. Trade and restaurants employ 267; 12 persons are in medical and health services; 10 furnish entertainment and recreation. Educational services, with 118, are the only other category engaging as many as 100 people. Of the total labor force, 659 (24 per cent) are classified as "laborers," and about 550 as "operatives and kindred workers," in contrast to the state as a whole, where 17 per cent are laborers and 15 per cent are operatives and kindred workers. Of 2,205 families reporting income (based on a 20-per-cent sample), 71 per cent receive less than $2,000 a year, 745 less than $1,000, and 435 less than $500. Thirty-five reported incomes of more than $10,000 and 170 reported more than $4,000. The median income was $1,557 (Table 1).

Broad outlines of life in Sabine County are typical of counties in the northeastern area of Texas, an area in which are concentrated those counties with a high percentage of low incomes and a comparatively high proportion of gainfully employed working in manufacturing.

1. They are not dominated by agricultural production as compared with the rest of the state. In fact, in 4 of the counties, 30 per cent or more of the gainfully employed are in manufacturing and in 5 others the number is more than 5 per cent. For the state, 13.5 per cent of the gainfully employed are in manufacturing; 17 of the counties here considered have a proportion in manufacturing 21 per cent larger than that for the state (Table 2, Map 2).

2. The distribution of incomes has a marked skew in each county. Typically, in San Jacinto County with 1,960 family incomes reported, 915 were less than $1,000; 110 were $4,000 or more; 5 were $10,000 or more. In Trinity County, with 2,650 incomes reported, 945 were less than $1,000; 180 were $4,000 or more; 20 were $10,000 or more (Table 1).

3. A notable characteristic of the population of these counties is

TABLE 1: Income of Families in Thirty-two Selected Counties, 1950

	No. of Families	*Less Than $500*	*$500 to $999*	*$1,000 to $1,999*	*$2,000 to $2,999*	*$3,000 to $3,999*	*$4,000 to $4,999*	*$5,000 to $6,999*	*$7,000 to $7,999*	*$10,000 and over*	*Med. Income*	*Percentage under $2,000*
Anderson	8,290	1,015	1,275	1,720	1,285	1,190	625	480	150	135	$1,943	55.5
Angelina	9,635	980	1,035	2,090	2,270	1,365	650	660	125	155	2,209	49.5
Bowie	16,045	1,905	1,795	3,330	3,500	2,400	1,195	1,015	230	155	2,190	50.9
Camp	2,330	445	525	545	320	200	105	50	25	20	1,259	70.3
Cass	6,515	1,305	1,150	1,605	1,090	620	280	215	75	45	1,436	67.2
Cherokee	9,225	1,215	1,440	2,445	1,480	915	470	410	150	155	1,645	63.4
Gregg	16,745	1,175	1,300	2,790	2,905	3,315	2,105	1,675	605	530	3,009	38.5
Grimes	3,780	535	750	875	480	310	110	85	45	60	1,322	71.4
Hardin	4,955	510	475	1,140	875	780	555	390	55	40	2,248	50.8
Harrison	11,420	1,320	1,635	2,700	2,050	1,540	775	675	235	125	1,949	58.8
Henderson	6,295	1,215	1,050	1,495	1,005	600	350	230	115	35	1,469	65.1
Houston	5,640	1,030	1,035	1,525	765	475	175	255	80	30	1,335	71.0
Jasper	4,825	600	745	1,395	785	515	290	240	65	60	1,733	61.3

Liberty	6,930	890	785	1,510	1,120	860	590	545	130	175	2,088	52.8
Marion	2,575	520	500	695	310	195	80	100	30	5	1,271	74.8
Montgomery	6,105	785	690	1,415	830	720	445	390	110	80	1,856	58.3
Morris	2,260	355	350	555	405	260	150	70	15	10	1,693	60.5
Nacogdoches	7,635	1,045	1,260	1,995	1,320	645	305	300	125	175	1,615	65.0
Newton	2,375	430	430	635	480	220	60	50	30	15	1,463	67.4
Panola	4,855	575	770	1,110	820	730	335	260	130	70	1,950	54.2
Polk	4,155	600	450	1,075	865	440	200	160	55	55	1,844	57.4
Rusk	10,980	1,315	1,530	2,295	1,595	1,710	1,075	755	210	225	2,116	51.9
Sabine	2,205	435	310	720	345	170	70	50	15	35	1,557	70.7
San Augustine	2,130	590	400	545	275	115	35	85	...	20	1,073	75.8
San Jacinto	1,960	395	520	570	195	125	35	50	20	5	1,054	78.6
Shelby	6,120	1,100	1,265	1,790	820	465	260	155	75	70	1,345	72.3
Smith	19,550	1,815	2,060	3,815	3,790	3,010	1,700	1,730	610	460	2,397	48.4
Titus	4,535	620	670	1,090	775	605	345	230	60	45	1,838	57.3
Trinity	2,650	500	445	715	380	245	65	85	10	20	1,394	70.9
Tyler	2,950	380	495	805	340	285	180	90	25	50	1,684	63.0
Upshur	5,410	905	1,035	1,425	780	550	255	215	95	60	1,439	66.7
Walker	4,580	595	690	1,350	735	440	255	235	55	30	$1,579	69.9

Source: U.S. Census, 1950, Vol. II; *Texas*, Tables 12 and 45.

TABLE 2: Occupational Distribution of Employed Male Population over Fourteen Years of Age in Thirty-two Selected Counties, 1950

	EMPLOYED					MAJOR INDUSTRY EMPLOYER
	Total	*In Agri-culture*	*In Manufacturing Number*	*Pct.*	*In Lumber & Furniture*	
Anderson	8,214	2,488	946	10.0	359	lumber & wood products (including furn.)
Angelina	9,565	1,036	3,934	33.6	1,828	"
Bowie	15,818	2,467	1,933	10.2	1,030	"
Camp	2,284	1,034	351	14.1	228	"
Cass	6,539	2,450	1,345	18.0	905	"
Cherokee	9,554	3,423	1,871	17.5	1,514	"
Gregg	16,543	738	2,539	12.1	301	machinery
Grimes	3,830	2,058	282	6.0	166	lumber & wood products (including furn.)
Hardin	5,039	386	1,668	28.1	1,369	"
Harrison	11,822	2,894	2,208	15.0	979	"
Henderson	5,869	2,432	524	7.9	166	"
Houston	5,745	2,768	790	11.3	644	"
Jasper	5,080	863	1,688	26.7	1,374	"
Liberty	7,356	1,263	1,566	17.6	1,202	"
Marion	2,523	803	667	20.0	508	"

Montgomery	6,395	829	2,203	28.3	1,881	"
Morris	2,330	715	555	19.6	167	primary metals
Nacogdoches	7,526	2,359	1,694	19.1	1,125	lumber & wood products (including furn.)
Newton	2,608	629	1,194	39.0	1,114	"
Panola	4,888	2,043	673	11.9	374	"
Polk	4,183	738	1,709	34.6	1,546	"
Rusk	11,222	3,026	1,034	7.9	549	"
Sabine	2,275	640	1,035	39.2	996	"
San Augustine	2,092	915	369	14.5	345	"
San Jacinto	1,839	884	503	22.3	481	"
Shelby	5,967	2,631	1,023	14.4	840	"
Smith	2,246	3,927	2,835	12.2	303	primary metals
Titus	4,445	1,404	588	11.2	135	other nondurable goods
Trinity	2,567	724	785	26.0	633	lumber & wood products (including furn.)
Tyler	3,130	717	958	25.3	876	"
Upshur	5,415	1,763	883	13.6	515	"
Walker	4,257	1,085	715	12.7	585	"

Source: U.S. Census, 1950; Vol. II: *Texas*, Table 43.

their lesser mobility, typified by the number of people in Sabine County who had lived in the same house for more than a year, mentioned above.

4. Of the 32 counties in the section, 28 having more than 5 per cent of their workers in manufacturing have as the major employer the industry processing lumber and timber. Immediately apparent is the fact that the economic life of the area is dominated by a single industry: the manufacturing of lumber and lumber products.

5. There is no town in the area with as many as 50,000 inhabitants. The following figures give the population and income picture for the seven cities with 10,000 inhabitants or more:

City	*Population*	*Median Income*	*Percentage of Incomes below $2,000*
Longview	25,000	$2,646	39.7
Lufkin	15,000	2,491	43.5
Marshall	22,000	1,767	54.5
Nacogdoches	12,300	1,599	57.7
Palestine	12,500	2,325	44.3
Texarkana	25,000	2,069	48.7
Tyler	39,000	2,367	42.5

Here, then, is a large group of people in a fairly limited section having the same climatic and geographical features as much of the rest of the state but whose incomes are notably outside the pattern for the state. The proportion of incomes available for consumption units is the most satisfactory indication of the general well-being of an area, and in a homogeneous environment a comparison of incomes raises few difficult questions, for the cultural environment within which the patterns of living—actual or aspired to—are accepted, is essentially the same.

A survey of the background of these people leads perforce to their lives as workers and, since their working environment has been largely conditioned by the forests in which they have lived and by the processing of its products, that environment, its history, and present-day achievements are of major interest.

Among the basic industries in the United States, lumbering comes next to agriculture, and, with the exception of agriculture, no industry has been more continuously studied by agencies of the federal government. Because of the size of the lumber industry, each decennial census has carried detailed information about its operation, as has each *Census of Manufactures*. The Forestry Service has published many reports. The Bureau of Corporations in 1915 made an investigation of control in the industry.[4] Suits against large holders of timber lands acquired under our public-lands policy and antitrust suits against the combinations and associations formed in the industry fill pages of our legal history.

The timber lands of Texas—18 per cent of its land surface—comprise more than 42,000 square miles, an area larger than the state of Ohio. There are 5,000 square miles of longleaf pine, 7,000 of loblolly pine (commonly called shortleaf) and hardwood, and 30,000 of shortleaf pine forests in the lignitic belt. The primary source of timber in the state was, and is, yellow pine, which in 1910 accounted for 97 per cent of the cut, in 1922 for 88.2 per cent, and in 1924 for 94.7 per cent. Other species, however, have been important also. As demand for dwellings in a new country becomes less pressing, the desire naturally arises for manufactures of lumber, especially furniture. Oak has always been preferred for making railroad ties, and in 1924, Texas mills were cutting 3.7 per cent of the nation's ties. They were producing also 6.3 per cent of the red gum, 5.7 per cent of the Tupelo gum, 4.1 per cent of the ash, and 1.2 per cent of the cottonwood used as paper pulp. In addition, some elm, hickory, sycamore (especially desirable for butcher blocks), walnut (shipped as logs), and magnolia (sometimes called sap poplar) were processed. An old standby of local importance was Osage orange or *bois d'arc* (highly prized by the Indians of the West, who considered it the choicest wood for making bows), mostly used for fence posts and as a sawmill product bought by wagon factories for fellies. In 1924 the cutting of cedar and maple was commercially reported for the first time.

[4] U.S. Dept. of Commerce, Bureau of Corporations, *The Lumber Industry*, Pt. II, 1913, especially pp. 104–106, 118, 140–172.

In the early settlement of a country, trees offer shelter and provide fuel, but they are also obstacles that must be removed so that food can be produced. Very early the need for untimbered prairies as well as the needs of industries made the processing of timber a highly profitable business, and the race to control stumpage—that is, areas covered by virgin forests—was on. After the Civil War, the processing of lumber in Texas became an important source of revenue for individuals, a source of housing materials for all sections of the state, and an employer for the steady flow of immigrants from the eastern states of the Confederacy. During the difficult period of postwar adjustment, lumber was an important factor in furnishing employment and providing some cash income. By 1870, reports were made to the federal government from each of 8 counties in which more than 100 lumber workers were employed. The Amsler mill at Prismoid had been in existence for six years, and four years later the Wingate mills began operation. The Gilmer interests had become established before the war, and earlier than 1880 Alexander Gilmer, an Irishman who first settled in Georgia, where he worked with his brother building shipmasts for the French Navy, had become a major entrepreneur of the Sabine area, with commercial and financial interests of many types. In the closing decades of the century, he was, if not the dominant personality in the lumber industry in Texas, one of the largest and most influential operators. His business was an example of the "personal company," for the Gilmer interests were not incorporated until 1906, the year their founder died.

Between 1905 and 1910 there was a vigorous movement among yellow-pine manufactures in the state to acquire timberland. During those five years the bulk of yellow-pine stumpage was blocked up in large properties and by 1910 one-sixth of the outstanding pine timber in the South was owned by twenty companies. Investigation by the Department of Commerce and Labor brought the general conclusion that "there is a very high concentration of ownership in the virgin stands of short leaf and loblolly pine in Texas, Arkansas, and Louisiana" and that "timber is more certainly gathered into large holdings in proportion as it is more desirable." In addition to owning the most valuable timber in a locality, "they [the large holders] control by blocking in a large amount of additional timber owned by small holders." Three companies, holding a total of from 5 billion to 13 billion board feet, held 11.2 billion—just over a million acres—in Texas. Of timber owned by companies holding 60 billion board feet or more, 36.5 billion were in Texas—55 per cent of the total timber in the state.

Landholders on the national scene owning more than 300,000 acres and holding timber lands in Texas were Southern Pacific, 117,000; Long Bell, 81,000; Central Coal and Coke, 248,000; and Kirby Lumber Company, 368,000. The holdings of the latter three were all in Texas and Louisiana, and the Kirby company was the largest holder of timber rights in the Southern pine area.

As an employer, the lumber industry has historically used more than 10 per cent of the industrially-employed workers in the United States and more than one-third of those in Texas. Until displaced by oil refining in 1929, the Texas lumber industry had for six decades hired more workers than any other manufacturing in the state. Though in only two census years—1890 and 1900—did the value of its product exceed that produced by any other industry, in 1909, when it ranked third in value produced, it employed one-third of all industrial wage-earners in the state. In 1940, it still ranked second in number of persons industrially employed. Because of its importance as an employer, the industry has been a major influence in setting the pattern of employer-employee relationships, in determining standards of industrial work, and in shaping the attitudes toward workers and the environment in which they and their families exist.

Its significance in these functions has been magnified by the large proportion of the total cost of production paid out in wages. In 1880, though there was not agreement as to the ratio of labor cost to the total cost of processing lumber, most firms calculated it from 35 per cent to 40 per cent and higher. One firm in Louisiana estimated it at 50 per cent; the Amsler mill in Texas at 40 per cent. Ten years later, wages in the United States were 58 per cent of total cost and in the Southern section of the industry 70 per cent, but a later judgment was that 60 per cent of the final cost of producing lumber went to wages. The 1939 census report gave consideration to the part that wages played in the total cost of manufactured products. The estimated proportion for all manufacturing industries was 16 per cent, with a range of from 5.1 per cent in the manufacture of tobacco to 27.6 per cent in timber. For chemicals it was 9.5 per cent and for oil refining 5.9 per cent. In 1917 the Assistant Forester of the United States noted that "it has been brought out before that the forests of the United States furnish more employment to labor than any other manufacturing industry, and that the element of wages in the cost of producing lumber is exceptionally large." Because wages form a larger part in the production and processing of lumber than in most other industries, the conditions of employment in this industry affected the lives of comparatively more individuals than did those of most other industries. Consequently, the final cost of the production of lumber and its auxiliary products was more dependent upon the effective direction and organization of the human factor than in most other industries.

CHAPTER TWO

Never before nor since have men so quickly and ruthlessly "slashed" a forest as they did the Southern coniferous forest, the most extensive of its kind. Rebel or Yankee, the Southern lumber baron operated under a "cut and get out" policy. Labor was cheap and plentiful, the terrain flat to gently rolling, and the weather never severe.—RUBEN L. PARSONS

DEVELOPMENT OF THE LUMBER INDUSTRY

SINCE THE INDISPENSABLE RESOURCE of the lumber industry is trees, the first aim of early entrepreneurs in the industry was to own or control virgin timberlands, enough at least, to make it profitable to organize and operate processing plants. In all sections of the United States, land was held by the government, and methods of transferring ownership from public to private hands became the engrossing interest of legislative and administrative bodies. Texas, which held title to its own public lands, up to 1880 pursued a very loose policy in regard to its lands. Through fraudulent classification or through careless valuation, lands were sold for far less than their value and wholesale theft of timber went unnoticed.

Following Texas' full restoration to the Union, legislation of 1879 provided only that timber could not be cut on lands from the public domain until the purchase price was fully paid. No limit was set upon the amount of timbered land one person could purchase, and no minimum price was prescribed other than the $1.00 per acre for school land in general. Valuation was left to county officials, and timber lands could be purchased on credit. Somewhat later, county valuation had to be approved by the Commissioner of the General Land Office.[1] Until 1882, Commissioner William C. Walsh stated in a letter to the Galveston *News*,[2] pine-timbered land was sold for from $1.00 to $2.00 per acre, and individuals and lumber corporations had been the chief beneficiaries. In that year, the price of timberland was set at $5.00 per acre, but no recognition was given to the difference in classes of such land, and it could still be bought "on time." In the following year pre-emption rights on the land were recognized by giving a settler the privilege of purchasing not less than 80 nor more than 320 acres for cash at a price ranging from $2.00 to $5.00 per acre, depending on the class of land. The $5.00-per-acre price tied up settlement of the land, and "as a result," reported the Commissioner of the General Land Office, "depredators are at work and legitimate timber cutting is checked."[3] In 1887, classification was authorized, with $5.00 per acre for the better land and $2.00 per acre for the poorer. Twelve years later, state agents were instructed to investigate the theft of timber on school lands, which, according to reports of the General Land Office, had been going on practically unhampered. In 1905, competitive bidding for timber land was introduced, but by that time the state had only 31,978 acres of public land and probably they were of little value.

Early Days of the Industry. Since long transportation hauls are not economically feasible for moving lumber, the processing of

[1] Material on land policy taken from E. T. Miller, *A Financial History of Texas*, University of Texas Press Bulletin No. 37, 1916; Aldon S. Lang, *Financial History of the Public Lands in Texas, Baylor Bulletin*, Vol. XXXV (July, 1932), Waco, Texas; Reuben McKittrick, *The Public Lands of Texas, 1823–1910*, University of Wisconsin Bulletin No. 905, Economic and Political Science Series, Vol. 9, No. 1, 1918; W. L. Bray, *Forest Resources of Texas*, U.S. Forestry Service Bulletin No. 47, 1904.

[2] March 1, 1882.

[3] Report, Commissioner General Land Office of Texas, 1886, p. 8.

lumber in Texas was for a long period of its early development a local industry, with small logging camps and water-run sawmills which supplied surrounding territories or vessels leaving nearby ports. Because of the large bulk and great weight of lumber in relation to its price, its early movement was restricted to watercourses, and Texas rivers and creeks are sluggish and often shallow. In 1915 the U.S. Department of Commerce listed in its *Directory of American Sawmills* 122 firms in Texas which from 1909 to 1915 had reported regularly to it; only 2 were listed as using transportation by water. In contrast, the state of Washington, with two pages of listings, showed 30 plants using water transportation. The exploitation of Texas forests did not, consequently, reach great volume until railroads passed through the area, furnishing not only transportation but a major market for the output of the industry. In addition, the entrepreneurs in the processing of timber were in many instances also the pioneer builders of railroads. Many common carriers of today started a few decades ago as part of a logging and sawmill enterprise.

Until 1910, the production of lumber in Texas yielded a surplus over that required by the inhabitants of the state. Markets were found in the Middle West, where the white pine of the Lakes forests was becoming insufficient. But lumber was also shipped from Gulf ports, especially Galveston and Port Arthur, to Hamburg, entry port for Europe. It went also, by water and overland, to Mexico and to South American countries. Later the West Indies and Cuba became leading customers for yellow pine. Locally, as population grew, so did the need for housing—private, commercial, and public. In 1905 bituminous coal mines in the state used 344,000 round timbers. Later, the production needed to meet the requirements of railroads for fuel, ties, cars, and other stock was augmented by the spectacular growth of the oil industry, which also required timber products.[4] For the years 1880–1907, 3.7 per cent of the total lumber cut of the nation came from Texas. States producing the largest shares at that time were, by percentage, Michigan, 12.5; Wisconsin, 9.4; Minnesota, 5.1; Pennsylvania, 7.3; and Washington, 4.8.[5]

[4] U.S. Forestry Service Circular No. 49, p. 4.

[5] *Ibid.*, No. 52, p. 18.

Growth of the Industry. In 1870 there were 324 lumber-producing plants in Texas, with a value of approximately $2 million.[6] Twenty years later there were 284 established lumber and sawmills producing 1.25 billion board feet, with a value of approximately $12 million.[7] Gross and net values of product of these mills ranked first among manufacturing industries in Texas and tenth in the nation. During the next ten years, the value of products of the industry increased by somewhat less than 20 per cent, and Texas was producing 3 per cent of the national output. By 1910 Texas output was 5 per cent of the national total. At that time, of 284 lumber mills and sawmills, 259 produced lumber and 25 produced shingles and miscellaneous items.

At the turn of the century, the lumber industry in the United States ranked fourth in value of product. In Texas, it ranked first, with 637 establishments producing $16 million of product, four times as much as in 1880. The sawmills, planing mills, and logging camps produced a variety of products:

Rough lumber	1,192,848	M.B.M.
Shingles:	210,633	M.
Cypress	23,807	
Other conifers	186,376	
Hardwoods	450	
Pickets and palings	897	M.B.M.
Laths	4,181	M.
Cooperage:		
Staves	7,236	M.
Headings	100,000	sets
Timber-camp products:		
Fence posts	14,000	
Railway ties (no.)	675,835	
Telegraph poles (no.)	2,070	
Rived and shaved shingles	2,313	M.
Piles	3,060	

[6] *U.S. Census, 1870, Industry and Wealth,* Vol. III, p. 574.
[7] *Biennial Census of Manufactures, 1890,* Pt. III, p. 611.

In the official census report of 1900, Texas was characterized as "an older state where it [the manufacture of lumber] has been prosecuted for generations."[8]

During the preceding decade (1890–1900) the production of lumber and timber had increased by 36.5 per cent, while production in planing mills had decreased by 40.6 per cent. This was due to the fact that planing mills were tied more or less to centers of population, and plants had been shifted to more isolated areas. In logging camps the average number of wage-earners was 8 for both the nation and the state. That Texas had a comparatively high degree of mechanization is indicated by census figures showing that capital investment per establishment and per worker was greater there than in the nation. On the other hand, value of product per establishment and per worker was less in Texas than in the nation. In sawmills the average number of workers per establishment was 10—3 more than that for the nation; capital invested per establishment was one-half more and value of product one-third more. None of the giant mills of the nation were in Texas, but of the 542 planing mills in the state, 179 produced each one million board feet of lumber. Thirty-six tie and timber camps indicate the importance of tie-cutting for railroads, but independent camps produced by no means all the ties used. Other auxiliary industries were developing: 4 establishments were carrying on wood-preserving processes, especially beneficial for ties, and 13 small plants were turning and carving wood.[9]

At the midpoint of the first decade of the century, the Bureau of the Census took careful steps to make available to the nation comparable figures for 1900 and 1905.[10] During the five-year period, the average size of establishment and value of product per wage-earner in the national industry had increased, and value of product per establishment was more than one-half again as large. Reports from

[8] *U.S. Census, 1900, Manufacturing*, "Selected Industries," Pt. II, pp. 862–885; Pt. III, pp. 803–897.

[9] James E. Defebaugh, *History of the Lumber Industry in America, 1906–07*, Vol. I, pp. 508–525.

[10] U.S. Census Bulletin No. 77, *Lumber and Timber Products*, 1905; Bulletin No. 48, pp. 35–57.

Texas in 1905 covered 294 sawmills and planing mills and 5 independent logging and timber camps, plus 262 camps connected with sawmills. For establishments, the average value of products was two and two-thirds as large as in 1900 and the average number of wage-earners was almost twice as great. In value of product, the industry ranked third in the state, but as an employer of workers it ranked first. By 1907, the Texas share of the national cut had grown from the 1.8 per cent it held in 1880 to 5.5 per cent.

Changing Economic Patterns: 1900–10. The first decade of the twentieth century produced great changes in the economic organization of the state of Texas. In industrial growth it followed the national pattern. The value of industrial products tripled and value added by manufacturing grew to two and a half times its 1900 amount. The number of wage-earners industrially employed almost doubled, and the increase in proportion to the population ten years of age and over who were gainfully employed was 6 per cent, one of the largest in the nation. The opening of the great oil fields of course precipitated new developments. Although oil and gas were largely to displace wood as fuel both in transportation and in manufacturing industries, the oil industry nevertheless became a major consumer for the output of the lumber industry.

This ten-year period marked the peak production of lumber for the United States and for Texas, but in Texas, as mentioned above, it also saw the end of surplus production over the requirements of its inhabitants.[11] In the following decade, the state passed into the deficit column—that is, it consumed more lumber than it produced—though the cut of lumber in the state was still 5 per cent of that for the nation. The output of rough lumber had increased by 70.3 per cent; that of shingles had decreased by 35 per cent; but the production of laths was fourteen times that of a decade earlier. The processing of timber was by far the most important employer, using one-third of all industrial wage-earners in the state. With value of product added by manufacturing somewhat less than one-fourth of the total value for the state, it was also the most important industry economically.

[11] *U.S. Census, 1909, Manufacturing*, Vol. X, pp. 487–508; also *Supplement for Texas*, pp. 771–798.

The pattern of the industry was becoming complex. In addition to the primary operations of logging, sawing, and planing, plants were turning out cooperage and other products; another 11 were turning and carving wood or building ships and boats; 8 were preserving wood or producing paper and wood pulp; and 2 custom sawmills were making specialized products. Three turpentine-distilling plants represented an auxiliary to operations in the pineries, but such activity was never a significant part of the Texas industry. In 1908, there were 200,650 gallons of turpentine and 28,661 barrels of rosin produced; six years later, the quantity of turpentine produced had nearly tripled and the production of rosin was up by one and a half times. After continuing to increase by approximately one-half, the production of both began to decrease steadily in the Sabine area.[12]

The Comprehensive Industry. Logging roads, an important adjunct of the lumber industry, operated about 1,400 miles of rails in the state. Though by 1910 many tram roads were becoming common carriers by perfecting their organizations and filing charters with the Secretary of State, there were, according to *Southwest*, 63 common logging roads still unincorporated and under the jurisdiction of private owners. Lumber plants were still a major consumer of their own product—fuel—burning 13,821 cords of wood in 1909, but they used also about 6,000 tons of bituminous coal and 7,000 barrels of oil and gasoline. The most important user of wood as fuel was the brick and tile industry, but the manufacture of ice and of bakery products each used more than was used in the processing of lumber. As would be expected from the increase in production, the consumption of primary horsepower had more than doubled in the five-year period, reaching 88,000 units, more than twice as much as was used by any other industry except the 45,200 units used in the production of cottonseed oil and cottonseed cake.

That the importance of the industry was more than statistical is suggested by the continuing interest in its operations which appears through the files of newspapers in the area. Lumber and timber exercised a powerful hold over the interest and imagination of the

[12] *U.S. Census, 1929, Manufactures,* Vol. III, p. 527.

inhabitants. The shutting down and reopening of the mills, logs coming down the Sabine, steamers clearing the water hyacinths from the channels, the arrival or departure of a sawyer, the passage of loads of logs on their way to the seacoast—all were items of major interest.

In 1910, a local paper noted that "Howard" arrived on a raft of logs, approximately a million feet, which floated down the Sabine River from Center to Orange, a distance of about 150 miles. Sometime later it wrote up the log drive of 10 million feet that took place after one company had purchased all the logs in the Sabine River. The same paper commented on an advertisement for teams with eight-wheel wagons to haul logs.[13]

A dramatic moment in the life of a town, one drawing curious crowds, might be Bob Ellis hauling Europe-bound square timber from 60 to 80 feet long and 16 to 20 inches square. A year later the same Bob Ellis was hauling timber one stick of which required twelve yoke of oxen and an eight-wheel wagon. Even in a town centering around the lumber industry, crowds gathered to watch as the giant logs passed down Main Street on the first lap of their journey. With a deep sense of international economic unity, the *Newsboy* chortled that "Mr. Englishman has to go down in his jeans when he buys them." A recognition of the economic life-and-death importance of the smoke rising from the mill is implicit in the grave pronouncement by the same newspaper that "in Texas a smokestack is as sacred as a church steeple."

Though the proliferation of activities and products comprehended by the industry continue to the present, the basic operations of logging, planing, and sawing have dominated and still dominate it.[14] Ancillary to the expansion of fruit and vegetable culture, the number of plants making wooden containers grew from 19 in 1919 to 26 in 1947. In 1929 there were 14 plants making caskets and coffins, but twenty years later none were reported.[15] Wood-preserving plants have been of increasing importance, with 4 plants in 1919 and 20 in 1947.

[13] Jasper *Newsboy*, Sept. 13, 1910; Feb. 28, 1912; July 12, 1911.

[14] *U.S. Census, 1919, Manufacturing*, "The Lumber Industry," Vol. X, pp. 420–474; "Texas," Vol. IX, pp. 1447–1483.

[15] *U.S. Census, 1929, Manufacturing*, Vol. III, pp. 507–518.

Development of the Industry

In 1947, 915 plants produced approximately $40 million worth of lumber and timber products, excluding furniture. Though 131 mills were idle, 67 had begun operation for the first time during the year. During the half-century since 1900 the face of the industry was much changed, but still 22,000 of a total of 31,000 workers in the industry were making "basic products." The following figures show the number of establishments resulting from, or allied to, the basic groups:

Making:	
Wooden boxes (excluding cigar)	26
Fruit and vegetable baskets	16
Cigar boxes	1
Wood products	39
Mirror and picture frames	3
Household furniture (upholstered)	31
Household furniture (not upholstered)	42
Wood preserving	20
Veneer mills	5
Cooperage mills	5
Plywood	1
Pulpwood	2
Prefabricated wood	12

There were, in addition, lath and shingle mills. Prefabrication of wood was reported for the first time, with Texas, Ohio, Indiana, and Illinois producing one-third of the total national product.[16] Bringing production figures up to date as of 1955, in Texas 1,044 establishments turned out lumber and wood products valued at $49 million and employed about 24,000 workers.[17]

Size of the Mills. Productive units in the lumber industry have never been large, measured by industrial standards. In 1947, only 3 mills were "large," sawing from 25 million to 30 million board feet, and 103 were "small," producing 3 million board feet each. The need to be near the source of raw material was one factor keeping plants small; another was the small investment needed to set up a mill. Under many conditions movable mills, since they could leave an area as soon as it was cut, were efficient. The large investment of

[16] *Biennial Census of Manufactures, 1947*, Vol. III, pp. 276, 283, 586.

[17] *Texas Business Review*, December, 1956.

the producer was in stumpage and not in plant. Furthermore, high transportation costs made it unprofitable to serve large markets from one mill. There were, on the other hand, some pressures for big operations. The rate of interest which had to be paid by "small men" was unprofitably large. The concentration of land ownership and stumpage discouraged individuals from building mills. Furthermore, being located in nonurban areas forced the mills to develop a local source of labor, and this was most satisfactorily done for large numbers.

In comparison with other industrial plants in the state in 1910, those processing lumber were large if measured by the average number of wage-earners, but if measured by other standards, such as average value of product and value added by manufacturing, they were small. The fact that the census figures did not isolate any establishments with output valued at $1 million indicates that there probably was one with such output. There were 8 establishments of that size in flour and grist milling, and 4 processing cottonseed oil and cottonseed cake. Approximately 65 per cent of each measurement mentioned here came from plants reporting from $100,000 to $1,-000,000. For all industries in the state, two-thirds of the wage-earners and of value added, and more than three-fourths of value of product came from such plants (Table 3). Ten years later there had been little change in the proportion of value which came from the largest plants. Establishments producing lumber turned out an average value of $40,300 which was quite small compared with the $137,000 of gristmill products and the $154,000 of cottonseed oil and cottonseed cake.

In 1900, with 52.5 per cent of all lumber enterprises individually owned, the industry was still dominated by such firms. But five years later a change in the character of ownership was apparent. Though the number of individually-owned enterprises was in about the same proportion to the total number of plants, the number of firms had shown a marked decrease and that of incorporated businesses was double that in 1900. But more significant figures show that corporations employed more than three-fourths of the workers and produced three-fourths of value and of value added by manufacture. At the end of the decade, as shown by the figures in Table 4, the one-fifth of establishments that had passed under corporate control produced approximately three-fourths of value of product and of value added in the industry, and employed three-fourths of the wage-earners. Though the lumber and timber-products industry followed the general industrial pattern in the state, individual firm ownership was more the rule in the production of lumber than in the total industrial pattern of the state.

That the industry is still, as it has always been, highly concentrated is indicated by the names of the counties having the largest number employed in the industry for more than three-quarters of a century:

1870	*1880*	*1940*	*1950*
Montgomery	Montgomery	Polk	Montgomery
Red River	Jefferson	Newton	Angelina
Bastrop	Orange	Montgomery	Polk
Orange	Cass	Jasper	Cherokee

Of 17 counties with more than 100 industrial employees in 1870, 8 were leaders in the production of lumber.[18] Ten years later, 10 counties had more than 100 workers employed in the production of lumber, and 5 of them had no other industry.[19] Reports of the 1900 census noted the concentration, saying that the industry was confined almost entirely "to counties composing the extreme eastern part of the state from Bowie County on the north to Jefferson and Harris Counties on the south," where 85.5 per cent of the total product of the state was produced. The report continues that "from Texarkana south to Jefferson lies the finest continuous area of shortleaf pine in the United States."[20]

In 1940, Polk County had more than 1,800 workers employed by the lumber industry; 6 counties—Newton, Angelina, Montgomery, Jasper, Cass, and Cherokee—had more than 1,000; 4 others—Bowie, Harrison, Liberty, and Sabine—had 500. Sixteen counties had more than 20 establishments engaged in the industry. Of the 76 plants employing 100 workers or more, 7 were in Montgomery County; 6

[18] *U.S. Census, 1870, Industry and Wealth*, pp. 572–573.

[19] *U.S. Census, 1880*, Vol. II, pp. 359–361.

[20] *U.S. Census, 1900, Manufactures*, Pt. II, p. 864.

each in Angelina and Harris; 5 in Bowie; 4 each in Cherokee, Jasper, and Nacogdoches; 3 each in Hardin, Harrison, Newton, Orange, and Polk. Five other counties had 2 each and 15 had one.[21]

The industry was and is highly rural. No major city reported as many as 500 employees in the industry, and no town of 10,000 or more had as many as 1,000 persons working in the processing of lumber and timber products.

Owing, in part, to factors already mentioned, the industry was highly competitive. But the pressure upon the holders of timber to translate it into cash caused a general tendency to produce lumber beyond the capacity of the market to absorb it. With the rapid growth of population in Texas after 1880, the demand for lumber was heavy and insistent—not for good lumber, for just lumber. The quality of production was often little considered. One result of hasty production was, of course, large waste. Good wood was used for fuel, while sawdust accumulated. In general, if lumbering is to pay as an enterprise it requires large tracts of land with a supply of timber which will last for a reasonably long period. The owners of small tracts either had to sell their timber on the stump or contract for its manufacture. Often stumpage was sold by the owner on contract which specified a definite time for removal. If the purchaser did not observe the time limit, he could lose his right to the timber. Such contracts led to the cutting of all usable trees within the specified period, with little or no consideration for aftereffects. High tax rates on timber land might force logging, but as taxes in Texas were not of a compulsive nature, this factor was probably not of great importance. Since the primary product—lumber—is tied largely to the investment of its use in housing, railroads, etc., instability was a marked feature in the industry.[22]

Organization of the Industry. The possibilities for operating small and fly-by-night plants, as well as other factors mentioned, caused cutthroat competition to develop in the lumber industry. Its counterpart, monopoly, already powerful in the ownership and control of stumpage, began to seek methods of controlling production

[21] U.S. Census of 1940, Monograph No. 24, pp. 592 ff.

[22] Herman Chapman, *Forest Valuation*, pp. 69, 72.

Table 3: Distribution of Plants by Size, 1910

	PLANTS		WAGE-EARNERS		VAL. OF PROD.		VAL. ADD BY MFG.	
	State	*L&T**	*State*	*L&T*	*State*	*L&T*	*State*	*L&T*
Less than $5,000	38.1	33.5	3.8	4.1	1.6	2.1	3.1	2.5
$5,000 and less than $20,000	33.0	34.7	11.1	10.8	5.7	8.9	10.2	10.2
$20,000 and less than $100,000	18.9	21.4	22.4	21.7	14.3	22.7	20.7	22.8
$100,000 and less than $1 million	9.3	10.4	49.7	63.4	41.0	66.3	45.9	64.5
$1 million and over	0.8	...	13.1	...	37.4	...	20.1	...
Av. per plant			15	29	59,480	40,302	20,645	26,530

* Abbreviation for "Lumber and Timber."
Source: U.S. Census, 1910; Supplement for Texas, p. 781.

Table 4: Distribution of Lumber Plants by Type of Ownership, 1910

	PLANTS		WAGE-EARNERS		VAL. OF PROD.		VAL. ADD BY MFG.	
	State	*L&T*	*State*	*L&T*	*State*	*L&T*	*State*	*L&T*
Individual	49.9	43.8	13,2	12.9	8.5	11.0	12.7	12.0
Firm	19.8	33.4	8.8	13.8	6.8	14.3	9.0	15.8
Corporation	29.5	22.8	77.9	73.3	84.7	74.7	78.2	72.3
Other	0.8	...	0.1	...	0.1	...	0.1	...

Source: U.S. Census, 1910; Supplement for Texas, p. 781.

and markets. The industry was early organized into numerous associations, local, district, or national in membership and scope of interest, and Texas producers were active in them.[23]

That the industry believed in the effectiveness of close collaboration is attested to by the number of associations that have come and gone.

In the 1880's the Southern Pacific Shingle Manufacturer's Association had both a president and secretary from Texas. In the same decade ten manufacturers of the Sabine area organized the East Texas and Louisiana Lumbermen's Association. Dues were based upon the number of board feet cut monthly, at the rate of 50 cents per 100,000. A few years later, the association expanded its membership to cover all of Texas and Louisiana. In 1883, reports were made to the R. G. Dunn credit-rating service by 26 mills in the Sabine area. Later the Yellow Pine Clearing House had reports of output. On December 27, 1890, the Beaumont *Journal* urged that

> if any sawmill firm in Texas has failed to join the Southern Lumberman's Association, let them send membership at once to J. J. Trump, Secretary, Little Rock, Arkansas. This Association is no trust or semblance of a trust, but an organization for the advancement and development of the lumber industry in the South. If you want to keep abreast of the time, the sooner you join the better.[24]

In the nineties the Lumbermen's Association of Texas was also active. In 1897 a letter addressed to members stated that "five dollars gives us ample funds to force an aggressive campaign on all wrongdoers."[25] The organ of the association was the *Lumber Review*. In the middle of the decade the Southern Cypress Shingle Association, with 95 per cent of the shingle manufacturers in Louisiana, Texas, and Arkansas on its membership roll, represented an $800 million annual output. By 1900 trade associations were the order of the day. When the Federal Trade Commission in 1922 reported on these or-

[23] Information about the various associations are from the Gilmer papers and periodicals of the industry.

[24] Dec. 27, 1890.

[25] Gilmer letter, dated March 23, 1897.

ganizations, the Southern Pine Association represented a larger production than any other group.[26]

At about the same time, the Attorney General of Texas appeared before the Legislature and charged that lumber manufacturers and retail dealers, through the National Lumber Manufacturer's Association, dominated one of the great resources of the country to their own personal advantage. Following the investigation by the Federal Trade Commission, a member wrote to the president of the National Lumber Manufacturer's Association saying, among other things, "I realize that it will be necessary to take into account the state authorities of Texas and Missouri—but through the help of Kirby [the dominant figure in the Texas industry] we ought to get a pretty definite angle on the Texas situation."[27]

The lumber operators also had an international social organization called "Hoo-Hoo," which held yearly meetings. While the purposes and activities of the society were avowedly social, the value of social collaboration as an asset to industrial and business cooperation has long been recognized.

The Yellow Pine Manufacturer's Association, founded in 1902, was the largest of fourteen groups forming the National Lumber Manufacturer's Association. In the twentieth century the Southern Pine Association has been the most significant organization of producers in the pineries of the Southeastern and South Central area. In 1938 its membership included only 10 per cent of pine lumber manufacturers in the South, but that percentage represented approximately 45 per cent of total production and 60 per cent of capacity in the Southern pine industry.

These associations have aided in organizing and stabilizing the market for lumber, have disseminated valuable information, and have stated the interests and opinions of the operators before the public. Plainly, the operators of establishments in the manufacture of lumber and timber products have been strong exponents of organization as a means of protecting their economic position and strengthening cooperation.

[26] Report on Lumber Manufacturers' Association, 1922.

[27] R. C. Bryant, *Lumber: Its Manufacture and Distribution*, p. 333.

UNTIL QUITE RECENT DECADES the history of northeastern Texas has been a history of the production of timber and lumber in the state—its development, its operation, and its decline. Entrepreneurs in the industry, aided and abetted by Texas' public-land policies, have owned or controlled the forest lands of the state, their basic capital resource. Until the recent interest in reforestation, timber-cutting, plus the effects of wind and water, meant the denudation of the land. Stripping forest lands may leave soil of little value, as it undoubtedly did on many acres of the Texas pinelands. When the land can be used for agriculture, tenancy is a probable aftermath, its character depending upon the nature of the soil.

At its peak the Texas lumber industry produced 5.5 per cent of the national output and not only supplied the needs of the state but served other areas as well. By 1910 the period of surplus production ended because of increasing demands within the state for a variety of products. Collaterally, the pattern of production became increasingly complex. In the late forties there were, in addition to establishments producing the primary products of lumber and timber, 14 types of plants making subsidiary products. Establishments in the industry have been, and still are, small as size is understood in American industry. There have been also a large number of personally-owned plants. At the mid-twentieth century, the lumber industry produced $50 million worth of lumber and furniture products and employed more than 30,000 workers.

Since 1890, operators in the Texas industry have represented an important segment of membership in many associations—national, sectional, and local. At present, the principal ones are the National Lumber Manufacturer's Association, the Southern Pine Association, and the Texas Lumbermen's Association.

CHAPTER THREE

Improved conditions make better men and better men improve conditions.—SIMON PATTEN

THE INDUSTRY AS AN EMPLOYER

AS HAS ALREADY BEEN STRESSED, the processing of lumber has held a major position in the hierarchy of Texas industries because of its importance as an employer of industrial labor. It bears repeating, however, that from 1870 until 1930 the lumber industry employed more workers than any other in the state. In 1940 it ranked second only to oil refining in the number industrially employed. The entrepreneur in the lumber industry presided over a diversity of occupations which, though not very complex, might extend over a fairly wide area.

The primary processes are still, as they have always been, "logging" and "milling." Over the years there has been little change in job classifications, based in general upon the type of work and to some extent upon wages paid. But classifications have by no means been rigid, and with the exception of a few jobs calling for particular skills, any employee might have a variety of work to perform. In 1915 a federal investigation, confined to establishments which did both logging and sawing and whose records were available, covered 6 logging camps in Texas.[1] Broad divisions of workers were as follows:

[1] U.S. BLS Bulletin No. 225, p. 193.

1. General repair, upkeep, and general service, which included skilled craftsmen such as blacksmiths, carpenters, and machinists at one end of the scale, and waterboys, stablemen, and unskilled workers at the other.

2. Cutting, which included only sawyers and foremen.

3. Hauling, skidding, and loading, which included workers in mechanical transportation such as engineers and firemen as well as teamsters.

4. Crews for railroad construction and operation (connected with mechanical transportation).

5. Crews for road and railroad maintenance.

Logging and Milling. Logging operations, as distinct from sawmill operations, begin at the tree and end at the sawmill. They are carried on "in the woods," often many miles from the mill, and may extend over a large forest area. Various kinds of work may be in progress at the same time. One crew may be building or repairing roads while other crews are felling timbers or moving logs to a point accessible to transportation.

Milling operations have been, in general, more uniform than those in logging camps and have offered a greater variety of both work and products. The core of milling is the sawmill, with subsidiary specialized plants—planing mills, lath (or stave) mills, and shingle mills. By the early years of the twentieth century, kiln-drying of green lumber had become a common, if not universal, adjunct. Necessary for the upkeep of plant and machinery are the millwrights, carpenters, machinists, blacksmiths, engineers, firemen, oilers, and electricians, with helpers as needed. Furnishing protection against fire, always a great hazard, are the water-carriers, hydrant men, and watchmen.

In the mill itself men on the log deck place logs on the incline so that they move easily into place for the saw; "dimension men" scale the logs; others work as sawyers, edgers, trimmers, filers, and clean-up men. These workers are classified broadly as benchmen, machine hands, and laborers, but a man may work at different machines without any change in occupational title. Workers designated as "live-roll men" and "transfer men" may be assigned from time to time to almost any job where there is need to fill in basic units.

Employment in sawmilling has differed in many respects from that in logging, where operations are more subject to the vagaries of weather. Wages in logging have been lower and higher, payment by the piece more common, and payment in general more complicated. In addition to regular wage labor, the full pattern of employment has included contract labor, gang work, unpaid family labor and, in the latter part of the nineteenth century, prisoners leased from the state penitentiaries. In 1880, prisoners of the penitentiary system who were "contracted out" included 263 leased for woodcutting and sawmill labor, and 215 for cutting wood for the Texas and Pacific Railroad. On the fringe of the industry were 1,738 "chopping" as an aid to construction of railroads.[2]

By 1910 there were three types of camps. The permanent camp had a life span equivalent to the period required to log the timber within its reach. It might have shops for making repairs which housed considerable machinery. Portable camps were comprised of small cabins or shacks which could be loaded on flatcars and moved as the site of the camp was changed. Wheel camps were built on railroad trucks and were ordinarily better constructed than portable camps. Furthermore, since they were not subjected to the severe strains of moving, their "life expectancy" would easily have been from ten to fifteen years, with a salvage value from 5 per cent to 15 per cent of cost. As the cutting of trees used up the forests near towns such as Orange and Beaumont, camps necessarily moved into sections farther and farther removed from centers of population, and it was necessary for the employer to furnish facilities for board and lodging. Many camps had "cook houses," and sometimes the employer included board as a part of wages paid. In 1907 a writer, taking a look backward, stated that in the "early days" workers in the woods received $2.00 per day and board.[3] The federal investigation of 1915, already mentioned, did not report any "cook house" in Texas, though 50

[2] Biennial report, *Texas Prison System*, pp. 51, 53.

[3] *Southwest*, Vol. 14 (May, 1907), p. 42.

were reported by 13 other states, and no wages reported from Texas included board. As a rule, logging workers in Texas, like other workers in the lumber industry, lived in the area with their families. By 1940, camps for loggers were rarely found in the South.[4]

The woods "foman" was The Bull—or Bull of the Woods. When a man had a "run-in" with him he told the other workmen that he had "locked horns with The Bull." Often the man who had charge of the tram had "Midnight" added to his name, as "Midnight Charlie" or "Midnight Mike," because he went out to the job between midnight and daylight and got back between dark and midnight.[5] The term "flathead" was applied locally to a man who cut pine logs only. The word was no reflection on his brains. It came from a grub. When a pine tree is cut, the flat-headed borer lays eggs in or under the bark. The egg hatches a white grub with a flat brown head. The grub cuts out the inner bark and eats it. Since both the grub and the man cut pine, both are "flatheads."

Even after the advent of railroads the two-wheeled carts and the eight-wheeled wagons drawn by oxen and mules furnished transportation for work in the swamps and bottoms. The caretakers and drivers of the large number of animals used were an important group. In 1890, 4,508 animals were used. In 1900, 1,479 mules, 3,802 oxen, and 1,158 horses aided in the production of lumber,[6] and during the next five years their number remained substantially the same. A man who drove mules was a "skinner," and one who drove oxen was a "puncher" or a "bull puncher." Mr. O'Quinn, a lumber-town expatriate, looking back through three academic degrees, gives the following account of the "bull puncher" at work:

> One could hear the puncher perhaps two miles from the skidway. He was incessantly "singing" to his oxen. I use the word "singing" here as it is used in connection with European street vendors. The puncher came

[4] *Wages and Hours of Labor in the Lumber, Millwork, and Furniture Industries*, U.S. BLS Bulletin No. 225, 1916, pp. 147–192, cited hereinafter as U.S. BLS Bulletin No. 225.

[5] Reminiscences of men who have lived in "lumber towns," contained in a letter to the author from Louis O'Quinn.

[6] *U.S. Census, 1900, Manufacturing*, Pt. III, p. 867.

into hearing perhaps an hour before he reached the skidway. He progressed about two miles per hour. As he came on in, his voice and whip were more and more audible. Many of them had deep melodious voices. Some of them cursed the oxen along with all else. The driving vocabulary was entirely different from that of a skinner. I recall some of the vocabulary, but cannot recall the meaning exactly: *woa back up, yea back up, gee back up,* etc. The whip was very different from that of a skinner. The puncher kept it flying almost constantly—talking to the oxen and letting fly with that whip. One unaccustomed to the thing would have been certain that the puncher was beating the oxen unmercifully. Actually he was not even hitting them. He had the art of coming within one-eighth of an inch of the hide without touching it. Then the long leather whip had a tip on it (often) made of cotton rope, so that if he accidentally touched the oxen he would not cut the hide. But the main point here is that no one who has lived around such would ever forget how the puncher sounded—giving commands, cursing, and cracking the whip. If he was feeling well, he was at his best on the last load—which he got into the skidway, if he could, just as it got too dark for a man to see his way around. If he came in after dark, he was carrying a lantern. (You have no idea what an important thing a lantern was then and there.) Perhaps I have not made this clear: The puncher was using his voice and/or whip at least fifty per cent of the time. The result was something that one never forgets.

As already mentioned, there has been a great deal of contract work and "gang" organization connected with logging. Work under a contract system has existed from the earliest days; it was more suited to logging than to mill work, and the system was widely used in the production of railroad ties. In 1890, of 4,244 workers, approximately one-third were working for contractors.[7] At the turn of the century logging camps employing 3,421 wage-earners paid out for contract work a quarter of a million dollars.[8] By 1914 logging by contract had become general throughout the Southwest, and men were paid for "just what they do and no more."[9] By 1927 more than $1,100,000

[7] *U.S. Census, 1890, Manufacturing,* Pt. III, pp. 867–868.

[8] *U.S. Census, 1900, Manufacturing,* Pt. III, pp. 805–897. U.S. Census Bureau, *Census of Manufactures, 1905,* "Lumber and Timber Products," Bulletin No. 77, 1907, pp. 17 ff., cited hereinafter as U.S. Census Bulletin No. 77.

[9] *Southwest,* Vol. 21 (November, 1914), p. 13.

was paid for contract work, but two years later the amount had decreased by approximately one-third.[10] In 1939, logging camps and logging contractors not operating sawmills employed 532 wage-earners in 42 camps,[11] and mills combined with logging camps had 14,498 wage-earners. In 1950, 6,157 wage-earners were reported as working in logging camps.[12]

The Tie-maker. As railroads penetrated the eastern pines, they became an important transportation link between the camp and the mill, and railroad workers became an important segment of the labor force. Tram roads were built and operated by the producing companies or by organizations such as the Sabine Tram Company, whose interest was largely in hauling and marketing. An important outgrowth of the mutual dependence of railroads and lumber processing was the making of crossties. During the 1880's, when the major part of Texas railroad mileage was being laid, advertisements for tie-makers appeared regularly in newspapers of east Texas. Changes in the rate of pay are of interest: in July, 1881, the Houston and Texas Central offered 25 cents per tie.[13] Five years later, the East Line Road in January wanted 500 tie-makers at 15 cents per tie. In July, the Santa Fe tried to obtain 1,000 tie-workers by offering 20 cents per tie. Tie-makers were not always, probably seldom, connected with lumber mills or logging camps, and a contracting system for their services was fairly well standardized. The making of ties was a continuously important sector connected with Texas lumbering. In 1905 it was reported that workers in logging and timber companies cut 4 million railroad ties.[14]

Though the wooden tie, because of a resiliency which has not been duplicated in any other material, remains practically unchallenged, notable expansion of its use ended with the completion of the railroad-building period. Methods of treatment which prolonged the life of ties lessened the need for replacement, and creosoting plants became

[10] *U.S. Census, 1929, Manufacturing,* Vol. II, pp. 446–449.

[11] *U.S. Census, 1939, Manufacturing,* Vol. II, Pt. I, p. 510.

[12] *U.S. Census, 1950, Population—General Characteristics,* Tables 20, 43.

[13] Files of the *Chronicle* (Houston).

[14] U.S. Census Bulletin No. 77, p. 19.

important to the fabricating of ties and posts. Hewn ties were thought to shed water better than sawed ties and therefore to last longer, but the preference became less marked, and sawed ties were simply one of the several timber products coming from logging camps and sawmills.

Railroads bought ties through their purchasing departments—some in the open markets, others by contract with persons or firms that might buy them in surrounding territory and deliver them at determined stations. The contractor usually divided the area into territories which he let out to subcontractors. Some contractors "subbed" out their territories to merchants and they in turn obtained ties from farmers in the surrounding areas, who cut and hauled them to the railroad. The final purchaser had the right to reject "culls." Still other contractors bought ties from anyone who would ship to them from any point along the railroad. When local farmers produced ties as a by-product, it was inevitable that the use of unpaid family labor should be connected with such a method of production. The same labor and method cut, in addition, other timber: 235,950 fence posts and 40,027 telegraph and telephone poles in 1905.

Tie-cutters were the dramatic figures of the "piney woods" workers. They were more migratory than the mill hands, and individual achievement was a legendary feature of their work. Henry C. Goodnow commented:

> However farfetched the stories may be, they simply serve to prove that the hewers are an interesting folk. If I were a philosopher, an an-thro-what-you-call-it, or a student of men, minds and morals, I would go to the tie woods to conduct my investigations. . . . They are nomads, the very nature of their calling makes them so, and being nomads, they are spendthrifts. They wander to every point where railroads run and timber grows. They see the world, but like the rolling stone, they gather no moss. Very small causes start them traveling, and it is commonly said that a jug of whiskey and a copy of the *St. Louis Globe-Democrat* will break up any tie camp in the world. The *Globe-Democrat* is the tie makers bible. All the big jobs are advertised in it, and through it they keep posted on all the events in the labor world.[15]

[15] Henry C. Goodnow, "In the Tie Woods of Texas," *Southwest*, Vol. 12 (July, 1904), pp. 14–15; (August, 1904), pp. 24–25.

The "high roller" might hew as many as forty ties in a given day, but the regular worker set himself a task within the range of his strength and tried every day to come up with that number. Twenty or twenty-five was a good day's work. The farmer tie-maker, who cannot be reckoned as a "regular," usually lived at home and made up his own and his neighbor's timber. Apprentice tie-makers were called "thumpers" and might expect to become hewers in about two months.

Since tie camps were of necessity in the woods, a commissary and boardinghouse were often necessary. Unmarried tie-makers, who according to Goodnow led "a sort of hermit existence," might have tents and cooking outfits. Writing in 1904, he was probably remembering the earlier tie camps with kindly nostalgia:

There are tie makers, tie hewers, and tie hackers, and in Arkansas "tie gitter outs." They represent every class and grade of society and I have known an ex-preacher, ex-congressman, and an ex-convict, and a millionaire's son in disguise (a youthful tramp) do work side by side, and they were all very good tie makers. Men from every state in the Union, and from almost every civilized country on the globe are found in the camps, and the range of subjects discussed around the camp fires are quite as cosmopolitan as the contents of a New York Sunday newspaper. Further, they are discussed with almost equal intelligence. Philosophy, law, politics, history, medicine, love and adventures by field and flood, all come in for a share of attention.

There are no available records to support this description. The tie-worker, like other lumber workers, seems to have been predominantly native-born white. That there certainly were "men of mystery" from the outside world and young men who were temporarily employed on their way up, is borne out by the statement in a letter to the author from a man who has lived among them:

Many of them were young men of some learning who had set out to seek their fortune. Then there were men who had got into trouble elsewhere and had "hidden out" in the rough-and-ready sawmill towns. In the village in which I came up, there were two men about whom nobody knew one thing in the world, not even their wives. Both were well-educated. One was a wonderful musician, and the other was an accomplished civil engineer. My father always thought that they had got entangled with the law in the East and had hidden out at the sawmill.

In the late nineteenth century, tie-makers were comparatively well paid. In 1885, when sawyers were paid $1.50 per day, first-class tie-makers made $3.00. By the piece they were paid 15 cents or 16 cents, and 600 pieces per month was a good output.[16]

The Size of Plants. Though the lumber industry has for many reasons never been characterized by large establishments as such things are rated in industrial society, the plants in the Texas industry, when measured in terms of workers employed, have until fairly recently been comparatively large. In 1870 the average number of workers in a plant was less than 15 for the state, though there was, of course, wide variation. For instance, in Bastrop County it was 12, and in Montgomery County, with the largest number of plants, it was 93. In that year the manufacturing of lumber was the largest of three major industries in the state and was the only one complex enough to call for occupational breakdown.[17] Listed by craft were lumbermen, millwrights, sawyers, shingle-makers, woodcutters, and coopers. There were 446 sawmill operators, 326 woodcutters, and 421 mechanics.

By 1880 the number of workers in the industry had about doubled that of 1870, and "sawing lumber" was one of two industries employing more than 2,000 persons;[18] 2,200 were classified as mill operatives, 721 as woodchoppers, and 223 as lumbermen and raftsmen. There were 45 sawyers, a group who were then, and have remained, highly-skilled and highly-paid workers. By 1890 the Texas industry ranked ninth among the states in average number of employees.[19]

At the turn of the century the lumber industry in Texas ranked first in value of product, and reports were made for three branches of it.[20] Of a total of 7,924 wage-earners, 3,421 were in logging camps, 5,657 in sawmills, and 2,331 in planing mills, both independent and

[16] U.S. Census Bulletin No. 77.

[17] *U.S. Census, 1870, Industry and Wealth*, pp. 359–361.

[18] *U.S. Census, 1880, Manufactures*, Vol. II, pp. 179–180.

[19] *U.S. Census, 1890, Manufacturing Industries*, Pt. I, pp. 238–241.

[20] *U.S. Census, 1900, Manufactures*, Pt. II, pp. 816 ff., 863–864.

in combination. There is of course considerable duplication. There were 36 tie camps and timber camps. The average-size sawmill, measured by number of wage-earners employed, was greater than the 7 for the nation. Five years later, though lumber processing had fallen to third place in the state in value of product, it was still the leader in the use of industrial labor.[21]

For the many reasons noted above, the decade ending in 1910 marks the end of an era. In taking the thirteenth census the U.S. Bureau of Census used a new index of occupations, one more revealing of work divisions. In that year also census reports include a supplement for the state of Texas. Moreover, the Thirty-first Texas Legislature established a Bureau of Labor Statistics, which began operation in 1909. Its function was to "collect, assort, systematize and present in biennial reports to the Governor statistical details relating to all departments of labor in Texas." Like many another report, the first report of the Bureau carried the statement: "The Legislature did not provide sufficient funds to carry on the work in the most efficient manner." Though it was then and has been throughout its history seriously handicapped by inadequate funds, it has always, especially during its early years, published important information "bearing upon the commercial, social, educational and sanitary conditions of employees and their families, . . . the labor of women and children and the number of hours exacted of them."[22] The Bureau also attempted to enforce the Child Labor Law, passed in 1903. Furthermore, by 1910 local protest against the conditions of wage-earners in factories and on farms was becoming articulate under the leadership of the Social Democratic Party. The prime centers of unrest were among agricultural tenants and laborers and among the wage-earners in the northeastern Texas timber industry. An aggressive attempt to organize the lumber workers was made through the Brotherhood of Timber Workers, a movement discussed later in this study.

A profile of the labor force in the industry processing lumber and timber in 1910 may be drawn from federal and state reports. In the

[21] U.S. Census Bulletin No. 77, p. 19.

[22] Texas Bureau of Labor Statistics, First Biennial Report, 1909–10, pp. 5, 34–64, 166–181.

ten years preceding, the number of wage-earners had doubled.[23] The 799 establishments employed 23,500 wage-earners, a third of the industrially-employed workers in the state. "Wage-earners" constituted 91 per cent of the total employed in the industry, compared with 83 per cent of persons engaged in all manufacture. Only three other industries—brick and tile with 90.6 per cent, machine and repair shops for railroads with 92.9 per cent, and cotton goods with 97.4 per cent—had as high as 90 per cent of their employees in the wage-earning group. Of nonwage-earners employed in all manufacturing industries, 9.4 per cent were proprietors and officials and 7.6 per cent were clerks. Since lumber firms had 6.1 per cent proprietors and officials and only 2.9 per cent clerks, it seems that they were comparatively large and did not have a great amount of clerical work to be done.

The following figures give the pattern of production workers by classification. For the mills were: laborers, 14,806; semiskilled operators, 968; sawyers, 718; and for the "woods" were: lumbermen and raftsmen, 2,286; woodchoppers and tie-cutters, 1,965; teamsters and haulers, 538; foremen and overseers, 113; on turpentine farms, 204 (189 male, 15 female); distilling turpentine, 46. The 4,902 workers listed under agriculture, forestry, and animal husbandry as lumbermen, raftsmen, and woodchoppers were probably to a large extent tie-makers. The spectacular and the dramatic in the feats of individual tie-cutters was still recognized. On several occasions the Jasper *Newsboy* publicized the claims of J. H. Mitchell to the championship among tie-workers.[24] He made 600 ties in eleven and one-half days with only one cull in the lot.

The workers were employed in comparatively large plants when measured by volume of business also; 63 per cent were in plants producing from $100,000 to $1 million of product, while the comparable proportion for all industries in the state was 50 per cent. There were also large groups in Texas camps: one-tenth in businesses with more than 500 employees; approximately 60 per cent in those employing more than 100.

[23] *U.S. Census, 1910, Supplement for Texas,* pp. 776–782.

[24] August 10 and September 13, 1910; July 12, 1911.

TABLE 5: Distribution of Plants According to Number of Wage-earners, 1910

Size of Plant by Number of Wage-earners	*Number of Wage-earners*	*Percentage of Wage-earners*
1–50	6,880	29.3
51–100	2,538	10.8
101–250	8,179	34.8
251–500	3,617	15.4
501–1,000	2,304	9.8

Source: U.S. Census, 1910; Supplement for Texas, p. 783.

Of the firms, 574 employed fewer than 20 workers, and considerably more than one-half of all firms were smaller than the average size in 1890. More than one-third of all workers were in plants employing from 101 to 250 wage-earners, while one-fourth of wage-earners in all industries were in such plants; 4 per cent worked in plants employing from one to 5 wage-earners. The average number of wage-earners per establishment in the lumber industry was 29, compared with 15 for all industries. The second highest average number was for foundry and machine-shop products, with 20 per establishment.

The first report made by the Texas Bureau (1909/10) included more than 1,600 employees in the lumber industry. One establishment in Jefferson County and one in Chambers County were small, employing fewer than 75 wage-earners. But figures for large plants were given also:

County	*Number of Establishments*	*Number Employed*
Newton	1	252
Orange	2	630
Panola	1	130
Polk	2	427
Walker	1	251

The Bureau undertook an extensive opinion survey of workers in the state, and it is of some interest that the views of no one from the lumber industry are included in the report. The Bureau listed union labor organizations in the state, but no organization among workers in the industry was reported, though the preceding decade had seen attempts to organize accompanied by much unrest.

By 1929, lumbering—with 21,000 workers—was one of two industries in the state employing more than 15,000 people.[25] In addition to those in the mills, there were 5,500 lumbermen, raftsmen, woodchoppers, and sawyers; 3,500 in lumber and furniture production; 1,700 preserving wood; and 1,100 making wooden boxes. During the preceding decade the number of wage-earners engaged in the primary processing of lumber and timber products had changed little, though the number of establishments reporting had decreased from 457 to 325, an indication of consolidation. There was an increase in the number of wage-earners in planing mills, those making wooden boxes remained about the same, and those in cooperage had decreased by more than one-half. The distilling of turpentine and rosin furnished employment for less than half the number employed in the Sabine area of Texas and Louisiana in 1919.

Toward the end of the thirties the forests of eastern Texas supported industries employing 15 per cent of all those in manufacturing industries in the state, and 4.4 per cent of the total employed by the nation's industry.[26] Just before the beginning of the Second World War, the number of workers employed by the lumber industry was the smallest since 1909. In the basic operations, more than 6,000 were raftsmen, lumbermen, and woodcutters.

In 1947 an intensive search to locate small mills produced a total of 30,694 workers, of whom 29,354 were production workers.[27] The pattern of employment showed great variety, though all except 9,000 were employed in sawmills and planing mills and in lath-making. An auxiliary activity, the making of furniture and paper and paper products, employed more than 40,000 workers. Of 915 establishments, 644 were planing mills and sawmills, 140 were doing specialized millwork, and 20 were preserving wood. As mentioned in another con-

[25] *U.S. Census, 1929, Manufacturing,* Pt. II (Vol. VII), pp. 444–538, 1562–1570.

[26] *Monthly Labor Review,* Vol. 50 (June, 1940), p. 1337.

[27] *Biennial Census of Manufactures,* 1947, Vol. III, p. 586.

nection, in 1947 there were 76 plants employing more than 100 workers, but of the total number of establishments, 574 employed fewer than 20 workers, and considerably more than half the plants reported upon employed a smaller number of workers than did the average-size plant in 1890. Only establishments engaged in handling food and related products reported a large number of plants employing more than 100 workers.

In 1950, wage-earners employed in the production of furniture, lumber, and wood products constituted 1.3 per cent of those engaged in the manufacturing of nondurable products—an increase of about 10,000 over the figure of 1940. Approximately 31,000 were still employed in the basic activities of logging and work in the mills. In 1955, a total of 1,044 establishments reported 21,000 workers.[28] Of these, 432 were in the production of lumber and basic products, and 259, employing 1,618 workers, were logging camps and contractors. Small plants were still a characteristic feature, for about half of the establishments had from one to 4 employees. But of 47 plants with more than 100 employees, 2 had from 500 to 1,000. Only 8 logging camps employed 20 or more. Three years later, employment in the manufacturing of timber and wood products showed a decrease of 7 per cent from the 23,100 employed a year earlier.[29]

The Operator. As an employer, the operator of a lumber-processing establishment often performed various functions. Not only was he the source of income, but he might be banker, landlord, community chest, storekeeper, and policeman. The operations of Alexander Gilmer, owner of several sawmills and lumberyards, were probably representative. Sometimes a worker would request that part of his wages go to pay off his debt to another person:

MR. A. GILMER

Please deduct one half of my wages each week until further notice and pay the same to Teague and Rim.

his
STEM *X* FOLEY
mark

[28] *U.S. Census, 1950*, Table 4.
[29] Reports of Texas Employment Office, 1958.

MR. A. GILMER

You will please hold of my wages $1.00 each week and give the same to C. H. —— until he has received in this way the sum of $19.00 and charge the same to me.

his
JOHN *X* MORRIS
mark

Sometimes the employer collected debts for outsiders. Gilmer collected amounts owed by his workers to Houston creditors for 3 cents on the dollar. Records for 1906 show that the Lemon Lumber Company paid $15.30 in taxes for Wilkerson, $4.01 for Jim Peveto, and $1.75 each (poll taxes?) for sixteen others. Fines also were paid to the proper authorities and deducted from wages.

Fares were advanced to workers going to jobs in towns away from the centers. Fares to the new town of Brookeland, at $2.55 each, were paid for men sent from Orange, and in some cases a wife was included at the same rate. The results were sometimes disappointing. In 1906, Gilmer notified the manager of the mill at Brookeland that he had sent 27 Negro and 15 white workers. A week later he writes:

> Please advise how many men we sent got there and give us names of those who did not and of any who left owing you. I understand some of them are back here and it might be they will go to Lemon and in that event we can get even with them.

At the same time, he sent a notice to the Lemon Lumber Company, a Gilmer plant, in which he stated, "Should any of the following men go to work for you we wish you would try to collect $2.55 for us."[30]

The Industrial Commission of 1912–15 found a marked tendency in the South toward the development of camps—especially those which were more or less permanently located near sawmills—into a "peculiar type" of town called "lumber towns." The development was the outgrowth of having logging crews carried to and from work locations many miles from the town on trains pulled by a donkey engine. The Commission found that, instead of improving the labor situation, the practice made it worse because it provided an abundant supply of cheap labor.

[30] Gilmer Letter Press, No. 77, pp. 272, 277.

In the latter half of the nineteenth century the lumber operator was commonly an individual entrepreneur, but corporate organizations began increasingly to displace the lumberman, not in number of firms but in the volume of business done. A characteristic feature remained, however: the small plant. In 1909 the 23 per cent of firms that were corporations produced 75 per cent of value of product and employed 75 per cent of the workers. In 1950 half the firms were still small—very small, having fewer than 5 employees. The large number of establishments in the early days meant many owner-operators in milling and logging, and there was undoubtedly a close personal relation between the employer and worker. But the growth of corporate organization brought a change, and even the "brass" at the plant was an employee. The owners were absentee stockholders living in one of the marketing centers—St. Louis, New Orleans, Houston, Beaumont. Managerial representatives of the company now formed the contacts between employer and workers. Although historically the same change in many industries was a major step toward clarifying the meaning of the job-wage system, it proved not so in the Southern pineries. The corporate employer came to exist in an already crystallized environment: a plantation system that had borrowed those features of an industrial setup which best served its purpose. The lumber town was no longer the abode of an owner and his "hands." It was the domain of a corporation.

CHAPTER FOUR

Children are the basis of the State; as they live or die, as they thrive or are ill-nourished, as they are intelligent or ignorant, so fares the State. How do the children of American workers fare?—U.S. COMMISSION ON INDUSTRIAL RELATIONS, 1916

A PECULIAR PEOPLE

TIMBERING in the Sabine pines lacked the drama of the Pacific Northwest and the Lakes states. The yellow-pine forests of Texas were brought into the great lumber empires of the nation after they had become names to conjure with in politics, finance, and industry. The addition of a few million acres to holdings already beyond the comprehension of even the owning corporations could stir little interest. The colorful denizen of the Northern woods—the lumberjack with his deeds of derring-do, his outrageous flaunting of accepted codes of conduct, and the flavor of the exotic brought from alien lands—is not a hero of Texas legends. Compared with the cowboy of picturesque skills and songs, and later the oil-field worker, the timber worker of eastern Texas sounds dull and colorless. His work in the Southern pines has never become a part of the legendary past of the nation. For one thing, it is not past. The actuality of the present mocks any romance that might be generated about the worker and his work.

The foot-loose, happy-go-lucky migrant of lumberjack tradition was a transient in the pineries of the Sabine area. There workers were not only native-born Americans but they were born within the area of the Southern "piney woods." They married girls from the pine area and their children played in pine-tree shade. They were family men who lived with their families. In the census of 1915, not a single instance of wages with board was reported from Texas, a situation true of only one other state.

Amazingly enough, there has been little interest in folk attitudes and their expression in the world of the Sabine lumber workers. But there is unquestionably a rich and untapped store of folklore concerning those who have lived in a world isolated and apart. The primary interest of this study, however, is not in the spectacular and the dramatic, intriguing though it is. It is concerned instead with the commonplace, the basis of daily living.

The Native-born Worker. In 1880, of the 2,182 sawmill and planing mill operatives in Texas, 2,119—all but 63—were native-born; of the 944 lumbermen, raftsmen, and woodchoppers, 860 were native-born.[1] In 1890, of a total employment of 6,400, only 336 were recorded as foreign-born. Almost half of them were in sawmills and planing mills, and 146 of them could not speak English. According to country of origin, they were distributed as follows: 57 Germans, 41 Britons, 26 Canadians, 16 Irishmen, 11 Scandinavians, and 183 from undesignated countries.[2]

In 1910 the Texas Bureau attempted to secure information about the nativity and race of persons employed in industrial establishments. The attempt was vitiated, however, by the failure to obtain significant information. Employees were generally identified as "American" or "miscellaneous." The terms used are, however, revealing. "American" evidently excluded all except well-established Anglo-Saxon stock. One can only be intrigued by a firm in Cherokee County employing 173 "miscellaneous" and no Americans (could they have been Indians from the nearby reservation?); by a firm in Liberty County with no Americans and 110 miscellaneous; and by

[1] *U.S. Census, 1880, Population,* Vol. I, Table XXXIX, p. 847.

[2] *U.S. Census, 1890, Statistics of Population,* Vol. I, Table 15, pp. 430–432; Table 33, pp. 657–660; Pt. II, Vol. II, pp. 612–613.

one in Nacogdoches County with one Italian woman and 124 miscellaneous. The federal census reported the following distribution of the 22,281 male workers employed in lumbering in Texas:[3]

	Native-born White	*Negroes*	*Foreign-born White*	*Other*	*Total*
Lumbermen, raftsmen, woodchoppers	2,521	1,351	831	2	4,890
Sawmills and planing mills					
Laborers	6,714	7,216	766	9	14,705
Semiskilled operatives	1,333	587	43	5	1,968
Sawyers	538	155	11	14	718

The "other" were probably Indians from the Alabama-Coushatta Reservation in Polk County. Foreign-born whites were predominantly Mexican and German, but there were 100 Italians each in Polk County and in Bowie County, 72 in Angelina, and 76 in Jasper. In Newton County there were 75 Austrians, and in Grimes County, 41 Hungarians and 127 Russians.

The natal homogeneity of workers in the industry is further empha-

	1900 *Number of Foreign-born*	*Percentage*	1909 *Number of Foreign-born*	*Percentage*
Angelina	171	1.3	225	1.3
Bowie	271	1.0	348	1.0
Cass	41	0.2	39	0.1
Cherokee	146	0.6	120	0.4
Grimes	841	3.2	606	2.9
Harrison	295	0.9	348	0.9
Jasper	19	0.3	336	2.4
Liberty	191	2.4	334	3.1
Marion	96	0.9	72	0.7
Montgomery	198	1.3	217	1.3
Newton	77	1.1	267	2.5
Polk	104	0.7	425	2.4
Shelby	48	0.2	71	0.3

[3] *U.S. Census, 1910, Supplement for Texas*, Table VII, pp. 602 ff.

sized by the small number of foreign-born in the counties in which lumber production was the important industry.[4]

Within the period, the foreign-born population in the state had increased from 5.8 per cent to 6.2 per cent. Since only 4 of the counties listed show an equal increase, it is interesting that in Newton County the proportion had doubled, in Polk it had tripled, and in Jasper it was seven times as great. In 1919, of a total of 4,600 lumbermen, raftsmen, and woodchoppers, 1,040 were foreign-born white; of 11,615 sawmill and planing mill "laborers," 809 were foreign-born white; of 884 sawyers, 11 were foreign-born white. Of 1,865 semiskilled operators in sawmills and planing mills, 73 were foreign-born white.[5]

The Negro in the Industry. For three-quarters of a century the lumber workers of Texas have not only been native-born, they have also been predominantly white. In 1950, only 37 per cent of workers in logging and 36 per cent of those in sawmills were Negroes, a proportion that had increased slightly since 1940. In 1880, the proportion of Negroes had been slightly less. The following figures show the number of Negro males employed in lumber production between 1890 and 1950:

Year	*Total Employed*	*Negroes*
1890	6,350	2,660
1910	22,281	9,309
1940	36,000	9,119
1950	30,912	13,043

The attitude of employers in the lumber industry toward Negro workers was curiously ambivalent—not to suggest that the attitude was either original or unique. Negro workers were, as a rule, in the lowest-paid groups, and they had little opportunity to rise to the highest-paid jobs. But the implicit assumption that Negroes were satisfied with the situation is contradicted by the fact that it was they who created labor shortages. In September, 1907, *Southwest* noted that many mills on the Trinity and Brazos Rivers were closed down

[4] Compiled from *U.S. Census, 1910, Supplement for Texas*, pp. 602–649.
[5] *U.S. Census, 1919, Compendium for Texas*, Vol. IV, Table 25, pp. 1022 ff.

temporarily because the Negro laborers "had gone cotton picking where they could make more." It noted further that operators in the Sabine area were trying out Mexican workers in sawmills. They were better workers than Negroes and "more satisfactory to handle."[6] At the same time a report of the federal Bureau of Labor stated that since 1900, Mexican immigrants had been working as unskilled hands as far from the border as Chicago, Iowa, Wyoming, and San Francisco. But, it added, "they compete little if any with what is called 'white labor' in the Southwest."[7] No mention is made of the use of Mexican labor in the east Texas lumber industry. Certainly the going wage would not have drawn Mexican immigrants in large numbers from the more highly-paid work in the mines of west Texas, New Mexico, and Colorado.

The St. Louis *Lumberman* pontificated that "there is a limit to the amount of wages that can be paid with safety to colored laborers around sawmills and wood camps. Too much pay breeds discontent and idleness among them,"[8] though at about the same time it was mourning the "great scarcity of labor impending." In regard to attempts to secure immigrants not primarily Mexican for the South, *Southwest* copied from the Nashville *Tradesman* a somewhat more penetrating statement: "There is under all this cry of getting a 'share' for the South of those immigrants now flooding our shores, a subtle and well covered plan to supplant the Negro with foreign labor."[9] The *Tradesman* objected not to the immigrant who came to the South as a farmer, but only to

> . . . those who will come purely as laborers and who are intended to supplant the Negro. The trouble with the Negro is not his own so much as it is that of the South. He has been left to pick up trades and acquire skill pretty much in his own way. Let it be said to the Negro's credit that wherever a serious effort has been made to teach him skill and efficiency in any field of labor, he has responded with a degree of aptness that is little short of marvellous.

[6] Vol. 15 (August, 1907), p. 42.

[7] Victor Clark, *Mexican Labor*, U.S. Bureau of Labor Bulletin No. 78, 1908, p. 466.

[8] Vol. 45 (April 1, 1910), p. 65.

[9] Vol. 13 (June, 1905), p. 5.

With the expansion of Northern industry after 1914, Negroes migrated in large numbers to Northern cities for "ridiculously high wages." Companies offered not only high pay but transportation. The St. Louis *Lumberman* estimated that 50 per cent of Southern lumber workers had left and said that there was a great scarcity of labor in Southern mills. Texas mills were less affected than those in other Southern states because of the smaller proportion of Negroes employed. Nevertheless, after 600 had left Houston in one week of June, 1917, action was taken to stop migration. At one point the sheriff and police chief forced the railroad agent to abandon plans to ship large numbers of Negro laborers. Prepaid orders for transportation were canceled, for it was thought the companies could not "trust individuals with transportation money."[10]

The winter of 1918 was severe and a writer in the *Lumberman* felt that it would not be difficult to persuade the Negroes to return if "certain entirely practicable inducements which should not be especially formidable were offered. The Negroes, although ignorant, will probably know enough to demand that certain hardships to which they have been subjected will have to be eliminated." He thought that they must have more nearly habitable quarters, commissaries that would not take all their earnings, and that life should offer them some excuse for "even a nigger to live."[11]

The conditions of the migrating Negroes led to the establishment of a Division of Negro Economics in the U.S. Department of Labor. Investigation brought forth the suggestion that there was not only "the Northern pull but the Southern push sending the Negro out of the South." The North, needing labor sorely, "sought it where it was available.... One of the long-standing griefs of the Negro is the small pay he receives in the South."[12] Several years later Carter G. Woodson, considering the situation, concluded that "the fundamental causes of the unrest were economic. It is highly probable that the

[10] Vol. 60 (July 1, 1917), p. 13; (Aug. 15, 1917), p. 20.

[11] Vol. 61 (April 18, 1918), p. 44.

[12] J. H. Dillard, *Negro Migration, 1916–17*, U.S. Dept. of Labor, Division of Negro Economics, 1919, pp. 100–103.

Negroes would not be leaving the South today if they were treated as men."[13]

Following the First World War a federal Employment Bureau was set up to direct the former servicemen and workers from contracting war industries into areas and jobs where they could be used efficiently.

The Southern Pine Association announced its willingness to cooperate in any movement to bring Negroes back to the South. It offered to advance the transportation costs for any number of Negroes destined for work at any particular place, the amount to be refunded by the employer when the Negro arrived. "The Association is taking this stand in order to generally relieve the labor situation throughout the State and to lessen the difficulty faced by pine lumbermen because of the great scarcity of Negro labor."

But toward the federal Bureau, the Southern Pine Association and leading Texas lumber operators expressed unequivocal opposition.[14] It was asserted that the peculiar labor condition in the South, especially in the lumber industry, would be hampered rather than improved by such a government bureau. J. H. Kirby, president of the Lumber Manufacturers' Association, speaking to and for the Southern pine manufacturers, charged the Department of Labor with sending carpetbaggers into the South to interfere in industrial conditions and forcing men to join the AF of L regardless of their wishes. He called on the Department to withdraw, to quit sending emissaries to the South, and to cease interfering in the South's industry. He told dramatically of refusing to sit with a Negro in a Department of Labor conference. He further charged that the Department of Labor was trying to organize the labor forces at the sawmills—particularly among the Negro element—in Alabama, Mississippi, Florida, and Texas.

About five years later Frank Tannenbaum expressed a contrary and certainly debatable judgment that the South needed "a sufficient

[13] *A Century of Negro Migration*, p. 169.

[14] *Lumberman* (St. Louis), Vols. 63 and 64 (July 21, 1919), pp. 27–28; (April 7, 1919), p. 15; (Aug. 11, 1919), p. 82.

migration to make the Negro a valued possession by the South and compel the welcoming of an immigration of foreigners." The South, he said, needed the foreigner for its spiritual as well as its economic well-being. It needed him to take the place of migrating Negroes, to develop industry, and to break the emotional concentration upon Negroes. "If the foreigner came in large numbers, the South would learn to fear and hate him" and "fear and hate are healthy things in a community" if they are not too single in their aim, for a community must have a scapegoat and a diversity of scapegoats is better than one. Dealing with foreigners would call for greater pliancy of temper than dealing with Negroes, and the pressure of foreign attitudes toward the Negro would break the customary pattern. The South, he concluded, did not have trouble enough and immigration would give it more conflict.[15]

In 1910, of 7,958 Negroes in the mills, 7,216 were laborers, and there were no Negro sawyers or operatives in sawmills and planing mills. In 1940, of the approximately 10,600 nonwhite wage-earners, a few more than 9,000 were laborers. Of 1,213 working in logging camps, all but 84 were laborers; 68 had attained the position of operatives. In sawmills and planing mills, 6,348 out of 7,829 were laborers. Twenty years later the number of Negroes employed had increased, but their social and economic position remained unchanged.[16] Of a total of 12,148 male laborers employed in the lumber and furniture industry, 5,545 were Negroes and 24 others were listed as nonwhite.

On the eve of the Second World War, of 34,500 workers employed in the lumber industry, 10,600 were classified as nonwhite. Of 1,297 Negroes employed in logging, all but 84 were still classified as laborers; 63 had attained the position of operatives. Of the total 7,862 paid Negro employees in sawmills and planing mills, 6,348 were still laborers; 969 were operatives and associated workers; 432 were craftsmen, firemen, and associated workers. The following figures give the classification of all workers by color and sex:[17]

[15] *Darker Phases of the South*, p. 173.

[16] *U.S. Census, 1929, Population*, Vol. IV, pp. 1562–1570.

[17] *U.S. Census, 1940, Texas*, pp. 546, 557, 577.

	White	Nonwhite	Male	Female
Logging	3,830	1,305	5,087	48
Sawmills and planing mills	13,372	7,894	21,060	206

Of the females, 8 in logging and 32 in mills were nonwhite. Of Negroes employed in sawmills and planing mills, 33 were employers on own account. Of the privately employed, 36 were in the managerial, professional, and clerical groups; 432 were skilled workers, and 969 were semiskilled; 6,410 were laborers and other unskilled workers. In logging, 195 were employers on own account and 5 were unpaid family laborers. Privately employed were 14 managers and skilled workers, 68 semiskilled, and 1,215 laborers.

In May, 1943, an executive order reaffirmed the policy of the United States that there should be "no discrimination in the employment of any person in war industries . . . by reason of race, creed, color or national origin." Shortly after, as a part of the program to distribute labor and stabilize wages, the National War Labor Board ruled in a case brought before it that wage classifications based on difference in races were invalid and ordered that equal pay be given to Negroes and whites for equal work. The company in the case was ordered to reclassify workers, giving a wage increase in each classification. Resulting increases to Negroes were made "with regard simply to the democratic formula of equal pay for work equal in quantity and quality in the same classification."[18]

By 1950, there had been an increase of more than 6,000 in the number of persons employed in logging and in sawmills and planing mills, but the proportion of Negroes was little changed. They represented 37 per cent of workers in logging and 36 per cent of those in sawmills.[19]

Women and Children in the Industry. Though the employment of women and children has been reported in each decade—11 in 1890, for instance—women have never played any significant part in the lumber industry as paid workers. The system of labor was so organized, however, as to permit women to assist as unpaid family

[18] *Monthly Labor Review*, Vol. 57 (July, 1943), pp. 3–33.

[19] *U.S. Census, 1950, Population—General Characteristics*, Texas, Table 3.

laborers or as aids to contract workers and piece workers. By the twentieth century the Congressional Commission on Industrial Relations heard the statement that in Harrison County "mothers with little babies have to get crossties for the railroad company for bread."[20] A song sung at east Texas play parties gives another glimpse:

> Old Joe Clark is a-cuttin' ties
> Old Lady Clark is a-haulin'
> Little Joe Clark in the middle of the road
> Is killin' hisself a-bawlin'.

Owing to the way tie-cutting was conducted, it was probably in this phase of lumbering that much "unpaid family labor" was used. Any figures concerning workers in this group are open to question. We may assume that few if any were adult male workers. In 1940 the figure given was 161, most of them young boys and youths. Only 16 were female—8 in logging, of whom one was a Negress, and 8 in sawmills and planing mills. Under the category of women and children the 1920 report listed 93 semi-skilled operatives, 153 laborers, 4 laborers in turpentine distilleries, and 18 lumbermen, raftsmen, and woodchoppers. Thirty years later 0.6 per cent of the 44,000 persons employed in furniture, lumber, and wood products were women, 2,000 of whom were in urban areas. In 1940, women in the industry accounted for less than one per cent of all employed women in the state, and in 1950 for about 2 per cent. Occupationally they were distributed:

	1940	*1950*
Laborers (sawmills and planing mills)	33	61
Lumbermen, raftsmen, and woodchoppers	47	101
Sawyers	4	56
Operatives (planing mills and sawmills)	15	95

Defining the term "children" as a part of the labor supply has been an evolutionary process ever since the days when an Englishman stated that seven years is the maximum age at which a child should expect to be supported, and Parliamentary action limited the work

[20] *Report of Commission on Industrial Relations*, Vol. 28, 1915, p. 9277.

hours of children to twelve per day. But census reports have isolated groups of workers by year from ten to seventeen years of age. That the reported number of employed wage-earners at these ages did not cover the total number working in industries closely tied to the family would seem to be beyond question. But since our interests do not lie primarily in the completeness of published figures, official statements are here accepted.

In 1880, 9 boys from ten to fifteen years of age worked as woodchoppers, lumbermen, or raftsmen, and 50 boys in that age group worked as sawmill and planing mill operatives in Texas.[21] Ten years later, 31 children between these ages worked in the lumber industry at jobs classified as "operatives," skilled and unskilled.[22] Fifteen years later the number had changed little.

Reports around 1905 indicate that child labor was characteristic of small factories.[23] A national survey found no children under sixteen and no women sixteen or over in the largest factories, though 40 per cent of all men employed were in these factories. That youthful workers were much more common in Southern plants than in Western ones is shown by figures regarding distribution. The largest numbers of children under sixteen years of age employed in the lumber industry were 230 in Arkansas and 226 in Louisiana; the smallest were 15 in Michigan, 18 in Minnesota, and 48 in California.

Texas passed a child labor law in 1903, but the agency charged with its enforcement reported that "the age limit prescribed by the law under which children are not permitted to be employed is shown fully below the standard of practically every other state in the union."[24] It stated further that public sentiment had changed in recent years, largely owing to the efforts of organized labor, undoubtedly supplemented by those of the general public and particular women who had an interest in the welfare of future generations.

At the time the first inspection was made by the Texas Bureau, the federal census reported that 1.3 per cent of the 23,518 workers in

[21] *U.S. Census, 1880, Manufactures*, pp. 180, 790, 840, 847.

[22] *U.S. Census, 1890, Manufactures*, Pt. III, pp. 615–842.

[23] U.S. Census Bulletin No. 77.

[24] Texas Bureau of Labor Statistics, *First Biennial Report*, p. 9.

lumber and products in Texas were under sixteen years of age, compared with 1.8 per cent in all industries. The actual number of youthful wage-earners was larger in the lumber industry than in any other, though the proportion was larger in four others. There were 58 lumbermen, raftsmen, and woodchoppers, 196 laborers in sawmills and planing mills, and 16 semiskilled operatives between ten and thirteen years of age, and there were 81 lumbermen, raftsmen, and woodchoppers, 450 laborers in sawmills and planing mills, 2 sawyers, and 56 semiskilled operatives between fourteen and fifteen years old.[25] The Texas Bureau found 50 children under sixteen working in one plant in Polk County. In the following year it reported that 55 children under sixteen had been removed from lumber-processing plants, almost a third of the total number of children removed from industry in the state. Both in 1913 and 1914, 53 children were removed from lumber mills and box and basket factories—about a fifth of the total number of children taken out of industry.[26] During the war years, the scarcity of labor for lumber mills, as noted already, led to the hiring of "stripling" boys.

Young persons were employed as signal men (whistlepunks) and wood bucks; to pile brush and remove grabs or tongs from logs; as laborers in camp railroad construction; as handy men and as fire wardens. They were employed in sawmills in the South as doffers, block-setters, log-turners and edgermen, stackers, and packers. The unofficial functions of some Negro children—and the amused tolerance with which they were accepted—are evident from the description of an observer:

> They are persistently in evidence during the middle of each working day in every sawmill town of the South. They are an almost indispensable object to the manufacture of lumber—these little "dinner carriers" as they called them. So dependable is their appearance on the roads to the mill at 11:30 each day, that clocks can be regulated by their comings and goings. They are a motley lot, ranging from six to sixteen, of both sexes. Some of them are not much larger than the baskets they carry, others, more enterprising, pushing homemade wagons with three or four dinner

[25] *U.S. Census, 1910, Supplement for Texas*, p. 777.

[26] Texas Bureau of Labor Statistics, *Biennial Report*, p. 141.

pails. Rain or shine, hot or cold, the same crowd makes the trip every day for $1.00 per month for each pail or basket carried.

If it is "nigger shootin' " time, every little "pic" has his nigger shooter; if it is marble time, great are the games that go on while their respective relatives or employers are eating dinner, and so on. If one boy makes a new whistle, horn or other noisemaking affair, it is a safe bet that to-morrow the gang will all have them.

One wonders, too, during the cane grinding season, how many tons of sugar are consumed by these little "grinders" for, as they go along the streets, they chew cane. Many of them pulling it with their teeth.

"Pecan time," as they call it, they are like squirrels. You cannot pass one who is not eating pecans, and so they thrive and grow fat, never hearing of the regularity of eating. And seldom it is that a Negro child dies—in spite of the fact that many eat as they please and when they please. They are exposed to cold and rains in the winter, to heat and sun in the summer. They fight, swim, fish, go berrying, etc.; but an accident to one of them is a rarity. Watching them pass, one wonders what would happen in one big plant, if they decided to strike at 11:30![27]

A child's Utopia! But a few comments suggest themselves. First, a query: was no one concerned in 1919 that these children were not in school? Second, even without acceptable vital statistics for the state of Texas at the time this was written, facts well known make it a strain on credulity to believe "seldom it is that a Negro child dies." Lastly, considering the wages paid to workers, it is incredible that these children were paid a dollar a month per basket.

In 1927/28 agents of the state Bureau visited 825 homes in 16 lumber camps. Of 3,610 persons, more than half were under twenty-one years of age.[28] Of 1,078 children of school age, 929 attended school during the year; 149 had never been enrolled in school.

By 1920, following a national trend, the number of children employed in Texas lumber and timber industries had decreased greatly—to 1.6 per cent compared to the 4.5 per cent of ten years earlier.[29]

[27] "If the Pickaninnies Should Go on Strike," *Southwest*, Vol. 26 (April 15, 1919), p. 14.

[28] *Biennial Report*, pp. 44–45; 120–125.

[29] *U.S. Census, 1919*, Vol. IV, Table 17, pp. 584–585.

In sawmills and planing mills (including box factories) and in logging camps their numbers were:

Employed in Mills

	LABORERS		SEMISKILLED	
	Male	*Female*	*Male*	*Female*
Ages 10 to 13	26	3	2	0
14	38	2	6	0
15	113	1	20	2
16	266	6	30	3
17	378	6	60	1
Total	821	18	118	6

Employed in Logging (Lumbermen, Raftsmen, Woodcutters)

	Male	*Female*
Ages 10 to 13	45	3
14	19	0
15	41	0
16	61	0
17	114	0
Total	280	3

Ten years later (1930) there was a total of 853 male and female workers between ten and seventeen years of age. Of this number, 48 were females, 21 of whom were laborers in sawmills and planing mills. Male employees showed the following distribution:[30]

	10–13	*14*	*15*	*16*	*17*	*Total*
Lumbermen, raftsmen, and woodchoppers	13	18	25	39	68	163
Operatives						
Sawmills and planing mills	4	3	13	17	43	80
Other lumber and furniture mfg.	2	. .	5	19	28	54
Laborers						
Sawmills and planing mills	14	9	53	127	237	440
Other lumber and furniture mfg.	2	1	9	16	40	68

The Children's Bureau, studying occupational hazards for young

[30] *U.S. Census, 1929, Population*, Vol. IV, p. 1608.

workers in 1930, found that at the time Texas was producing 4.7 per cent of the national lumber production, it employed 3.3 per cent of minors between ten and seventeen years old, 5.3 per cent of those from ten to fifteen, and 2.7 per cent of those sixteen and seventeen years of age.[31]

In 1933 the NRA code of fair competition for the lumber and timber products industry provided that

> . . . no individual under eighteen years of age shall be employed except that boys sixteen years and over may be employed in the wooden package division and in non-hazardous occupations during school vacations or if there are no wage earners of eighteen years or over in their families.[32]

In 1941, the Wage and Hour Contracts Division issued an order which in effect raised to eighteen years the minimum age for employment in occupations connected with logging, lumber mills, sawmills, lath mills, and shingle mills. Up to that time no state had an eighteen-year minimum.

By 1947 the war had ended, but during the period of conflict the number of children employed had increased. Nearly 200 between fourteen and fifteen years of age were employed, 134 of whom were in the woods as lumbermen, choppers, or raftsmen. Of an additional 527 between sixteen and seventeen years of age, 263 were in the woods.

By 1950, child workers were almost gone—only 6 were employed between fourteen and fifteen years of age, and only 11 between sixteen and seventeen. Figures on school attendance indicate that the children were not idle.

The Job Level. A notably large proportion of the workers in the lumber industry have been at the lowest job level. The census classification of "laborer" does not include the lowest-paid workers listed in wage reports. It may be assumed, however, that the classification includes all those receiving laborer's wages or less. In 1910, of 17,390 wage-earners in the mills, 14,705 were "laborers." Ten

[31] Children's Bureau, *Occupational Hazards for Young Workers*, Report No. 4, Logging and Sawmilling Ser., 1942, p. 8.

[32] *Ibid.*, p. 9.

years later, of a total of 19,000 wage-earners, 11,600 were classified as "laborers." By 1930 the proportion was 25 per cent—4 per cent higher than in the nation. By comparison, 28 per cent were so classified in Louisiana; in California, 21 per cent. In 1940, of 12,704 wage-earners in sawmills and planing mills, 10,594 were "laborers." In the fifties more than one-third of all "laborers not classified" employed in manufacturing in the state were in lumber, furniture, and lumber products. An additional 6,151 lumbermen, raftsmen, and woodchoppers constituted somewhat less than one-third of "classified laborers." That classification is a method of determining wage rates is self-evident, and having large numbers of workers at the lowest rates is an effective method of keeping rates and total wages-paid at a comparatively small amount.

In 1950, 57 per cent of the workers in sawmills, planing mills, and other millwork were classified as "laborers." According to the 1954 *Biennial Census of Manufactures*, more than a third of "not classified" laborers in manufacturing in the state were in the lumber, furniture, and lumber-products industry, and 6,151 lumbermen, raftsmen, and woodchoppers made up a little less than a third of the "specified" laborers.

Educational Level of the Workers. The educational level of the workers in the industry has been and still is low. Records of the Gilmer mills show how many men could only make their mark instead of writing their name, men who worked steadily and made comparatively good wages. Since so large a proportion of the workers in each county listed worked in the production of lumber and since practically all the workers were male, figures on the literacy of the male population may be accepted as applicable to all the workers in the industry (Table 6).

By 1950 the designation "illiterate" had been abandoned by the Bureau of the Census, and the number of school years completed became the measure of educational attainment. It is assumed, however, that those who have completed fewer than four grades are "illiterate." Figures for the counties listed in Table 6 show that all except two have 20 per cent or higher who have completed fewer than four years of schooling; the comparable figure for the state is 17 per cent. The schooling of males twenty-five years of age and above, in selected counties, is shown in Table 7.

WORKERS IN THE TEXAS LUMBER INDUSTRY have always been in many ways a peculiar people, influenced by historical roots, by isolation from the main stream of national life, and by the nature of their economic environment. A typical group portrait would show two of each three persons to be adult white males, with a considerable sprinkling

TABLE 6: Illiteracy of Males of Voting Age, by Percentage, in Selected Counties, 1900–20

	1900	1910	1920
State	15.4	10.9	9.6
Angelina	15.6	11.0	6.9
Bowie	21.4	14.5	11.4
Cass	22.2	17.7	13.3
Cherokee	18.1	11.0	11.3
Gregg	28.0	18.0	13.2
Grimes	31.7	25.9	17.2
Hardin	7.0	9.7	12.9
Henderson	14.2	11.6	8.0
Jasper	24.2	14.1	12.0
Liberty	23.5	21.7	15.7
Marion	32.2	19.0	17.9
Montgomery	21.0	18.5	15.2
Newton	18.3	10.3	14.1
Polk	21.3	18.8	13.9
Sabine	20.4	8.2	13.0
San Augustine	28.7	17.7	16.9

Source: U.S. Census, 1899, Vol. I, Table 92; *U.S. Census, 1909—Supplement for Texas*, Table I; *U.S. Census for 1919*, Vol. III, Table 9.

of young boys and teen-age youths. One of three would be a Negro. Women could not be in this picture of workers, though behind the scene they have been hard-working and have often helped to increase family output and income. A few faces would bear marks of alien birth—Mexican, German, or Italian. Most of the figures, however, would be not only American-born but region-born—emphatically

TABLE 7: Schooling of Males Twenty-five Years or above, in Selected Counties, 1950

County	*Total No. of Males 25 or Older*	*No School Year Completed*	*1 to 4 Years Completed*	*Median School Years Completed*
Angelina	9,845	275	1,680	8.1
Bowie	16,445	370	2,340	8.7
Cass	6,830	170	1,260	8.0
Cherokee	11,100	420	2,170	7.7
Gregg	16,980	455	1,545	9.6
Grimes	4,095	335	890	7.0
Hardin	5,260	260	1,040	7.6
Henderson	6,620	155	1,205	8.2
Jasper	5,065	240	995	7.6
Liberty	7,155	415	1,340	7.9
Montgomery	6,175	300	1,350	7.7
Newton	2,545	100	570	6.9
Polk	4,965	230	880	7.6
Sabine	2,280	80	485	7.2
San Augustine	2,235	120	490	7.0

Source: U.S. Census 1950; Texas, *Population—General Characteristics,* Tables 20, 43. The median school year completed for all males over twenty-five in the state was 8.9.

what their more militant fellow lumberjacks of the Northwest have called "the homeguard."

For the great majority of them there has been only unskilled work, but among them have been craftsmen who ranked among the best in the national industry: saw filers, sawyers, and engineers. Their level of literacy and education has increasingly been lower than that of other workers in their own state. In 1910, in nine of seventeen counties in which these workers were concentrated, more than 15 per cent were illiterate, compared to the state figure of 11 per cent. In 1950, only two counties of the seventeen had median school years completed by male adults equal to the 8.9 for the state.

CHAPTER FIVE

Though the forest, together with the fat soil sustaining it, had at first glance no recorded past, no hallowed antiquity, it promised a glorious future. . . . It implied new chapters in the history of commerce and agriculture, politics and statesmanship, technology and culture. Here was a great possibility for security, wealth and happiness.—R. G. LILLARD

A DAY'S WORK, A DAY'S PAY

FIGURES ON WAGES in the early days of lumbering are scant and certainly of scant reliability. But since our chief interest is more in comparison than in absolute accuracy, the credence to be given specific figures is not of primary significance. Did workers in the Texas lumber industry receive as high wages as lumber workers in other areas? How did their wages compare with wages of other workers in the state? For this use there would seem to be no valid reason for not accepting the available data. Any bias would tend to be general. Furthermore, reports covering sparsely settled areas such as Texas would tend to emphasize the earnings of workers employed in the more accessible plants, and they would probably be the better paid.

In considering wages in lumber, it should be pointed out that the industry was, and is, a rural, nonfarm industry and may have drawn workers largely from surrounding farms, whose living came in part from those farms. Presumably the group inhabiting the area might have had their incomes from lumber raised to an acceptable level by the addition of farm incomes. But, as noted in Chapter One, a study in 1949 by a Subcommittee of the Joint Congressional Committee on the Economic Report of the President[1] found the areas of lumber production to be made up of counties in the lowest fifth of family-living indexes in the nation in 1945, and Texas ranked sixteenth among the states in percentage of improvement in family living between 1940 and 1945. In the judgment of the Committee, the dividing line setting off low-income families was an income of $2,000 for urban families and $1,000 for farm families. In the latter category were about two million nonfarm families in the South and one million rural nonfarm ones.[2]

But the Committee, reporting to the Eighty-fourth Congress in 1955, further pointed out that, at that time at least, returns from farms in the area were so little that the problem of low incomes was even more emphasized. Of commercial farms in the Oklahoma-Texas Cross Timbers and Prairies, 50.2 per cent were low-production farms, having from $250 to $2,499 value of sales, in excess of other family income, with the operator working off the farm less than a hundred days.[3] The report continues that in the Southwest Sandy Lands, 64.4 per cent of the farmers were low-production commercial producers. In Texas, rural income for farms having less than $2,000 income was distributed as follows:[4]

Income	*Percentage of Farms*
Under $500	7.0
$500–999	6.3
$1,000–1,499	9.4
$1,500–1,999	10.6

In agriculture, then, northeastern Texas is a serious low-income and level-of-living area. Moreover, the extent to which wages for work

[1] JCP, *Low-Income Families*, 1949, pp. 44–45.

[2] *Ibid.*, p. 278.

[3] Joint Committee Print, *Characteristics of Low-Income Population and Related Federal Programs*, 84th Cong., 1st Sess., 1955, p. 198, cited hereinafter as JCP, *Characteristics of Low-Income Population*, 1955.

[4] *Ibid.*, p. 200.

in the processing of lumber might be part of total income for the individual and for the family would seem to be limited by two factors. As the "company town" became a dominant feature in the organization of the industry the worker had no easy access to farm work and he could not be a farm operator. And since—as appears from a study of the number of days plants operated—mills operated almost continuously, work on farms by adult laborers could be done only when there was individual unemployment in the mills. The same situation existed in the logging camps. If farms added to the income of lumber workers, they were, in general, operated by the family without the assistance of its adult males.

Sources of information regarding wages during the twentieth century are numerous. The Wages and Hours Division of the U.S. Bureau of Labor Statistics has made periodic studies of employed workers. The reports of the *Biennial Census of Manufactures* become more detailed with each study. Under the Bureau of the Census, individuals —among them Davis Dewey and Paul Brissenden—have made analyses of incomes of principal groups of workers in the nation, and Congressional committees have investigated their living and wages. Students such as Paul Douglas and Whitney Coombs have traced the historical trends of wages. In some reports information about employees in the processing of Texas lumber is specific; in others it is included in figures for the national or sectional industry. Furthermore, many terms used in early studies were not clearly defined either by precise denotation or by connotation. For example, the average wage, which is calculated by dividing the sum of a list of given wages by the number of cases, is unduly influenced by the extremes at either end of the list and is not a very enlightening figure for any purpose, though it may be assumed that at any given time the meaning was understood for practical purposes. As the use of statistics has become more carefully analytical, the "average" has been displaced by the "median," which is the point on a given list of cases which represents an actual wage received, below and above which are the same number of individual wages paid. With these advantages and limitations in mind, then, let us start with the year 1870, the beginning of the period covered by the present study, and see how Texas lumber workers have fared financially in comparison with lumber workers in other sections of the country as well as with their own fellow Texans.

Wages and Hours: 1870–1930. In 1870 the lumber industry in Texas paid an average annual wage of $222.86, which was low compared with that paid by other employers in the state.[5] The only workers who received less were those employed in the making of bricks—an industry which, like the processing of lumber, included a comparatively large group of unskilled workers—and those in the working of saddlery and harness. Boatbuilders and shipwrights, a small, highly-specialized group, received more than two and one-half times as much as lumber workers. Mechanics in the state received from $1.00 to $5.00 per day, depending upon the character of the work and the skill required. Ten years later, when the number of workers employed in lumbering had doubled, the average yearly wage had increased to $230.69, somewhat more than the $215 average paid by the industry in the United States.[6] The average daily rate of wages in Texas was $1.32, but the number of hours worked was not reported.

In 1890 wages in the lumber industry (284 mills reporting) were:[7]

Category	*Average No. of Months Worked*	*Average Monthly Earnings*
Officials and firm members		
175 adult males	8.19	$122.29
Clerks		
132 adult males	10.16	69.46
1 adult female	5.00	50.00
Operatives, skilled and unskilled (adult males)		
in woods—2,033	9.30	39.11
transportation—896	9.23	42.61
Planing mills—1,027	10.65	$ 39.18
Other mills—5,288	9.31	37.39

[5] *U.S. Census, 1870, Wealth and Industry*, Vol. III. See also *Texas Almanac*, 1872.

[6] *U.S. Census, 1880*, Vol. III, p. 179.

[7] *U.S. Census, 1890, Manufacturing*, Pt. III, "Selected Industries," pp. 593–645.

Two notable features of the preceding figures are that (1) no group was able to work full time and (2) the pay of the office force was high compared to that of other workers.

For the 1890's much information regarding the pay of workers is available from the records of the Alexander Gilmer mills. In the middle of the decade the wage scale showed a range from $7.00 per day for saw filers to $1.25 per day for common laborers.[8] Sawyers were paid $5.00 per day and filers' helpers $2.50—as much as engineers and shipping inspectors; setters and edgermen received more than $2.50 per day. Foremen, paid $35 per week, received less than filers who worked full time.

Employment offered a variety of jobs and several methods of payment. In addition to straight-wage work in mills and logging camps, a man often did piece work. Payment by the piece was evidently practicable for many jobs in the industry, especially those connected with logging, and it enabled the workers to increase their income.

Piece-work Jobs	*Rate*
Making and stacking pickets	$2.50 per thousand
Raising logs (ordinary)	.15 each
Raising cypress logs	1.00 each
Unloading	.10 per thousand feet
Catching logs	.10 each
Bringing logs to mill (towing)	.05 each

Loggers handling forty-foot logs received double price.

One of the most common payments was for making and stacking pickets and another was for raising or catching logs which had sunk in the sluggish waters of the Sabine and its tributaries. Raising cypress logs required skill because of their weight, and the pay was seven times as high as that for ordinary logs. Records of the Gilmer company indicate the possibilities for a worker. One J. Dyson received the sum of $18.60 for raising 124 logs in 12 days. Straight-time wages for the period, allowing for a free Sunday, at $1.25 per day would have been $13.75. On January 17, 1895, Isaac Dyson

[8] Letter, Gilmer records, dated January 6, 1898.

received $62.88 for raising 393 logs, and on February 8, $40.95 for raising 256 logs. The rate was 16 cents per log, which seems to have been a cent higher than that for ordinary logs, for in April he raised 94 "sinkers" at 15 cents each. Log-scaling at time rates was $2.00 per day.

The following figures, taken from the Gilmer accounts for the six months ending June 30, 1896, indicate that piece work, especially raising logs, was both available and profitable.

Jan. 6	J. Dyson	27 logs @ 15¢	$ 4.05	Raising
Jan. 18	J. Dyson	124	18.60	
Feb. 4	C. Bozier	7	1.05	
Mar. 3	J. Dyson	98	14.70	Catching 45 @ 15¢ Raising 40 @ 15¢ Tongs, $2.00
Apr. 22	John Lunsford . . .	244	36.60	
Apr. 27	Smith Goodman . .	16	2.40	
May 1	J. A. Jet	10	1.50	Catching
May 1	J. A. Jet	54	2.70	Towing
June 2	J. A. Jet	84	12.60	Catching
June 16	C. Benson	142	24.14	
June 16	J. Lunsford	773	115.95	
June 16	S. Goodman	390	58.50	
June 30	Chris Benson . . .	59	8.85	
June 30	S. Goodman	48	7.20	Raising 28 logs @ 15¢ Three cypress logs @ $1.00

Payment for finding a pair of tongs was considered reward money.

"Making and stacking pickets" was a one-man job paid at piece rates. In 1896, the rate at the Gilmer mills was $2.50 per thousand. During the seven-week period from February 10 to March 30, one Tobe Lindsey received the sum of $152 for making and stacking pickets. A time worker getting $1.25 a day and working a six-day week would have received $52.50 for that period. The advantage of piece work—for Tobe Lindsey, at least—seems evident.

But not all work was individually done. Partnerships were common. For instance, the record of partners Dave Snell and Don Smith for August, 1896, show that they received $87.85 for raising ordinary logs and cypress logs.

In 1898, Mr. Gilmer reported the following daily wage scale for planing mills in the Orange County area.[9] Foremen were paid by the week ($35).

Filers	$7.00
Assistants to filers	2.50
Sawyers	5.00
Setters	2.75
Carriagemen	1.50
Edgermen	2.75
Men on log deck	1.25
Trimmermen	1.25
Engineers	2.50
Firemen	1.50
Watchmen	1.50
Boommen	2.00
Shippers (inspectors)	2.50
Assorters	1.50
Common laborers	$1.25—$1.50

The workday was 11 hours, and wages for the preceding week were paid in cash each Monday—possibly to lessen the possibility that the men would squander their wages on Saturday night.

In 1915 *Southwest* recalled that in the early 1900's a standing reward of $5.00 was offered to anybody who could get the lantern of a night watchman on duty and take it to the office of the foreman in the morning.[10] The watchman was invariably discharged, and the people who chose this way of augmenting their income could not have been very popular in the village.

At the turn of the century the average daily wage for ordinary labor was $1.00 in Texas.[11] In Minnesota and Oregon it was more than $1.50. With an average annual wage of $391 per earner, Texas ranked seventeenth in the nation. In the expanding Pacific Coast industry

[9] Gilmer Letter Press, No. 44, p. 689. Calculations have been made from day-books and payrolls of the Gilmer company.

[10] Vol. 22 (March, 1915), p. 32.

[11] *U.S. Census, 1900, Manufacturing*, Pt. III, pp. 805–897.

the average wage was $542 in Washington, $496 in Oregon, and $491 in California.

Hours of work in the industry were consistently long. On July 12, 1901, the Orange *Leader* reported that Lutcher-Moore had put its plant on a 10-hour basis and had been followed by other companies in Orange, which was the first town in the yellow-pine district to reduce working hours and the first to have a weekly cash payday. Prevailing hours of work were 60 per week, but more than a fifth of the total number of employees worked from 60 to 72 hours.[12] Compared to the general pattern of industrial employment, they worked long hours, but none were reported as working 72 or more, while more than three-fourths of the workers in oil, cottonseed, and cottonseed cake did work 72 hours or more.

In its second survey, the state Bureau found the lowest pay in the lumber industry to be 75 cents per day in Hardin County; the highest was $10 per day to saw filers in Newton County, and the next highest was $9.00 in Polk County.[13] Since laborers received, on the average, from $1.35 to $1.75 per day, a ratio of one to seven between the highest- and the lowest-paid workers prevailed. All workers were paid by the day except "stackers" in Newton County, whose rate was 20 cents per thousand. In Jefferson County a large establishment employing 840 persons paid $3.00 for an 11-hour day. In Newton County all workers worked an 11-hour day. In Polk County wage-earners worked 10 hours a day, 60 hours a week; office men (clerks, cashiers, and office help) worked 12 hours per day, 72 hours per week; engineers, electricians, and machinists put in a 70-hour week. The manager received $7.00 a day with no hours specified. "Clerks" received $3.35 a day, approximately $1,000 a year.

By comparison, a paper- and pulp-making establishment had a 12-hour day, a 72-hour week; wages ranged from $1.50 to $3.75. In coal mining, an industry somewhat similar to lumbering in its organization, hours were 10 per day for a 5-day week in Milam County; in Palo Pinto County the 48-hour week and a daily wage were universal.

[12] *U.S. Census, 1910, Supplement for Texas*, p. 778.

[13] Texas Bureau of Labor Statistics, *Biennial Report*, 1911/12, pp. 166–180, 188–280.

Cottonseed-oil mills had generally a 72-hour week. But the longest hours were in petroleum refineries, where many worked 84 hours a week and the engineers and watchmen worked 98. Skilled craftsmen in petroleum refining worked a 54-hour week, as did workers in telephone and telegraph offices, express companies, and some railway shops. There was a standard 8-hour day in painting shops, sheet-metal works, breweries, and the building trades.

In 1913/14 the Texas Bureau reported on more than 8,000 workers in the lumber industry.[14] Angelina County had 1,000 employees in 4 plants; Hopkins, Houston, Jefferson, and Trinity Counties had more than 500 each; Polk, Sabine, and Tyler Counties more than 300 each. The common minimum daily wage was $1.50. There were 2 large plants closely connected to lumbering, a cooperage plant in Bowie County employing 200 men and a turpentine plant in Newton County employing 375. In the latter the maximum wage was $2.50, the minimum $1.50, and everybody worked a 10-hour day, a 60-hour week.

At the same time, U.S. Bureau of Labor Statistics investigations covered 12 sawmills employing 2,900 of the 21,500 lumber employees in the state.[15] Average full-time weekly earnings of the workers were $10.32, 8 cents less than the national average, in which the range of difference was from 7 cents in South Carolina to 14 cents in Oregon. The national average is affected by the large number of "laborers" in the Southern industry compared with the number in Pacific Coast states. In Texas, typical of Southern distribution, of 2,906 workers in 12 mills, 1,832 were classified as "laborers." Only foremen, bosses, and skilled craftsmen were paid at an hourly rate of more than 20 cents.

The 1915/16 reports of the state Bureau on plants manufacturing lumber and its products were limited to those in the Beaumont–Port Arthur area because of the inaccessibility of plants in less settled districts.[16] The reports were concerned with occupational status, with-

[14] *Biennial Report*, 1913/14, pp. 34–65.

[15] U.S. BLS, *Wages and Hours of Labor in the Lumber, Millwork, and Furniture Industries, 1907–1913*, Bulletin No. 153, 1914, cited hereinafter as *Wages and Hours of Labor*, 1914.

[16] *Biennial Report*, pp. 26–102.

out relation to specific establishments. In planing mills the highest pay of wage-earners was $22.50 per week to engineers; skilled workmen, such as bench carpenters and glaziers, averaged somewhat less than $20; "laborers" got about $9.00. The highest returns went to the office and sales force: managers and bookkeepers received as much as $44, salesmen averaged $30, and male stenographers got from $20 to $25. In the sawmills, saw filers were still highly paid—$49 maximum and $27.27 average—but even they received somewhat less than bookkeepers, who were paid from $25 to $46.15, with an average of $36.18. Of 34 loggers, 12 received less than $13 and only one earned more than $16. Machinists received from $12 to $38.50. A semimonthly payday was the rule throughout the industry. Within the same thirty-mile radius, oil refineries were paying wages ranging from $6.00 to $48, but the modal group—887—received from $20 to $25 per week. It is indeed puzzling that workers remained in the lumber industry when the wages paid to "laborers" in oil refining were $25 per week, while wages of 34 loggers in the area ranged from $12 to $16.50.

The high pay of the office and sales forces is an index of the scarcity of such workers in a frontier society. As noted above, bookkeepers were paid a maximum of about twice as much as the best-paid mill men. Skilled carpenters averaged $19.03 per week and salesmen $30. The scarcity of highly-skilled workers and the strong pull of West Coast wages are emphasized by the $45.90 per week paid to saw filers and the $42 paid to sawyers. Within a year, in spite of the war in Europe, weekly and average full-time yearly earnings of sawmill laborers in Texas fell by approximately 10 per cent. In 1915, the federal Bureau gives somewhat detailed information for 6 Texas logging camps, employing approximately 1,600 workers. Since information from other states is equally detailed, some comparisons can be made.[17] The highest-paid Texas workers (not including foremen) were loadermen, at from $90 to $100 per month, and railroad engineers, blacksmiths, and machinists at $3.50 per day, or $90 per

[17] U.S. BLS, *Wages and Hours of Labor in the Lumber, Millwork, and Furniture Industries, 1915*, Bulletin No. 225, 1916, pp. 193–245, cited hereinafter as *Wages and Hours of Labor*, 1916.

month. Those paid at an hourly rate of 35 cents or more were machinists, loadermen, and engineers. The hourly rate for blacksmiths —34.6 cents per hour—was lower than the 40 cents paid in California, the 38 cents paid in Georgia, and the 35 cents in Arkansas. The hourly rate for machinists was 13 cents less than in Arkansas, 9 cents less than in Idaho and Mississippi, 5 cents less than in California, and 1.4 cents less than in Florida. The 60-hour week prevailed, though two engineers worked 70 hours. The highest average wage per hour—55 cents, based on piece work—was paid to band sawyers, whose average for the nation was somewhat less. The range in the nation was from 44 cents in West Virginia to 80 cents in Montana.

The entry of the United States into the war in 1917 increased the already great pressure upon the lumber industry to produce. The need for workers, however, seems to have had little effect upon wages paid in Texas, though in the Western mills wages rose rapidly and markedly. The methods used to hold workers in the South and avoid the need for higher wages are described in Chapter Three of this study. When the war had ended, a national survey of logging camps was made. In Texas, hookers were paid 15 cents more per hour in 1919 than in 1915, drivers (teamsters) 10 cents more, and engineers 8 cents more. Wages of the highest-paid laborers had increased by 7 cents, but their hourly wage was still only 27.4 cents, compared with 46.1 cents in California, 56.1 cents in Oregon, and 53.7 cents in Washington; only in Alabama and Florida were the wages of "laborers" less than in Texas. A comparison of wages paid in Texas and on the West coast are shown for the immediate prewar and postwar years:[18]

	Texas		*California*		*Oregon*		*Washington*	
	1915	*1919*	*1915*	*1919*	*1915*	*1919*	*1915*	*1919*
Doggers	17.6	34.0	22.9	36.9	23.1	44.2	22.0	51.9
Edgermen	24.6	47.3	33.3	49.9	35.4	80.2	34.3	70.5
Laborers	15.7	31.7	19.8	35.7	20.4	52.5	19.9	50.1

[18] U.S. BLS, *Industrial Survey in Selected Industries in the United States, 1919*, Bulletin No. 265, 1920, pp. 348–368; *Wages and Hours of Labor*, 1916, pp. 234–236.

This disparity in wages was not a regional feature, for in the chemical industry "laborers" in Texas received an hourly average of 39.1 cents—8 cents more than in the lumber industry; primary-process men received 68.7 cents, compared with the 72.9 cents average for the United States; heater men, 58.7 compared with 60.9. In the overalls industry in Texas, male laborers employed as cutters received an average hourly wage of 64.6 cents, 3 cents more than the average for the nation.

In January, 1922, a survey by the state Bureau covered wages and working conditions of employees in the lumber camps of eastern Texas.[19] Of 91 sawmills investigated, 14 were practically closed down, but 12,765 persons were covered in 77 mills. Presumably the study included salaried workers. Within the year, the average daily wage had decreased by more than 25 per cent. Distribution of wages paid to operatives for the week of greatest employment during the year was:

18 employees	$ 6– 8 per week
292	8–10
1,788	10–12
3,391	12–15
3,775	15–20
1,155	20–25
357	25–30
278	30–40
132	40–50
301	50 or more

Somewhat more than 7,000 employees received from $12 to $20 a week—from $612 to $1,020 for a full year's work. Five years later, 196 of the 9,207 establishments in the United States producing value of more than $5,000 were in Texas.[20] They employed 18,200 wage-earners at an average annual wage of $878. The highest weekly full-time wage in sawmills was paid in California—$29 for 57 hours; the lowest was in Georgia—$12.80 for a 61-hour week. In Texas, average full-time earnings per week were $18 for a 61-hour week. While wages

[19] *Biennial Report*, pp. 13 ff., 74.

[20] U.S. BLS, *Wages and Hours of Labor in Lumbering Manufacturing, 1929*, Bulletin No. 497, pp. 3, 26, 625, cited hereinafter as *Wages and Hours of Labor*, 1929.

in Texas were falling, as shown by comparative figures, those in the nation were rising. Average earnings for 1925 and 1928 were:

	PER HOUR *United States*	*Texas*	PER WEEK *United States*	*Texas*
1925	35.7¢	30.0¢	$20.74	$18.48
1928	37.1	29.0	21.00	17.43

For the nation, average full-time hours per week in 1928 were 56.6, a decrease of 1.5; average earnings per hour had increased by 1.4 cents, and full-time earnings per week by 26 cents. At the same time wage rates for unskilled labor in Texas cities, hired for work in constructing, repairing, or cleaning streets, ranged from 72.9 cents per hour in Jefferson, to 18.8 cents in Laredo;[21] from 50 cents to 19 cents was the general range, and the 48-hour week was fairly general.

In 1930 in Texas, of 11 lumber mills, 9 operated 60 hours per week as a full-time schedule; one operated 50 hours, and one 52.5 hours. One operated 60 hours at night. In Idaho alone was the 48-hour week universal, but it was only in the Southern states that all establishments operated more than 60 hours per week.

For the two years 1928 and 1930 the federal Bureau published the following comparative figures:[22]

	No. of Establish-ments		*No. of Employees*		*Average Full-time Hours per Week*		*Average Earnings per Hour*		*Average Full-time Earnings per Week*	
	1928	*1930*	*1928*	*1930*	*1928*	*1930*	*1928*	*1930*	*1928*	*1930*
Texas	11	11	2,502	2,350	58.3	58.7	29.9¢	29.6¢	$17.43	$17.38
Wash.	21	21	7,283	6,398	48.1	48.1	55.2	54.9	26.55	26.41
Calif.	14	14	3,496	2,650	56.1	53.7	51.0	54.2	28.61	29.11
Nation	319	324	58,007	50,951	56.6	56.5	37.1	35.9	21.00	20.28

The range of average full-time earnings was from $13.67 in South

[21] *Ibid., Wages and Hours of Common Street Laborers*, Bulletin No. 484, 1928, p. 38.

[22] *Ibid., Wages and Hours of Labor in the Lumber Industry in the United States, 1930*, Bulletin No. 560, 1932, pp. 6, 28, 30, cited hereinafter as *Wages and Hours of Labor*, 1932.

Carolina to $28.61 in California in 1928, and from $12.64 in Georgia to $29.11 in California in 1930.

Wages and Hours: Effects of the Depression and the Second World War. That the lumber industry, in common with all others, felt the Depression appears in the decline in the number of employees and in the amount of work available. The number of hours actually worked per wage-earner per week in Texas was 36.5—60.9 per cent of full time. Washington and Montana had fewer average hours per week per wage-earner but in Washington, because of a shorter standard work week, its 35 hours represented 72.9 per cent of full time. The hourly wage for all wage-earners in the industry in Texas was 22.1 cents, compared with 25.6 for the nation. During the decade of the thirties, reports of the Texas Bureau covered so few workers that they are scarcely representative, but such figures as they do give support the federal figures.

In 1937, when the Fair Labor Standards Act was passed, the average annual wage in the Texas lumber industry was $643—$380 less than the average wage for 11 manufacturing groups in the state.[23] Through virtue of the act (with later amendments) the lowest wages were raised and wage distribution was changed. In October, 1938, a 25-cent minimum went into effect. Average hourly earnings in the Southern lumber industry were raised from 27 cents to 31 cents, and half the workers were paid 30 cents per hour.[24] Two years later the minimum was raised to 35 cents. By November, 1941, wage adjustment and the general movement upward had raised the average to 38 cents and within a short time to 42 cents. By 1946, average hourly earnings had increased by 70 per cent, while earnings in all manufacturing increased by 50 per cent.

Though the pressure for an increased supply of lumber for a nation again at war had an impact upon the wage level in the Southern in-

[23] *Monthly Labor Review*, Vol. 50 (June, 1940), p. 1480.

[24] U.S. Dept. of Labor, *Economic Factors Bearing on the Establishment of Minimum Wages in Logging, Lumber, Timber and Related Industries*, Wage and Hour Division, 1943, pp. 2, 10, 35–36, 40, cited hereinafter as *Economic Factors*, 1943.

dustry, it was not great enough to draw the labor required to fill military needs. As a result, in the Southern pine area 1,000 sawmills, having an annual output of 2.5 billion board feet, were closed down. The inability to meet national requirements was attributed to (1) the unusually high turnover of labor, accelerated by rising wages in other industries and the need for military personnel; (2) the lack of skilled and experienced labor in some areas; (3) the relatively low wage level. Since manpower shortage was the reason most frequently given for inadequate production, the government took action to help the industry solve this difficulty. In September, 1942, an employment stabilization plan for lumber production was put into effect by the War Manpower Commission in twelve states, one of which was Texas. A worker had to get a certificate of separation before leaving his lumber job to work elsewhere. In the following year the National War Labor Board authorized the setting of a 50-cent minimum wage for lumber workers in District VIII, the Dallas district comprising Texas, Louisiana, and Oklahoma. The wage set had little effect in the West, where average hourly earnings in sawmills and logging camps in February, 1943, was more than $1.00; but in Texas the average was 43.9 cents. Since 2 per cent of employees were getting less than 35 cents, and 44 per cent were getting less than 40 cents, the increase in income was great for workers at the lower levels. It is probable that tying workers to jobs prevented them from going elsewhere and deprived them of the power to bargain for higher wages.

In the immediate postwar period, average hourly earnings in Southern lumber increased 8 per cent, while in manufacturing they increased 30 per cent. By 1950, the median annual income of male workers in logging was $1,151; in sawmills and planing mills, $1,545. Only private household servants—with $763—had a lower median.[25] Since household servants are all "laborers," no wages would be above a low general level. The median of all male workers in the state was $2,332. In the spring of that year, the highest hourly wage rate in Southwest mills was $1.56, paid to band-saw operators in independent

[25] *U.S. Census, 1950*, Pt. 43, Texas, Table 86.

mills;[26] other groups receiving more than $1.00 were head circular-saw operators, millwrights, saw filers, planer operators, and set-up men. In logging only fellers and buckers by hand received more than $1.00. The lowest wage—70 cents—was paid to watchmen. From a survey of mills by number of employees, there is evidence that for most types of work, but not all, the mills employing 101 employees or more paid the highest wages. It does seem from the following figures that where incentive pay was given, workers averaged considerably higher than those paid straight time:

	Hourly Incentive Pay	*Hourly Straight-time Pay*
Loaders (car and truck)	$1.14	$ .72
Lumber stackers:		
Air or storage drying	1.00	.73
Kiln drying	1.07	.74
Fellers and buckers (hand)	1.11	.82

But in spite of the favorable differential, only about a third of those surveyed were paid on an incentive basis.

In the fall of 1949, average hourly earnings for all workers in Texas sawmills was 75 cents; 89 per cent made less than $1.00 and 13 per cent less than 60 cents. In December, 1949, 0.4 per cent of workers in sawmills in the Southwest were paid the highest wage—$1.70 and over—and 11.4 per cent were paid more than $1.00. Three months later, 0.7 per cent were paid the highest wage and 12.2 per cent received more than $1.00.

By March, 1950, the average straight-time hourly wage in Texas, which had been 75 cents the preceding fall, was raised 3 cents; in Louisiana it was raised 12 cents.[27] Furthermore, 31 per cent of Texas lumber workers were still getting less than 75 cents. In no other state

[26] U.S. BLS, *Wage Structure: Lumber in the South, 1949 and 1950*, Wages and Hours of Labor Ser., Report No. 76, 1950, pp. 14, 25–26, 44, 53, 129, cited hereinafter as *Lumber in the South*, 1943. See also *Monthly Labor Review*, Vol. 3 (September, 1950), pp. 313–317.

[27] U.S. BLS, *Wage Structure: The Southern Lumber Industry*, Wages and Hours of Labor Ser., Report No. 45, 1953, pp. 6, 53, cited hereinafter as *The Southern Lumber Industry*, 1953.

did the proportion exceed 12 per cent. In 1949 only two Southern states, Kentucky and West Virginia, had higher straight-time average hourly earnings than Texas, but in the following spring only two of thirteen states, Alabama and South Carolina, had a lower average than Texas. The surprising conclusion is that Texas in 1949 was one of the highest-paying states but by 1950 it was one of the lowest-paying.

Two years later the federal Bureau found 794 sawmills with 8 or more workers employing 41,460 persons in the Southwest (Arkansas, Louisiana, Oklahoma, and Texas). Of these, 88 plants were studied. The highest straight-time average hourly wage—$1.66—was paid to head band-saw operators in stationary mills. Average hourly earnings for fellers and hand buckers who worked for incentive wages was $1.33—51 cents more than average hourly wages for straight-time workers. Average straight-time hourly earnings of more than 12,000 production workers was 92 cents, and 85 per cent made less than $1.00 per hour. At the time "laborers" in machinery were making $1.17 per hour in Dallas; in Houston, $1.37.[28]

After the amendment to the Fair Labor Standards Act increased the minimum wage from 75 cents to $1.00 per hour, the Wages and Hours and the Public Contracts Division with the Bureau of Labor Statistics surveyed the effect on wages paid to 150,000 workers in approximately 4,500 Southern sawmills employing 8 or more workers.[29] In April, 1956, average straight-time hourly earnings in Southwestern mills were $1.08, raised from the 94 cents of a year earlier. They were $1.07 for the total South, $1.10 for the border states, and $1.06 for the Southeast. Again it must be noted that the low wage is not a regional characteristic, for average hourly earnings in other Southwestern industries were fertilizer, $1.45; footwear, $1.23; processed waste, $1.01; and wooden containers, $1.05. Of twenty-nine jobs in Southern sawmills only three averaged more than $1.00 an hour before March 1, 1957, and workers earning less than $1.00 per hour made up 74 per cent of all employed in the industry.[30]

[28] *Monthly Labor Review*, Vol. 77 (June, 1954), p. 653.

[29] *Ibid.*, Vol. 80 (March, 1957), p. 326.

[30] *Ibid.* (April, 1957), p. 442.

Premium Pay for the Skilled Worker. Another significant feature that emerges from a study of wages is that industries vary not only with respect to average earnings but also in the extent to which individual earners are dispersed around the average wage. In many ways information concerning the extent of such dispersion gives a better basis for comparison than does any type of average. When individual earnings are widely scattered and no pronounced concentration exists, the "average" may approximate the earnings of only a few of the workers. The converse is true when individual earnings are highly concentrated as group earnings. The dispersion of earnings around the median over a period of time allows a comparison between groups as to the distribution of workers through a range of wages paid.

Minimum-wage requirements reduced the spread of earnings, at least temporarily. When the minimum wage was raised, high concentration developed in the wage structure. In December, 1949, the largest concentration in Southern lumber was the 20 per cent in the class earning from 60 cents to 65 cents. A short time later 67 per cent of the workers earned between 75 cents and 80 cents per hour, and in 1953, 46 per cent were in this class. The mean was 86 cents and the median 81 cents.

As has been suggested, a frontier area does not lack labor. But it does lack skilled laborers and literate laborers, clerks, and bookkeepers, as did the lumber industry. Skilled workers in Texas were drawn from older areas and held by good wages against the pull of the uniformly higher pay of the industry farther west. Sawyers and saw filers were scarce, essential, and locally unavailable. In 1890, workers in these classifications were getting from $4.00 to $6.00 per day. The median wage for saw filers was $7.00 a day, almost six times that for common labor and twice that for foremen, who received $3.50 per day.

In July of 1890 Mr. Gilmer wrote, "Need sawyer, will not quarrel about wages." A week later he wrote, "Have had bad luck with sawyers but have one now. If he is not satisfactory will hire you." A few days later he wrote to one Flipsey in Michigan, "Need sawyer, come at once." A week later he asked a Beaumont man to send a Negro sawyer "until I can get one." By 1895 the depression was affecting all areas of the economy. Gilmer answered a query from Minnesota, "No sawyer needed, two out of work now." That sawyers were persons of importance is indicated by a typical item in the Orange *Leader*[31] that Fred Ahrens, band sawyer of Duluth, Minnesota, had taken a position with a local firm. He had come in as a factory representative to put in band saws and had been persuaded to stay. The head saw filer in the firm was also from the Lake area in Michigan.

As might be expected, with the expansion of the industry the wages of these workers rose. In the first decade of the twentieth century they approximately doubled. When the state Bureau made its first investigation of wages in 1910 it found saw filers in Newton County getting $10 per day and in Polk County, $9.00.[32] *Southwest* reported at the time that $10 per day was sometimes paid for "higher grade men in band saw mills," with a going rate of $7.50 per day.[33] The federal Bureau reported comparative hourly wages for band sawyers as 54.5 cents for the nation, 58 cents for Texas, 65 cents for Oregon and Louisiana, and 63 cents for South Carolina.[34] But compared to the earnings of other craftsmen in Texas, this wage was not high. In Dallas the hourly rate for skilled trades under union organization was 75 cents for plasterers and bricklayers and 69 cents for gas-fitters. But by 1912 these trades worked a standard 44-hour week, making a full-time wage of $33, while lumber production paid $36 full time for a 60-hour week.

In 1912 the Texas Bureau reported a maximum daily wage of $12 (paid to, we may presume, a sawyer or saw filer) in Angelina County and in Nacogdoches County.[35] In Polk, Sabine, Trinity, and Walker, $10 was the maximum. Nationally, only one band sawyer earned less than 25 cents an hour; in Texas none earned less than 50 cents and the majority earned more than 60 cents. Wages for sawyers in the state were still rising, and comparative figures again show the pull of

[31] November 16, 1898; July 6, 1899.

[32] *Biennial Report*, 1909/10.

[33] Vol. 7 (April, 1910), p. 65.

[34] U.S. BLS, *Wages and Hours of Labor in the Lumber, Millwork, and Furniture Industry, 1890–1913*, Bulletin No. 129, p. 25.

[35] *Biennial Report*, pp. 74–92.

Western wages. In 1913 the average wage was 61.6 cents, an increase of 2.5 cents, compared to a national increase of approximately 1.5 cents.[36] The highest weekly wage, $46.41, was paid to band sawyers in Montana, and more than $35 was paid in Arkansas, Louisiana, Minnesota, and Oregon, compared to the $32.66 paid in Texas. For all, full time was 60 hours per week.

Two years later, when $10 per day was being paid in Nacogdoches and Walker Counties and $8.00 in Hardin, Liberty, Jefferson, and Tyler Counties,[37] the maximum wage paid skilled workers in the lumber industry was one of the highest in the state. For clerical work in merchandising, the maximum was generally higher, but among skilled operatives in manufacturing only printing and publishing, machine shops, foundries, and carbonic-acid gas plants had a higher maximum.

Payment by the piece was used to tie the wages of sawyers to their performance and make their earnings flexible. In 1915 the federal Bureau, studying wages and hours in the lumber industry, found that all sawyers working in Texas logging camps were paid by piece rate.[38] In mills they averaged 55 cents per hour, $32.66 per week. The national average hourly pay was lower—53.7 cents—and the weekly wages the same. It is evident that the average number of full-time hours per week employees in Texas were allowed to work was somewhat lower than the national average, which is always heavily weighted by the Southern industry. Only in Arkansas, Minnesota, and Texas were full-time hours per month less than 260—4.5 hours less than the national average. Piece workers throughout the country commonly worked in plants with a 60-hour full-time week for operatives, but under a piece-work system individual sawyers might work fewer hours with no decrease in pay.

Though their average earnings had decreased nationally by about 5 per cent in the preceding two years, band sawyers, receiving $33 per week, were still the highest-paid workers in the industry. In Texas

[36] U.S. BLS, *Wages and Hours of Labor*, 1914, pp. 29, 34.
[37] *Biennial Report*, 1915/16.
[38] U.S. BLS, *Wages and Hours of Labor*, 1916, pp. 12–38.

their earnings had decreased more than twice as much as the national average, approximately 12 per cent, while in neighboring Louisiana they had decreased only 5 per cent. In the state, sawyers in planing mills worked 229 hours per month, the national average also, compared with 251.3 in Arkansas and California and 245 in Mississippi. Weekly earnings were higher in Arkansas ($37.65) and Mississippi ($33.16) than in other states, but the higher wage was the result of longer hours, not a higher rate.

The assassination of an Austrian archduke, followed by the march of armed men throughout Europe, affected the wages of sawyers markedly. Lumber was needed to fill military requirements. In 1916, saw filers in the Beaumont area were paid as much as $45 per week and sawyers $42. One-third of the sawyers received 60 cents or more per hour and all circular sawyers more than 50 cents. As shown by the figures below, wages of band sawyers in Texas were $5.00 more than the national average but $3.00 less than those paid across the Sabine:

	Average Wages per Week	*Average Hours per Week*
Nation	$33.53	61.1
Texas	38.69	60.1
Louisiana	41.67	60.8
Arkansas	39.79	60.9

During the war period their wages in Southern mills increased greatly but not so much as in the Northwest. By 1919 the average for the state was 5 cents higher than that for the nation. Comparative figures were:

	1919	*1915*
Nation	$0.773	$0.537
Texas	0.827	0.550
Oregon	1.125	0.605
Washington	1.229	0.680

After the war their wages did not return to the prewar level. Ten years later, band sawyers in Texas received $.827 per hour, and only three states—Oregon, Wyoming, and Minnesota—paid more. The national average was .$773. Average hours worked per day were 7.9 in Texas, 5.5 in Washington, and 8.1 in Oregon, where all worked between 8 and 9 hours.

As has been indicated, sawyers were of several kinds. In 1925 their wages according to classification were listed as:[39]

TYPE OF SAWYER	TEXAS Per Hour	Per Week	NATION Per Hour	Per Week
Head circular	$0.960	$57.60	$0.816	$47.49
Head band	0.866	51.70	0.887	50.60
Gang	0.671	45.63	0.581	33.64
Resaw	0.517	32.31	0.489	27.34

Highest average earnings per week ($63.54) were paid in Florida for a 60-hour week at $1.05 per hour. In both California and Washington wages were much over $1.00 per hour, but the work week was 48 hours. Head circular sawyers in Texas had the highest actual earnings per week in the nation ($55.60), but they worked 57.5 hours, compared with 55.5 hours for the nation. In Washington, earnings of $54.38 were paid for a week of 48.8 hours, which was 103 per cent of full time. By the midtwenties, overtime with pay higher than the standard rate was a common feature on the Pacific Coast.

The passage of the Fair Labor Standards Act a decade later had no direct effect upon the wages of highly-skilled workers, though there was, as stated above, some indirect effect through the compression of wages to lessen differentials.[40] The average hourly wage of circular band sawyers was $1.07 in the fall of 1949 and $1.13 in March, 1950, when the 75-cent minimum became effective. With relation to the base, wages of all groups fell after the setting of the 75-cent minimum, owing not to a decrease in higher wages but to an increase in the lower wages. In some cases compensating action was taken. Some firms reported that the narrowing of wage scales was partly offset by reducing overtime for the less skilled workers and allowing their more skilled ones some overtime, resulting in larger actual earnings. Since a standard of 40 hours was set in the fall of 1940, hours of work for both skilled and unskilled were sharply reduced.

[39] *Ibid., Wages and Hours of Labor in the Lumber Industry, 1925,* Bulletin No. 413, 1926, p. 29, cited hereinafter as *Wages and Hours of Labor,* 1926.

[40] *Ibid., Lumber in the South,* 1943, pp. 1, 15, 20.

By 1953, skill differentials were being reinstated, but the incentive wages which had given skilled workers an advantage were disappearing because of the installation of power saws, which displaced the less-efficient incentive workers more than they did the time workers.

Low Wages for the Great Majority. At the other extreme of the wage scale were massed a group called, in general, "laborers," though the lowest wages were not paid to those so classified. Broad categories are operatives, semiskilled operatives, and laborers, and the federal Bureau of Labor Statistics defines "laborers" as all workers who have no craft skills. Though job names in the lumber plants were varied, it is probably valid to assume that all those receiving wages through the range defined as "laborers" or below were unskilled workers. Clustered at these lowest wage levels were the great majority of workers.

In 1909, "mill hands" in Walker County were reported to the state Bureau as receiving from 75 cents to $1.75 per day.[41] At the same time, the federal Bureau stated that of a total of 727 male "laborers" only 8 earned 25 cents or more per hour. The largest group earned from 14 cents to 16 cents, with full-time earnings of approximately $9.00 for a 60-hour week. At the same time laborers under union scales in the building trades in Dallas received 25 cents per hour for a 48-hour week, $12 per week full-time earnings. By 1912 the 44-hour week was standard for them.

By 1915 the pattern of wages seems to have been set on lines which have since been recognized.[42] The skilled groups received wages comparable to the highest paid in the states of the Northwest, while laborers were paid wages comparable to those paid in other areas of the Southern yellow-pine region. In that year 57 per cent of the workers in 12 Texas sawmills were classified as laborers. Their average hourly rate of pay was 15.7 cents, little different from that for the nation, and full-time weekly earnings were $9.41—$470.50 for a 50-week year. The following figures show that their wages compared favorably with those in three Southeastern states:

[41] *Biennial Report*, pp. 166–180, 188–280.
[42] U.S. BLS, *Wages and Hours of Labor*, 1916, pp. 34–35.

State	*Year*	*Average Full-time Hours per Week*	*Average Hourly Wage*	*Average Full-time Weekly Earnings*
Texas	1913	60.2	$0.172	$10.35
	1915	60.1	0.157	9.41
Alabama	1913	64.8	0.126	8.12
	1915	65.2	0.106	6.91
Georgia	1913	63.6	0.131	8.31
	1915	64.9	0.106	6.82
Mississippi	1913	60.1	0.136	8.17
	1915	60.6	0.126	7.61

The years of military aid and war had some influence in raising the minimum wages paid in the Texas industry, but the gap between them and those paid in the expanding Western areas continued to widen until by the midtwenties the average wage was 26 cents per hour in Texas—$15.62 for a little more than 60 hours—while on the West coast Oregon and Washington were paying 48 cents for 48 hours, approximately $23 per week, and California was paying 45 cents for a 56.4-hour week, or $25 per week. Not only, it may be noted, were hourly wages almost twice as much, but hours worked per week were 20 per cent less. The lowest wage, 20.1 cents per hour for a 60.4-hour week, was paid in Alabama.

In 1927 the Texas Bureau surveyed 16 lumber camps employing 4,000 wage-earners,[43] of whom 3,400 were unskilled laborers receiving an average daily wage of $2.59. Many, of course, received much less. A comparison of the daily rate of wages with annual earnings shows that the unskilled laborers not only received the lowest rate of wages but were also the least regularly employed. Federal reports at the same time showed that laborers in Texas lumber (not logging) with hourly wages of 24.2 cents were among the lowest-paid in the nation, with only five other states paying less.[44] Weekly earnings were $11.57 in Texas, $15.05 in the nation. In Washington, no laborer received less than 30 cents an hour, and more than half were paid from $20 to $25 or more per week. Only 3 laborers in Texas

[43] *Biennial Report*, pp. 44–45, 120–125.

[44] U.S. BLS, *Wages and Hours of Labor*, 1929, pp. 35–40, 54.

were reported as earning as much as $20 per week. Two years later Texas was reported as one of seven states where average actual earnings were below $10 per week, but no specific information regarding Texas "laborers" was given.

Passage of the Fair Labor Standards Act and the setting of an hourly minimum of 35 cents had a tremendous effect upon incomes of the lowest-paid workers, and Southern lumber was one of the industries most affected. In addition, within a short time military and war requirements again put pressure upon the demand for lumber and consequently upon the supply of labor available. In 1942, under the employment stabilization plan mentioned above, a 50-cent minimum wage was set to prevent the drawing off of workers.[45]

Several federal agencies investigated the effects of successively higher minimums. In their first survey, published in 1943, the greatest concentration of wage-earners in the industry, 43 per cent, was found to be in the Southern states, and 13 per cent in the four Southwestern states.[46] Of all wage-earners in logging, timber, and related industries in the country, 4.4 per cent were in Texas. The largest group of workers in Southern mills—almost one-half of all—was found to receive wages of from 40 cents to 50 cents per hour; almost 30 per cent received from 50 to 60 cents per hour. The average hourly wage in Southern mills and lumber camps was 48.3 cents compared with $1.04 in Western mills. In Texas establishments, average hourly earnings, adjusted by raising all employees to the minimum, was 43.9 cents; 2 per cent earned less than 35 cents and 43.6 per cent less than 40 cents. Since the effect of the 1949 amendment was limited by the provision that "employees of small logging camps and small forestry operations are exempted if no more than twelve employees are engaged in such operations," many Texas mills were not covered by the law.

At the beginning of the fifties, 30.1 per cent of workers in Texas sawmills were paid less than the 75-cent minimum and 69 per cent less than 80 cents.[47] The proportion that had been paid less than 75

[45] *Ibid., Wages in the Basic Lumber Industry, 1944*, Bulletin No. 854, 1945.
[46] U.S. Dept. of Labor, *Economic Factors*, 1943, pp. 10, 35–40.
[47] U.S. BLS, *The Southern Lumber Industry*, 1953, p. 6.

cents just before the minimum was changed was 61.8 per cent. Furthermore, 31 per cent of Texas lumber workers were still getting less than 75 cents.

With the setting of the $1.00 minimum in 1956, the increase in straight average hourly earnings might be termed dramatic. From the early thirties to the midfifties, the average annual increase in earnings was 3.6 cents; in the few months from late 1955 to April, 1956, it was 16 cents. In the fall of 1955, about three-fourths of nonsupervisory workers earned less than $1.00 and more than one-third earned 75 cents. Since sawmills with fewer than 8 employees were exempted, it is possible that many of them were forced to close, but even if they did, the effect of their closing upon the total number employed would have been inconsiderable. Certainly if the low wages paid before 1937 had been essential to the operation of the industry, the effect of the closing of the plants would have been notable if not spectacular.

None of the proverbial and historical "low-paid" groups have dominated the Texas lumber industry. Women workers have not been employed; Negroes have been a minority; children, while comparatively common workers, could scarcely have set levels in an industry where physical strength and size are major requisites; there has been no pressure of immigrant workers. The wages that have been paid were paid to adult white males who have been of native American stock for at least three or four generations.

Although the industry may be termed a "Southern industry" dominated by Southern wages, "regional difference" is too glib an explanation to account for the wage differential in Texas lumbering. The tendency to low wages is not necessarily a Northern versus a Southern feature. Nor is it due alone to retarded industrial development. In the processing of tobacco, for instance, wages in Pennsylvania are lower than in Florida. Within the Texas lumber industry two wage contours appear—one rooted in the Southern complex of a plentiful supply of untrained labor and the other drawn to the Western industry by the scarcity of skilled labor in Texas and the necessity to hold it against the compulsion of the Westward movement and the high wages of skilled labor in the Pacific Coast industry. Furthermore, the "level of wages" is greatly affected by the large proportion of workers at the lowest scale and the notable gap between their wages and those of sawyers, filers, and other trained workers. Historically the pattern was set early: high wages paid to a few skilled workers such as sawyers to prevent their migrating to the Western forests and very low wages paid to a large basic group classified as unskilled laborers.

Wages paid workers in the processing of lumber in Texas were, until the opening of the twentieth century, equal to those paid in other areas of the nation and in other industries. The Western forests were not yet being heavily worked, and the local demand for lumber in building was being increased by the needs of a developing oil industry. Moreover, with the deforestation of the Great Lakes regions the trained lumberjacks of the Lakes camps were becoming available. The state drew skilled workers from the land of Paul Bunyan through high wages made possible by the expansion of the industry. But there was neither need nor desire to draw unskilled labor; the supply of that was kept plentiful by the westward march from the Old South. Texas was a territory in which migrants, both Negro and white, felt at home. In the piney woods they could forget the advice of Colonel Suggs that "it is well to be shifty in a new Country."

By the time of the war years of 1914–19 there had developed a pattern of high wages for a few skilled craftsmen and low wages for the great body of workers. Two world wars, both of which put pressure on the industry, improved the wage scale of the lowest-paid little, if at all. In 1917, steps were taken to prevent Negro workers in Texas lumber mills from responding to possibly higher pay elsewhere, and during the 1940–45 conflict, workers were tied to their jobs with a minimum pay of 50 cents an hour.

During the first war period, wages for all groups in the booming Western industry rose rapidly and remained at a high level. But in Texas wages at the lower levels fell and continued to fall. The difference between the pay of laborers and that of skilled workers was equally great in the two sections but in Texas it was more meaningful than appears from the figures. The difference between poverty wages and wages from three to seven times as great is more divisive between groups of workers than that between a living wage and wages from three to seven times as high.

In the postwar period, wages did not in any section drop to prewar level. Weekly wages of skilled workers in Texas remained about equal to those in the Pacific Coast industry, but in the latter area the wages were paid for a work week standardized at 48 hours, while in the South and the Southwest they were paid for one that remained at approximately 60 hours. Though the first war period showed a not inconsiderable increase in wages for nonskilled workers, it was lost during the early twenties and, comparatively speaking, their situation was worse than it had been and continued to grow still more so until the midthirties. It did not improve until federal legislation made improvement mandatory.

The last quarter-century has seen the persistence of the pattern of low wages. The laborers have lost ground compared to the same groups in even the Southeastern states. The Fair Labor Standards Act has made the 40-hour week standard and has raised wages somewhat but not proportionately. Though small mills were exempt from coverage by the act, they could not remain unaffected, for they had either to hold their own workers or accept those whom no other mill would employ.

The lower wage cannot be explained as a regional difference. Methods of transportation and marketing tend to unify wages, and where they are high in a given industry in one section they tend to be high in that industry throughout the nation. For instance, in the fifties straight-time hourly earnings for chemical and petroleum products averaged for the South only a few cents below those of the Northeast and Middle West and but 28 cents below those of the Far West—always the highest-paying area.

It seems a bootless task to attempt to use wages considered in this study to formulate any generalization about the pay of these workers. It can only be said that wages were low because there was continuously a superfluity of laborers who would accept the going rate.

But, after all, the money rate of wages is only the skeleton for a pattern of life. The thing that determines the living of the workers is what they can buy with what we have come in recent years to call revealingly "take-home pay." Various aspects of this important question are the material for the following chapters.

CHAPTER SIX

That it is not the wage rate but the annual take-home pay which is actually most important to employees, however they may look upon it, has become axiomatic.—EDWIN E. WITTE

WAGES—MINUS...

IN COMPUTING WAGES RECEIVED, figures giving simply rates and averages are of questionable value because they do not take into account some other basic features of income. The annual wages for an individual are the product of the rate per hour multiplied by the total number of hours worked. The calculation of hours must subtract those days not worked because of the closing down of the employer's plant, which would be lost to all employees equally. The same would be true for officially-granted holidays, legal or otherwise. But some losses that occur with uneven and irregular incidence can greatly affect the income of individuals. Among these are days not worked because of illness or accident. Also when individuals work only intermittently, either because work is not available for all who are attached to the payroll, or where work is distributed among available workers, the effect upon the income of the workers and their families is highly significant. When any or all of such losses are compensated through workmen's compensation or unemployment insurance, the decrease in actual income is lessened, of course. Where there is a policy of paying rates higher than the standard ones for work beyond an established day or week, the distribution of available work—and consequently of income—is probably made less uneven.

In calculating earnings, then, regularity or irregularity of employment is a factor of major importance. Lumber plants in Texas, as already noted, were not seasonal in operation as were those of the Northwest and the Lakes states. Watercourses did not freeze and seldom was cold so bitter as to stop work in the woods. Heat and mosquitoes were more probable hindrances. Occasionally there were storms such as that of 1900 when, in the words of a lumber worker, "trees blowed down in Hardin County that never blowed down before." When railroads became the important means of transporting timber and lumber, mills became largely independent of the weather and could depend upon a steady flow of logs. Toward the close of the nineteenth century the installation of electricity changed hours of operation and patterns of work, not only for plants but for individuals, and mills could work extra time to fill rush orders.

Plant Operation: 1898–1956. In January, 1899, the Orange *Leader* noted that during the preceding year, none of the leading lumber producers in the city had operated full time, which may be assumed as 300 days. Figures on the number of days several firms were in operation indicate the general picture: Orange, 255 days; Lutcher-Moore, 272½; Gilmer, 217; and Bancroft, 228

Ten years later *Southwest*[1] commented that "many mill men feel constrained to run part-time if for no other reason than in order to insure dependent employees of living wages . . . on the other hand other mills have felt no such responsibility; some have instituted wage cuts [which] employees accepted with as good grace as possible." The next year, most mills used a long holiday period, December 26 to January 18, to make repairs.

Files of the Beaumont *Enterprise* and the Jasper *Newsboy* for 1909 give some suggestion of the extent to which nonoperation of plants existed. During the last week in February the Orange mills, which had been closed since January for lack of logs, were running at night

[1] Vol. 15 (January, 1908), p. 79.

after rains had brought a supply. The Orange Sawmill Company was supplied for several weeks by logs raised from the Sabine River. But three months later the mills were again operating on short time. In September, shutdowns were due to lack of water. A month later mills were closed for what was probably a "once in a lifetime" cause.[2] Conditions arising from a prohibition election at Kountze precipitated a grand-jury investigation. Six hundred witnesses were called and sawmills in the area were forced to close. As the year ended, the Orange Sawmill Company, which had been idle much of the past year, started up as the result of a small rise in the Sabine, which broke a mile-long jam on the river and brought a good supply of logs from 70 to 100 miles up stream. During the next two years the Yellowpine Mill at Orange closed for 7 months and the Kirby mills, 3 miles north of Jasper, shut down indefinitely. At the same time, many mills were operating at night—not, it seems, an unusual situation, though *Southwest* commented that night operation was a business and social crime—"a crime against the operators themselves, against their employees who will be called to work during the night hours and against the industry itself." Such a situation may be a partial explanation of why more workers were consistently attached to the industry than it could normally use. In 1915 in Texas, 12 lumber establishments operated from 236 to 304 days in the year; the average number of days of lumber operation for the state was 260.3; for the nation, it was 265.

Mills of the Sabine area were, as pointed out, closed down only occasionally because of "bad weather." Of the 12 establishments mentioned, only 3 gave weather as a cause of shutdowns. As shown by figures on the following page, other time lost for each of the plants was due to reasons within the industry itself.[3]

The national average for days lost in lumbering was 29.4 for slack work and 7.4 for other reasons. There was little official free time in Texas establishments, and what there was, was without pay. Holidays and vacations amounted to 2 days in one plant; 3 days in 6; 4 days and 5 days in 2 others; and 7 days in one.

[2] *Southwest*, Vol. 9 (September, 1909), p. 63; (October, 1909), p. 41.
[3] U.S. BLS, *Wages and Hours of Labor*, 1916, p. 21.

Cause	Days Lost
Slack work	72
Slack work and fire	61
Bad weather	47
Slack work and bad weather	39
Log shortage	32
Slack work and repairs	22
Slack work, log shortage, and repairs	17
Log shortage and repairs	17
Repairs and bad weather	14
Repairs	8
Repairs and log shortage	6
Repairs and slack work	6

Logging operations were everywhere more subject to weather than was milling, and they varied with the kind and size of timber and with the climate and topography of the region. For instance, in Texas in 1915, 6 logging establishments operated, respectively, 269, 270, 299, 298, 270, and 244 days during the year, an average operation of a high 270.9 days. In Washington the one establishment reporting operated for 218 days, and in Montana one operated for 231 days. In Texas no weeks were lost that year because of weather conditions. In 4 California plants, weather caused a loss of more than 100 days.

From April 1, 1927, to March 31, 1928, mills in Texas operated an average of 299 days, while the national average was 270 days.[4] For lack of market, mills were closed 7 days in Texas, 12 in Washington, 22 in Montana, 14 in Oregon, and 4 in California. For lack of logs, they were closed one day in Texas, one in California, 32 in Michigan, and 31 in Wisconsin. By this time 4 holidays were granted in Texas and 8 in California.

In 1956, of workers in Southern sawmills which employed more than 8 persons, 18 per cent had paid vacations and only 11 per cent had paid holidays.[5]

It seems clear that days lost because of the failure of a plant to operate were of relatively little importance in determining the wages of Texas workers. But the instability of the plants themselves has of recent years been disastrous to any pattern of steady employment.

[4] *Ibid., Wages and Hours of Labor*, 1919, p. 6.

[5] *Monthly Labor Review*, Vol. 80 (March, 1957), p. 328.

Between August, 1955, and August, 1956, 103 Southern sawmills employing nearly 4,600 workers disappeared, and a federal survey reported that Southern sawmills normally have a relatively high rate of turnover. In calculating earnings, then, merely to record the time lost by establishments reveals little.

Hours Worked. Since wages are the product of hours worked multiplied by rate of pay, the significant figure is the number of days the individual works. Even though a plant was in operation, the number of wage-earners it employed might fluctuate widely and rapidly. The average number of hours worked at a given rate does not indicate the wage of any single worker, of course, but it does suggest a general situation for the group. Month-by-month variations in the number employed or figures on the hours or days of those working during a month avoid the padding which results from merely reporting the number on the payroll. Fortunately, information about actual earnings versus full-time earnings has been gathered periodically.

A revealing example of the irregularity of employment of individual workers appears from the payroll books of the Gilmer company, which gives the number of persons receiving pay during each month over a five-year period.[6]

Year	*Jan.*	*Feb.*	*Mar.*	*Apr.*	*May*	*June*	*July*	*Aug.*	*Sept.*	*Oct.*	*Nov.*	*Dec.*
1891	153	146	132	128	120	156	177	190	170	173	149	149
1892	188	78	70	49	55	52	49	56	68	73	86	93
1893	82	89	94	51	36	32	38	41	26	28	56	33
1894	34	49	80	64	62	79	88	89	110	96	134	116
1895	117	130	127	116	125	129	125	160	150	134	127	120

In 1891, employment in May was 63 per cent of that in August. In the following year, employment in April was 26 per cent of that in January. From January, 1892, when 188 workers were employed, until September, 1894, when 110 were employed, at no time did the number employed reach 100. The figures are a reminder of the depression of 1893 and high-light its impact upon the town of Orange.

Entries for 60 workers in January, 1892, suggest what "being on the payroll" might mean to the individual employee: 2 persons

[6] Tabulations from Gilmer payrolls.

The lumber industry owes much to the ox. COURTESY TEXAS FOREST SERVICE

REPRINTED FROM ST. LOUIS *Lumberman*, AUGUST, 190

A floating boardinghouse.

REPRINTED FROM ST. LOUIS *Lumberman*, FEBRUARY, 190

Building a railroad through a cypress swamp.

Company Town REPRINTED FROM ST. LOUIS *Lumberman*, AUGUST, 1901

the Company Store. REPRINTED FROM ST. LOUIS *Lumberman*, FEBRUARY, 1905

Coördination

COURTESY TEXAS FOREST SERVICE

Double-handed through the pine knots. COURTESY TEXAS FOREST SERVICE

COURTESY SOUTHERN PINE LUMBER COMPANY

Mules also play an important role in lumbering.

COURTESY TEXAS FOREST SERVICE

"Big ones" on the way to market.

PHOTO BY JACK F. LAWS. COURTESY SOUTHERN PINE LUMBER COMPANY

he cry familiar to all men in the forest.

PHOTO BY JACK F. LAWS. COURTESY SOUTHERN PINE LUMBER COMPANY

The "Bull of the Woods" and his helpers: men, mules, machinery.

PHOTO FROM MOWAN STUDIO. COURTESY ANGELINA COUNTY CHAMBER OF COMMERCE

Lumber for work, lumber for play.

"Lickin' " exhibition.

COURTESY ANGELINA COUNTY CHAMBER OF COMMERCE

Loading up. COURTESY TEXAS HIGHWAY DEPARTMENT

PHOTO BY JACK F. LAWS. COURTESY SOUTHERN PINE LUMBER COMPANY

Surveying the stand. Saw weighs about seventy-five pounds.

worked 31 days, 14 worked more than 20 days, 18 worked less than 2 days, and 16 worked less than 7 days.

In 1909, the expansion of the industry brought comparatively steady work. Employment in the lowest month of the year was 98 per cent of that for the highest, compared with 85 per cent for all industries in the state.[7] Workers seemed to remain attached to the industry, for six years later, when average hours of operation per plant were 260 a month, the average per employee were 185.1—9 less than that for the nation.[8] Only 22 per cent of the workers reported on worked full time, though Alabama mills reported 90 per cent working full time and Georgia reported 86 per cent. Since actual hours per employee were 71 per cent of full-time hours, actual earnings would be less than three-fourths of full-time earnings. Average full-time earnings for Texas workers would have been 51 multiplied by $12—$612 for the year. But average hours per month per employee were 185.1, giving an income of approximately $435 for the year.

Following the close of the First World War information as to hours worked by occupational groups was gathered. The following figures are based on a 60-hour week, which was general.[9]

Average Hours per Day	*Texas*	*Nation*
Logging camps		
Drivers	5.4	6.2
Engineers	7.5	7.0
Hookers	2.5	5.2
Laborers	3.8	5.1
Lumber mills		
Doggers	4.6	6.6
Edgermen	4.7	7.6
Laborers	4.9	5.9
Machine feeders	4.8	6.8
Sawyers (band)	7.9	8.8
Setters	4.9	7.4
Trimmer operatives	5.8	7.8

Only engineers in logging worked as many hours as the average for the nation.

[7] *U.S. Census, 1910, Supplement for Texas*, p. 783.
[8] U.S. BLS, *Wages and Hours of Labor*, 1916, p. 62.
[9] *U.S. Census, 1919*, Vol. X, p. 424.

In the mid-twenties employment in plants reporting from Texas showed a minimum 87 per cent of maximum.[10] A good year is indicated in 1928 by the 310 days of operation of plants and with minimum employment 94 per cent of maximum.[11] But within another twelve months the minimum had dropped to 88.1 per cent of maximum. In planing mills the minimum of 82.5 per cent compared with 89.3 per cent in the United States.[12] Of workers in the Texas industry, 22 per cent worked full time and 29 per cent less than half of full time. Average full-time hours per month for establishments were 268.4 in Texas and 274.5 in the United States.

At the beginning of the fifties, underemployment and unemployment still characterized the lives of Texas lumber workers.[13] Of 6,120 employees in logging, 290 did not work at all in 1949; 310 worked not more than 13 weeks; 880, not more than 26 weeks; and 1,500—approximately 25 per cent of the total number—worked not more than half time. In 1953, employment was notably steady;[14] approximately 27,500 Texas lumber workers were employed for 7 months and the minimum was 96 per cent of that number.

Actual Earnings. The difference between actual earnings and potential earnings may be stated as that between wages received and the wages which would have been earned by working full time. In 1915 the differences for grades of workers in the lumber industry in Texas were:[15]

	Av. Hourly Wage (Cents)	*Av. Hours Full Time per Establishment*	*Actual Hours per Employee per Month*	*Percentage of Full Time*	*Approx. Actual Weekly Earnings*
Doggers	17.6	258.3	198.5	77	$10.52
Edgermen	24.6	258.3	191.5	74	16.44
Laborers	15.7	260.3	185.1	71	11.81
Machine feeders	16.1	260.5	215.2	82	7.29
Sawyers	55.0	257.8	229.0	89	15.84

[10] U.S. BLS, *Wages and Hours of Labor*, 1926, pp. 3, 12.
[11] *Ibid.*, *Wages and Hours of Labor*, 1929, p. 19.
[12] *U.S. Census, 1929*, Vol. II, pp. 440–534.
[13] *U.S. Census, 1950, Population—Detailed Characteristics*, p. 575.
[14] Reports, Texas Employment Office, 1953.
[15] U.S. BLS, *Wages and Hours of Labor*, 1916, pp. 30–46, 54–64.

Though sawyers were comparatively well paid in all states, in Texas, as already noted, they worked long hours for the weekly return. Of 34 employed in 1928, 14 worked 60 hours a week. In Washington, Idaho, and Oregon full-time hours that year were between 48 and 49.[16] Two years later actual and full-time earnings per week for head band-sawyers were:[17]

	Full Time	*Actual*
Texas	$49.45	$37.67
Washington	57.02	53.51
California	55.65	51.16
Louisiana	53.09	45.02
Nation	$49.53	$44.07

By 1932, for head band-sawyers in Texas with 60.6 per cent of full time, actual earnings were $22.85; full time would have been $37.72;[18] only two other states had a lower percentage of full time for sawyers. At the same time, 83 per cent of laborers in Texas sawmills worked full time, compared with 87 per cent in the United States. The average number of days worked per week was 4.3. Earnings—which would have been $13.94 for full time—were $11.57. That year laborers worked 90 per cent or more of full time in Oregon, California, Washington, and Wisconsin. Though the work week was 60 hours, 40 per cent of laborers worked 48 hours or less; and 44 per cent worked more than 60 hours. Of the 319 mills in the nation only 19 paid overtime rates higher than regular, and none seemed to be in Texas.

Paul Brissenden, after carefully weighing the evidence given in reports of the Census Bureau, found a marked divergence between possible full-time earnings and actual earnings in the lumber and lumber-products industry.[19] Figures for a quarter of a century give the following picture:

[16] *Ibid.*, *Wages and Hours of Labor*, 1929, pp. 19, 44.

[17] *Ibid.*, *Wages and Hours of Labor*, 1932, pp. 27–28.

[18] *Ibid.*, *Wages and Hours of Labor in the Lumber Industry in the United States, 1932*, Bulletin No. 586, 1933, p. 24, cited hereinafter as *Wages and Hours of Labor*, 1933.

[19] *Earnings of Factory Workers*, U.S. Census Monograph, No. X, 1929, p. 96, cited hereinafter as *Earnings of Factory Workers*, 1929.

Earnings	*1899*	*1904*	*1909*	*1914*	*1919*	*1921*	*1923*	*1925*
Full-time	$428	542	520	596	1,200	1,030	1,153	1,154
Actual	$346	435	426	458	1,000	775	1,078	1,126

In lumber and planing-mill products (not including planing mills combined with sawmills) the difference was:

Earnings	*1899*	*1904*	*1909*	*1914*	*1919*	*1921*	*1923*	*1925*
Full-time	$556	654	719	811	1,327	1,549	1,622	1,661
Actual	$449	525	590	624	1,088	1,165	1,517	1,621

As indicated above, the difference in the distribution of wage payments between the skilled and unskilled—i.e., between sawyers and laborers—was emphasized by the comparative regularity and irregularity of employment between the two groups. Individual earnings were, of course, increased by longer or extra hours of work. Though in Texas mills premium pay for overtime was seldom, probably never, given, work beyond the standard week was not uncommon. In fact, as mentioned earlier, sawyers were held in Texas by the extra hours obtainable, even though work was at lower hourly rates than were paid elsewhere. Laborers consistently worked fewer hours than sawyers. Until 1915, hours per work week were remarkably uniform throughout the country, being somewhat more than 60. At that time average full-time hours per sawmill per month were 264.4 for Texas —6.6 more than the average for the nation. Of 23 band sawyers in 10 establishments, 2 worked more than full time; 5 worked full time; 14 worked from 75 per cent to 100 per cent of full time. Of 1,727 laborers, only 109 worked full time and 117 more than full time; 221 worked less than 25 per cent of full time.

The difference between the hours the plants operated and the hours of work done by groups of employees is indicated by figures of monthly payrolls.[20] In Texas, establishments operated 258.3 hours; in the nation, 265.5. Comparative average hours worked for groups were:

[20] U.S. BLS, *Wages and Hours of Labor*, 1916, pp. 62–64.

	Texas	*Nation*
Doggers	198.5	206.1
Edgermen	191.5	225.1
Laborers	185.1	194.1
Band sawyers	229.0	229.5
Trimmer operators	234.7	234.6

The situation persisted and in 1928 of a total of 915, only 243 laborers worked the full-time week of 60 hours.[21] Four years later they worked 3.9 days per week compared with 4.6 for band sawyers.[22] In only one other state—Maine—did laborers work so small a proportion of full time.

Accidents and Compensation. Another factor entering into the determination of annual wages was unemployment due to sickness or industrial accidents. Since the lumber industry has had a heavy incidence of accidents and fatalities, it has been and still is described as "hazardous." In 1952 the federal Bureau of Labor Statistics, reporting on occupational hazards, stated that there has been some lessening of the "average lumber workman's chance of sustaining an injury on the job" but that it is still seven times as great as that of a workman in all manufacturing industries.[23] Reliable figures for the Texas section of the industry are not available, but there is no basis for assuming that if they were they would show Texas to be safer than the rest of the nation. Owing to the size of trees and the use of heavy machinery on the West Coast the rate and severity of accidents have been greater there than in the South; on the other hand, protection for workers has been more adequate there and compensation for injuries has been more generous.

From 1880 to 1900 there was no protection for workers in the Texas industry though casualty insurance by private companies was available. The financial settlement for each accident was determined by private agreement or in the courts. The Gilmer company carried

[21] *Ibid., Wages and Hours of Labor,* 1932, pp. 21, 48.

[22] *Ibid., Wages and Hours of Labor,* 1933.

[23] U.S. Children's Bureau, *Occupational Hazards to Young Workers,* Report No. 4, Logging and Sawmilling Industries Ser., 1942, p. 21, cited hereinafter as *Occupational Hazards to Young Workers.*

insurance on its workers as early as 1890.[24] It is probable that some of the other companies processing lumber also carried insurance.

Gilmer records for 1899 note that Charles Stafford had both legs broken and lost one of them. Treatment for six months cost $375, and his wooden leg, made by a sign painter at the "Magic Glue Pot," cost $2.00. According to the Orange *Leader*, Stafford was paid a fixed sum for the remainder of his life. Also in 1899, Vertes Looney received $25 as compensation for the amputation of a toe. Jack Davidson, a sawyer, received compensation of $25 per week (presumably while incapacitated). A few years later, a worker named Bilbo got $150 compensation for wages lost, $50 more the following month, and such work thereafter as he could do. One of the problems connected with court settlements is suggested by the search for Harry Livingstone, wanted as a witness in a damage suit in 1898. In the West such a search was an endless and usually futile task. Attempts were made in 1891 to pass a law giving some protection to workers. The lumber interests acted immediately to check the attempt. An immediate call went out from lumber operators M. T. Jones and Sam Allen to Mr. Gilmer, urging him to rally opposition.[25]

DEAR SIR:

We notice in today's *Post* that the judiciary committee #2 of the House reports favorably on a bill to protect employees of corporations and manufacturers against accidents growing out of defective appliances and the carelessness of fellow employees.

This seems very dangerous legislation to the manufacturing interests, and unless something is done the probabilities are the bill will pass the legislature and become law. We have not seen a full text of the bill, but we think best to act immediately.

It might be well for you to get your employees to petition the legislature against the passage of such a bill, and bring it along with you.

Advise us here as to how many can come to Austin on a telegraphic call.

Yours truly,

M. T. J.

S. C. A.

[24] Gilmer records and letters.

[25] Letters from Gilmer records.

Gilmer also received a letter concerning the bill from S. T. Swinford of the Warren Lumber Company, March 2, 1891: "Have written Mr. Lutcher to meet you and me and Mr. Bancroft at your office. I wish to bring matter of damage bill pending before legislature." And again from M. T. Jones, February 14, 1891: "The legislature proposes to look after the other fellow's interest against us." A decade later the "Fidelity Insurance Company was founded locally to protect sawmill laborers in case of accident."[26]

General recognition of hazard is implicit in the Fay Egan catalogue advertisement of a circular cutter head for hand-planers and surfacers, which presented pictures of a workman's hand with two fingers gone—"all lost on a hand jointer with a square cutter head."[27]

The St. Louis *Lumberman* reported the sources which were responsible for 39 per cent of all accidents in Southern logging: 21 per cent were in the logging camps, where almost one-half of this figure occurred in the cutting of lumber; 33 per cent occurred in the skidding and loading by power; 18 per cent were on the logging railroads—and 72 per cent of that figure occurred in the operation of cars and maintenance work.[28]

The same paper, noting popular attitudes in connection with a suit against the Kirby company for injuries on a logging road, said: "It has always been the practice of sawmill companies to force trial of lawsuits in counties where company headquarters are located to avoid prejudice that usually causes a sawmill town jury to bring a verdict for the plaintiff. . . . Saw and planing mills have shown a strong disposition to improve conditions especially in accident prevention."[29]

By the second decade of the century interest in industrial injuries—their costs to the nation and to the individual workers—was arousing national concern and in many states compensation laws were passed. In 1917, Texas enacted a law which gave limited coverage. For the lumber workers the most objectionable features of the law were the exclusion of plants employing 3 or fewer and the require-

[26] *Leader* (Orange), Jan. 10, 1902.
[27] *Lumberman*, Vol. 45 (April 1, 1909), p. 28.
[28] *Ibid.*, Vol. 46 (Nov. 1, 1910), p. 46.
[29] *Ibid.*, Vol. 45 (March 10, 1910), pp. 28, 64.

ment that the worker give written notice of claim to coverage at the time he was hired.

At the Fourth Southern Logging Conference in New Orleans in 1914, C. P. Myers of the Kirby Lumber Company discussed the extent of the problem. He did not include injuries in unpreventable catastrophes:

> Since receiving this letter I have checked up on hospital records and find that from January 1 to June 1 we had employees in the hospital aggregating 600 days or an average of 4 men in the hospital each day from Jan. 1 to June 1. From June 1 to September 1 we have had in the hospital employees an aggregate of 44 days or an average of 1 man less than one-half the time for the three months' period. Of these, two were for injury, one 22 days on account of having been kicked by a mule, and the other one day on account of slight injury to the eye. I do not think that you need any better proof of what can be accomplished with reasonable effort.
>
> I have had prepared a list of over 2500 accidents, classified under 59 different headings, and of these are reclassified under 17 [*sic*]. I find that these 17 classes amount to 2307 of the 2574 accidents, most numerous of which are injuries to the hands or fingers being cut or mashed, which amount to 753, and injury to the foot by being cut, mashed, or sprained amounting to 546. Practically all of the accidents of the hand or foot are no doubt of a preventable nature. I have here a recapitulation showing the manner in which different injuries occurred, which will be taken up in detail later.[30]

Mr. Myers stated that from September 1, 1912, to September 1, 1914, there had been in his company a total of 2,574 minor accidents hospitalized.

In 1913, the Texas Commissioner of Labor Statistics found a strong disposition among operators of sawmills and planing mills to "improve conditions especially in accident prevention." But, he continued:

> This character of industry is productive of a large percentage of accidents and a large amount of accidents occurring are due largely to absolute carelessness on the part of the employers. We, as a general rule, find the

[30] *Ibid.*, Vol. 54 (November, 1914), p. 22.

management of this character of industry ready to provide all suggested guards and protective devices but when any changes in improvements or repairs are to be made on machinery they will not replace them and the ultimate result is an accident to someone.[31]

Of twelve lump-sum settlements made by the Texas Industrial and Accident Board in December of that year, five were in the lumber industry.[32] They were paid by the Lumbermen's Indemnity Exchange. The operators' concern over accidents was expressed in their meetings, and in 1920, the Assistant Secretary of the Lumbermen's Mutual Casualty Company stated to a National Safety Conference meeting that 80 per cent of the accidents in the industry were preventable.[33]

In 1919, the Director of Safety of the Southern Pine Association reported 16,950 accidents with 125 lives lost in the area.[34] In 1927, the first official report of accidents in lumber-making in Texas by the Industrial Accident and Hygiene Service of the federal Department of Labor gave 12 deaths in sawmills employing 8,500 workers; in planing mills, one.[35] Three sawmills reporting 246 full-year workers had one death, representing a rate of 8.12 per 1,000 hours of exposure, and 17 sawmills reported 12 deaths, 2.81 per 1,000 hours of exposure. Three persons were permanently disabled in planing mills and 83 in sawmills, 4.58 per 1,000 hours of exposure. There were in addition 1,461 who had disabilities extending beyond one day.

After the passage of the Walsh-Healey Government Contracts Act in 1936 and the Fair Labor Standards Act in 1938, a study was made by the U. S. Children's Bureau of the sources of industrial hazards.[36] The first three industries in frequency of disabling injuries were logging, coal mining, and sawmilling. In severity of injuries, milling was exceeded only by logging, and ranked fourth in the number of fatalities, being exceeded by logging, coal mining, and fertilizer manufacturing. Though work in Western sawmills was more hazardous

[31] *Biennial Report,* p. 153.

[32] *Southwest,* Vol. 55 (January, 1915), p. 26.

[33] *Lumberman,* Vol. 65 (Oct. 4, 1920), p. 27.

[34] *Ibid.,* Vol. 64 (Jan. 28, 1920), p. 28.

[35] U.S. BLS, *Statistics of Industrial Accidents in the United States to the End of 1927,* Bulletin No. 490, 1928, p. 50.

[36] *Occupational Hazards to Young Workers.*

than that in Southern mills, the number of injuries in Southern mills was more than double that for manufacturing as a whole. The study pointed out that "portable sawmills are especially prevalent in the South. The equipment is often old, sometimes makeshift and crude and there seldom are devices for safeguarding the workers."[37] Though sawmilling was found to be less dangerous than logging, which had a very high injury rate, it ranked third after logging and coal mining in frequency of disabling injuries. While logging operations in some areas tended to be safer than those in other parts of the country, the frequency and severity rates in even the safest areas exceeded by far the corresponding rates for manufacturing as a whole. The 1939 federal Bureau report on industrial accidents said: "Since 1926, when the Bureau began to compile industrial injury rates for manufacturing industries, logging has consistently had the highest number of injuries per million employee hours worked."[38] In 1936–38 its frequency rate of 109—the highest of seventy-nine industry classifications—exceeded the combined rates for anthracite and bituminous coal mining. In logging, the average time per permanent partial disability was 1,832.3 days; in all manufacturing, 984.8 days. In the following year the average number of days lost per accident by lumber workmen in the South was 92, and those with permanent partial disability lost an average of 944 days—more than two and one-half years. Minor accidents caused total disability for an average of 17 days.

In 1952, logging topped the list of all industry, manufacturing, and nonmanufacturing in frequency rate of injuries. While the severity rate in lumber and wood products was 4.6, in no other manufacturing industry was it more than 2. Death or permanent total disability resulted from 0.5 per cent of the accidents. The frequency rate of injuries in "lumber and wood products, except furniture," was 49.6; in logging, 92.1.

In the mid-thirties compensation for industrial accidents in Texas applied to all employers having more than 3 employees. There was a waiting period of 7 days before a worker was eligible to receive com-

[37] *Ibid.*, p. 46.

[38] U.S. BLS Bulletin No. 667, pp. 21–23, 189.

pensation, and the waiting period was uncompensated unless disability lasted for 4 weeks or more. Compensation was 60 per cent of wages with a minimum of $7.00 for a number of weeks, depending upon the seriousness of the disability. For young people illegally employed there was no compensation. For wage-earners at the lowest levels, the right to take legal steps is almost nothing more than a gesture, though the amount which may be taken in lawyer's fees is limited by statute.

As the number of portable mills increased, so did the chances for accident, for all employees worked in close proximity to machinery. The equipment was often crude and makeshift, and devices for safeguarding workers were rare. For all lumber and wood products except furniture, the frequency rate was 43.6 and the severity rate 4.1; the average number of days lost for all cases was 92 and for permanent partial disability about 2.5 years; one-half of 1 per cent of injuries resulted in death or permanent total disability.[39] These mills, which were common in the Sabine pineries, were because of their size often exempted from coverage by the state compensation laws.

A figure of some interest is the high percentage of males unable to work in the population of the thirty-two counties in which the production of lumber is concentrated (Table 8). It can scarcely be ignored that the large number of men working in the most dangerous industry in the country results in many men's being incapacitated for holding available jobs.

The proportion in the state is 6.3 per cent of total population, 6 per cent of urban, 8.4 per cent of rural nonfarm, and 5.6 of rural farm populations. Only three counties—Bowie, Gregg, and Walker—have a proportion lower than that of the farm population; six have

[39] The injury frequency rate is the average number of disabling work injuries for each million employee hours worked. The severity rate is the average number of days' disability resulting from work injuries for each million employee hours worked and reflects both the severity of injuries and the frequency of occurrence. A disabling injury is any injury occurring during the course of, or arising out of, the employment which results in death or permanent physical impairment or makes the injured worker unable to perform the duties of any regularly-established job which is available to him in hours corresponding to the regular shift.

TABLE 8: Males Unable to Work in Thirty-two Lumber-Producing Counties, 1950

	Males 14+	*Unable to Work*	*Percentage*
Anderson	11,200	949	8.4
Angelina	12,701	775	6.1
Bowie	21,495	1,163	5.4
Camp	3,044	264	8.7
Cass	9,133	802	8.8
Cherokee	14,176	904	6.4
Gregg	21,501	1,104	5.1
Grimes	5,391	482	9.0
Hardin	6,905	534	7.7
Harrison	16,022	909	5.7
Henderson	8,436	576	6.8
Houston	8,126	751	9.2
Jasper	6,820	486	7.1
Liberty	9,472	648	6.8
Marion	3,459	227	6.5
Montgomery	8,657	767	8.9
Morris	3,295	349	11.0
Nacogdoches	10,653	782	7.3
Newton	3,663	387	11.0
Panola	6,558	537	8.2
Polk	5,715	504	8.8
Rusk	14,914	918	6.2
Sabine	3,033	316	10.4
San Augustine	3,034	257	8.5
San Jacinto	2,430	194	8.0
Shelby	8,217	852	10.3
Smith	26,406	1,772	6.7
Titus	6,114	520	8.5
Trinity	3,617	307	8.5
Tyler	4,096	313	7.6
Upshur	7,228	548	7.6
Walker	8,959	425	4.7

Source: Compiled from the preliminary report of *U.S. Census, 1950; Population—General Characteristics*, Texas, Table 43.

a proportion less than that for the state. Four have more than 10 per cent; 16 more than 8 per cent; 21 more than 7 per cent. For comparison, some other counties had as follows:

County	*Percentage*	*County*	*Percentage*
Atascosa	7.0	Dallas	3.0
Bastrop	9.0	El Paso	2.0
Bexar	4.5	Harris	3.0
Brazoria	3.5	Lubbock	2.5
Coleman	7.5	Nueces	2.0
Cooke	6.5		

There is no doubt that when a population has a high proportion of adult males unable to work, it has a marked effect upon median incomes and upon family living.

Media of Payment. Another factor which affects wages is the amount of actual money received and the regularity with which it is received. In the lumber areas of east Texas, wages were frequently paid in media other than money, and this became increasingly so after the turn of the century. Merchandise checks, coupons, disks cut out of pasteboard and stamped with the name of the company and the amount were often used. As recorded in the files of the Industrial Commission, the "K. Lumber Co." paid more than 90 per cent in merchandise checks, and these were accepted by the company in payment for rent, lumber, or supplies at the company store.[40] Used elsewhere they were discounted from 10 per cent to 20 per cent, for the discounter likewise had to spend them at the store or for products of the company. The time certificate, another medium of payment, was issued only in such emergencies as burials, weddings, discharge, or departure. This certificate stated simply that on the day of issuance John Doe had worked so many days, for which he had so much money coming to him, and that this money would be paid by the company on a certain future date. For the privilege of cashing before that date the worker had to pay a straight discount that ran from 10 per cent to 20 per cent; whether the time certificate fell due in one day or thirty, the same discount was charged. The "G. Co." had a somewhat different system—the issuance of daily pay checks dated ahead of the regular payday. If the men chose to hold them until payday, they received full value, but if they cashed them at the bank before that

[40] Unpublished records of the Industrial Commission, 1912. On file on microfilm in University of Texas Library, Austin, Texas.

time, or purchased with them, they had to accept a straight discount of 2.5 per cent.

Paydays at the "K. Lumber Co." were not only irregular; they were also far from frequent. In one instance, when the men were paid off in July, they were told that the next payday would be in December. In the meantime, however, they could secure merchandise checks up to the amount of their wages. Mining companies over the nation used scrip which did eventually become money, but the merchandise check never turned into copper, silver, or gold. The company did not redeem it, and took it back only in payment for rent, lumber, or supplies. It was worth only 80 cents or 90 cents on a dollar when presented anywhere other than at the company store, for merchants and professional men could not cash the checks. They had to turn them in at the company store for higher-priced supplies, or at the sawmill for lumber, hence they were compelled to demand the percentage. When asked by the representative of the Industrial Commission whether it often happened that a laborer got for $2.60 in merchandise checks only $1.80 in cash, the cashier of a company answered: "Quite often; the people are ignorant." It seems beyond question that when wages are paid not in cash but in "commissary money" (called "robissary money" by the workers) for a considerable length of time, as was done in a number of the lumber towns of Texas, the system put laborers practically into economic bondage to the owner of the commissary, where they had to buy everything at the price set. If they wished to buy elsewhere they had to cash checks at a discount, which meant a considerable deduction from wages received. One result of this system was that the employer operated at least partly on forced loans from his employees. Not only was no interest paid to the lenders but they had to pay for the privilege of becoming creditors!

As late as 1937 a bill read in the Texas House of Representatives and referred to the Committee on Labor stated in part:

> The fact that in some parts of the State certain parties are paying their laborers and other employees in scrip, chips, punchouts, coupons, or store orders redeemable only in merchandise at the commissary store owned by the employer and some of the parties are refusing to redeem such evidence of indebtedness unless the laborer discounts the coupons

or other evidence of indebtedness ten per cent or more which is a great injustice to the laborers of this State, creates an emergency and an imperative public necessity that the constitutional rule requiring bills to be read on three several days in each House be suspended . . . and shall take effect and be in full force from and after its passage.

The use of coupons and scrip for payment of wages is still legal in Texas but some protection for the workers was written into law in 1937. The employer must redeem them at face value in lawful money of the United States if they are presented at a regular payday. If payment in "good and lawful money" is refused, the wage-earner can bring suit and if he wins the case there is added to the amount a penalty of 25 per cent of the amount due and a reasonable fee for the plaintiff's attorney.

The use of coupons in lieu of cash wages had its difficulties for the employer as well as the employee. Since money issued by even the national government is not immune from nefarious activities, counterfeiting and bootlegging of company checks were to be expected. In one case the Trinity Lumber Company at Groveton was called on to redeem over $1,000 more than it had issued.[41] The Texas Rangers found perfect dies of plaster of Paris for reproducing the one-dollar and the fifty-cent checks used by the company and the bogus checks were so well made that they could scarcely be detected by expert examination. Other references in the newspapers indicate that this was not an isolated occurrence.

Medical Deductions. The pay of the workers was further affected by deductions for hospital and medical services furnished by the employing company.[42] By 1914 such deductions were well established and were taken from wages. In 1923 they amounted to $1.50 a month for heads of families and $1.00 a month for single men. Since they were general in the lumber camps, a man who worked for more than one company in a month might have to pay several deductions. Collection was without the consent or collaboration of the workers. Deductions for the cost of workmen's compensation carried

[41] *Southwest,* Vol. 13 (September, 1905).

[42] Gilmer records. See also the biennial reports of the state Bureau of Labor Statistics for the period.

under the Texas law were also made until 1917, when such action became illegal.

In summary, it bears repeating that wage *rates* tell only a part of the story. Actual earnings varied from potential full-time earnings because of irregularity not only of operation of plants but of work available for a large proportion of employees. Listed money wages were merely statements of hope for the workers. Irregular operation of establishments affected all workers, of course, but the working hours of individuals were sporadic, especially for the undifferentiated groups, and they were a large proportion. The extent of variance measured by the percentage of full time worked has been high in Texas compared to that in the nation. The high accident rate, which affected both skilled and unskilled, also made earnings uncertain.

The worker in the lumber industry lives dangerously, far more so than does a member of any other manufacturing group. The result is lowered incomes for the family and dependent adult males. The extent to which injury results in loss of income is a matter of legal provision within the state or of protection arranged by employers individually or collectively. Even after the passage of a compensation law in 1917, limited coverage deprived many workers of all income in case of an accident.

Until the recent past, "take-home pay" of the workers has been limited by deductions to pay for hospitalization furnished nominally by the employer and for workmen's compensation insurance. Moreover, the custom of paying wages in coupons, scrip, and other nonmonetary media denied the workers freedom of individual decision to buy in the cheapest market. Consequently they failed to secure even a meager knowledge of the financial structure of modern industrial society. Even now the law setting restrictions upon payment in scrip, coupons, etc., is not prohibitory and inevitably protects the more literate rather than the most ignorant and helpless.

One reason for low individual wages was undoubtedly the number of workers continuously attached to the industry. Wages were depressed by the persistent policy of keeping more workers on the payroll than could be used at even peak periods of production. The irregularity of work and income resulting from this practice is indicated by the difference between what wages *might* have been for the hours of plant operation and what they *were* for the actual hours worked. Payrolls were cocoons in which were hidden much disguised unemployment. Connected with the pronounced immobility of the unskilled wage-earners and largely resulting from it was their lack of bargaining power. The scarcity and mobility of the skilled gave their pay an upward pressure which was strong in the frontier days and continues, with diminishing intensity, to the present.

CHAPTER SEVEN

"Two things," said Kant, "fill me with breath-
less awe:
The starry heaven and the moral law."
But I know a thing more awful and obscure—
The long, long patience of the plundered poor.—
Edwin Markham

WHAT THE DOLLAR WOULD BUY

In order to evaluate the wages of any group over a period of time, it is important to consider what a dollar will buy. Goods, not money, are the living of the family and the individual. Any study of money wages, therefore, requires some comparative statements about the purchasing power of a dollar. Knowledge concerning the level of living of workers is the base for calculating the change in real wages.

Happily, some information is available as to the way the workers of Texas have lived. Little of it applies specifically to those in a given industry and the figures are generally from city areas. But it may be reasonably accepted that the workers in the lumber industry did not eat and live at a level differing greatly from that of other workers within their wage bracket in the state or region. Several studies give information relating to the principal items of food bought by the lumber workers and the quantity that could be purchased with the money received.

The 1901 Federal Survey. In 1901, the Bureau of Labor Statistics of the U.S. Department of Labor made its first attempt to gain information about how the average working man's family in the United States lived. The country was divided into five areas: the

TABLE 9: Average Quantity per Workingman's Family of Certain Principal Items of Food Consumed in 1901, by Geographical Divisions

Item	*Unit*	*North Atlantic Division (1,415 Families)*	*South Atlantic Division (219 Families)*	*North Central Division (721 Families)*	*South Central Division (122 Families)*	*Western Division (90 Families)*	*United States (2,567 Families)*
Fresh beef	pound	352.2	306.8	363.5	317.4	348.4	349.7
Salt beef	pound	75.3	9.4	21.3	3.5	3.8	48.6
Fresh hog products	pound	103.4	85.3	152.6	128.1	28.4	114.2
Salt hog products	pound	95.2	222.0	87.3	248.7	76.6	110.5
Other meat	pound	98.1	28.1	68.8	11.2	37.8	77.7
Poultry	pound	67.2	73.6	71.3	53.0	53.5	67.7
Fish	pound	98.9	66.1	56.5	39.5	57.5	79.9
Eggs	dozen	85.8	90.6	88.3	85.0	39.8	85.2
Milk	quart	396.3	191.9	348.2	220.8	324.4	354.5
Butter	pound	118.9	102.1	124.0	88.9	108.9	117.1
Cheese	pound	15.9	15.2	17.4	18.9	3.8	16.0
Lard	pound	73.8	119.5	89.1	143.3	48.5	84.4
Tea	pound	12.9	8.2	8.5	4.9	5.6	10.6
Coffee	pound	38.5	60.7	57.5	71.4	25.2	46.8
Sugar	pound	282.8	240.4	253.1	245.8	267.2	268.5
Molasses	gallon	3.2	4.6	3.4	6.2	4.0	3.6
Flour, meal	pound	624.0	851.8	718.2	979.5	452.3	680.8
Bread	loaf	310.2	197.0	165.6	199.8	255.2	252.7
Rice	pound	22.2	49.1	21.8	47.2	10.3	25.1
Potatoes	bushel	13.8	11.1	18.3	13.3	10.3	14.7

Source: U.S. BLS, *Retail Prices, 1890 to December, 1912,* Bulletin No. 132, p. 31.

North Atlantic, the South Atlantic, the North Central, the South Central, and the Western. Of the 2,567 families covered by the study, 122 were in the South Central district which comprised Louisiana, Arkansas, Texas, and Oklahoma. It seems valid to assume that families from eastern Texas are represented and that their expenditures are generally typified by the average for the section. In each of the several regions the average amount spent for food by the average family in 1901 was:[1]

South Central	$292.68	North Central	$321.60
North Atlantic	338.10	Western	308.53
South Atlantic	298.64	United States	326.90

TABLE 10: Average Amount Spent per Workingman's Family for the Principal Items of Food Consumed in 1901, by Geographical Divisions

Item	*North Atlantic Division (1,415 Families)*	*South Atlantic Division (219 Families)*	*North Central Division (721 Families)*	*South Central Division (122 Families)*	*Western Division (90 Families)*	*United States (2,567 Families)*
Fresh beef	$54.27	$41.08	$46.06	$37.84	$54.13	$50.05
Salt beef	8.18	1.13	2.20	.33	.66	5.26
Fresh hog products	12.83	10.48	18.39	15.60	4.04	14.02
Salt hog products	12.19	26.79	11.25	28.09	11.06	13.89
Other meat	12.26	3.86	8.68	1.40	5.35	9.73
Poultry	10.18	8.44	9.34	5.93	7.15	9.49
Fish	10.06	5.21	5.67	3.95	6.90	8.01
Eggs	18.44	15.55	15.24	13.20	11.01	16.79
Milk	24.29	13.02	19.67	12.25	20.46	21.32
Butter	29.77	25.76	28.48	21.74	31.81	28.76
Cheese	2.55	2.65	2.87	3.36	.69	2.62
Lard	8.15	12.72	10.34	14.31	5.44	9.35
Tea	6.33	4.40	4.22	2.69	3.43	5.30
Coffee	9.70	10.58	12.91	12.22	8.06	10.74
Sugar	16.67	14.15	14.63	15.70	14.49	15.76
Molasses	1.51	2.01	1.53	2.93	3.28	1.69
Flour and meal	16.24	21.10	16.47	22.68	8.85	16.76
Bread (bakery)	15.41	9.34	8.11	9.55	11.93	12.44
Rice	1.94	2.77	1.92	3.70	.91	2.05
Potatoes	13.77	9.29	13.01	11.54	9.84	12.93
Other vegetables	16.08	20.75	22.03	16.62	35.41	18.85
Fruit	15.31	15.22	17.15	11.52	40.53	16.52
Vinegar, pickles, and condiments	4.06	3.21	4.80	4.41	1.49	4.12
Other food	17.91	19.13	26.63	21.12	11.61	20.40
Total	$338.10	$298.64	$321.60	$292.68	$308.53	$326.90

Source: U.S. BLS, *Retail Prices of Food, 1890–1907,* Bulletin No. 77, pp. 181–332, especially p. 205.

[1] U.S. BLS, *Wages and Hours of Labor in Manufacturing Industries, 1890–1907,* Bulletin No. 77, 1908, pp. 181–332, especially p. 203.

That the amount spent in the South Central states was the lowest in the nation might be the result of several situations. One of them—that the prices of food might have been lower in the Southwestern states than in any other section—is discussed at some length in this chapter. Other factors that may have had some bearing on the low rank of the South Central District will be taken up later in this study.

The Bureau surveyed the food habits of the people and the prices paid for commonly-used items. The amounts consumed by families in the five areas and the prices they paid for these commodities show some interesting differences (Tables 9 and 10).

In the region claiming our particular attention the average family used in a year 128.1 pounds of fresh hog products and 317.4 pounds of fresh beef products. Throughout the nation as a whole, comparable families used 114.2 pounds of fresh hog products and 349.7 pounds of fresh beef. South Central families consumed 220.8 quarts of milk and ate 89 pounds of butter compared with the national average figures of 354.5 and 117, respectively. South Central families used 6.2 gallons of molasses; national-average families used half as much. South Central families used 25 pounds more coffee than the national average. Foods used in the South Central region in amounts larger than the average for the nation were: fresh and salt hog products, lard, coffee, molasses, flour, corn meal, and rice.

Notable differences as shown in Table 10 are the small amounts spent for fresh beef and "other meats" in the South Central area as compared to the United States, and the offsetting large expense in the South Central area for salt hog products; also the comparatively small amount spent in the South Central area for butter and the large amount spent for lard. Workers in the South Central area spent about half as much for tea as the national average and somewhat more for coffee; considerably more for flour and corn meal and markedly less for bakery bread. The amounts spent for sugar and potatoes are approximately the same.

The coffee in common use (one reason for its popularity may have been the stick of candy buried in each package) was Arbuckle's, which cost 20 cents per pound in Dallas and 17.5 cents in San Antonio. Another cheap coffee throughout the nation was Rio, which was 20 cents in Dallas. Those were the two most inexpensive coffees in all areas of the United States, but coffee prices ranged from 35 cents per pound for Mocha and Java to 14 cents for Rio. Round steak was 10 cents a pound in Dallas and San Antonio; the national price ranged from 9 cents to 21 cents. On the other hand, smoked and sliced ham cost 20 cents a pound in Dallas and 25 cents in San Antonio—the highest in the nation. Pork was 12.5 cents a pound in Dallas and San Antonio; molasses in New Orleans was from 50 cents to 65 cents a gallon, compared with 46.94 cents in the nation. Cheese was 20 cents a pound in Dallas and San Antonio, compared with the national average of 16.38 cents. Creamery butter at 32.92 cents per pound in Dallas was about median for the nation; granulated sugar at 6.5 cents was somewhat high. Fresh milk not bottled was 6.25 cents a quart in Dallas, 7.14 cents in San Antonio, 5.97 cents in Rochester (New York), and 6.07 cents in Seattle. A report on prices in Houston did not become available until 1918, but Dallas was the market for much buying, and prices in the two cities were probably very much the same.

Many of these prices seem beyond reasonable explanation. Why should ham be higher in Texas than anywhere else? Did the faithful razorback fail to produce hams and force his human compatriots to import them from other sections? Why should milk be more expensive? By 1901, certainly, the Longhorn was no longer synonymous with Texas cattle. Why was molasses in New Orleans—almost a trade name for molasses—50 per cent higher than in other sections? The answer cannot be found in transportation costs, for the railroad net in Texas was well established by 1900, and Dallas undoubtedly had as good rail service as had Denver or Salt Lake. Moreover, it is almost certainly true that the three items mentioned were locally produced.

The federal Bureau made a regular inspection of food prices, and in 1912 it made a year-by-year calculation of the relative cost of food for the average family from 1890 to 1912. In 1890 prices were 63.8 per cent of those in 1912; during the depression years of the nineties, they were more than 70 per cent. During the same twenty-year period the cost of food for South Central families was rising with

relation to the average cost for the nation, but they increased steadily after 1898.

It is an established principle of consumption patterns that the lower the family income, the larger is the percentage of that income spent for food. Assuming an average wage of $1.50 per day for workers in the lumber industry—a generous assumption, according

TABLE 11: Approximate Cost of a Year's Food Supply for an Average Workingman's Family, at Average Prices of Each Year, 1890–1912, by Geographical Divisions*

Year	*North Atlantic Division*	*South Atlantic Division*	*North Central Division*	*South Central Division*	*Western Division*
1890	$319	$274	$299	$260	$309
1891	320	277	307	274	314
1892	319	276	299	267	304
1893	327	280	312	278	300
1894	311	271	293	268	288
1895	304	266	285	261	281
1896	300	265	276	255	277
1897	305	265	282	259	279
1898	314	271	292	267	288
1899	313	278	293	270	299
1900	322	284	301	275	301
1901	338	299	322	293	309
1902	357	315	339	317	324
1903	356	312	339	321	323
1904	362	313	341	323	327
1905	360	315	342	324	329
1906	373	327	354	334	338
1907	388	343	370	349	358
1908	396	353	386	367	364
1909	411	375	409	392	386
1910	423	404	432	418	408
1911	422	389	424	419	409
1912	466	417	463	441	429

* Based on the average annual food cost per family in 1901 (Table 10) and the course of retail prices of food as indicated by the relative prices weighted according to family consumption. Cents are not shown in entering the approximate amounts in this table.

Source: U.S. BLS, *Retail Prices and Cost of Living, 1890 to December, 1912,* Bulletin No. 113, Retail Prices and Cost of Living Ser. 5, 1913, p. 35.

to figures already given—the return in 1901 for full-time work, 6 days per week for 50 weeks, was $450. Expenditures for food represented 65 per cent of full-time earnings of laborers.

Following its report of 1901, the Bureau made a regular check on prices. Using prices of 1890–99 as a base, it found that in the years between 1890 and 1912, retail prices of food rose by 63.8 per cent in the South Central area and 51.3 per cent over the nation (Table 11).

TABLE 12: Weighted Average Price for 1912 Compared with That of the Twenty-two Preceding Years

Price in 1912 higher than in	*North Atlantic Division*	*South Atlantic Division*	*North Central Division*	*South Central Division*	*Western Division*	*United States*
			PERCENTAGE			
1890	45.9	52.4	55.0	63.8	38.6	51.3
1891	45.6	50.9	51.0	60.8	36.4	49.1
1892	46.1	51.5	54.7	65.1	41.0	51.8
1893	42.4	49.3	48.4	58.6	42.8	48.1
1894	49.9	53.9	58.2	64.6	48.8	55.4
1895	53.0	56.7	62.3	68.8	52.5	58.8
1896	55.1	57.6	67.7	72.7	54.8	62.0
1897	52.7	57.4	64.0	70.6	53.6	59.5
1898	48.4	53.8	58.4	65.5	48.8	54.7
1899	48.7	50.3	58.2	63.2	43.2	53.0
1900	44.4	46.8	53.8	60.3	42.7	49.7
1901	37.7	39.7	43.9	50.7	39.0	42.1
1902	30.4	32.6	36.6	39.3	32.4	34.6
1903	30.8	33.8	36.5	37.4	32.7	34.4
1904	28.7	33.4	35.6	36.5	31.2	32.7
1905	29.3	32.5	35.5	36.3	30.4	32.5
1906	24.9	27.8	30.7	32.2	26.8	28.2
1907	20.0	21.8	25.1	26.3	19.7	22.5
1908	17.5	18.1	19.8	20.2	17.7	18.5
1909	13.3	11.2	13.3	12.4	11.0	12.4
1910	10.0	3.3	7.2	5.5	5.0	7.0
1911	10.2	7.3	9.1	5.3	4.8	7.8

Source: U.S. BLS, *Retail Prices, 1890 to December, 1912,* Bulletin No. 113, p. 21.

In the following year prices continued to rise. Using average prices of 1890–99 as a base, they changed by percentages as follows:

	1912	*1913*
Bacon	186.1	214.3
Flour	130.1	126.8
Corn meal	152.9	158.5
Eggs	202.9	205.2
Fresh milk	134.8	140.2
Sugar	115.1	102.9

At about the same time—in 1913/14—the common minimum daily wage in the Texas lumber industry was $1.50—$9.00 for a full-time week, $450 for a 50-week year. Within two years, average full-time weekly earnings of lumber workers in Texas decreased approximately 9 per cent, while average annual expenditures for twenty-two items of food in Dallas rose from $395.41 in January, 1913, to $410.63 in December, 1915.

The 1912 Survey. In 1912, the federal Bureau reported again on food expenditures. Using fifteen basic items, it found that total expenditures for food in each section represented the following percentages of total income: United States, 63.97; South Central, 67.95; North Atlantic, 64.11; South Atlantic, 66.43; North Central, 63.10; Western, 57.97.

Prices of the fifteen basic items of food were weighted according to average consumption in each division. In 1913 a rather inclusive study, made by the same agency, of the consumption of wage-earner families gave results as shown in Table 13.

To summarize the findings, in comparison with the consumption of wage-earning families throughout the nation, notable differences in the consumption of South Central families are: the greater use of fresh pork products; more than twice as much bacon and ham, and almost one and a half times as much lard; less bakery bread and much more flour and corn meal (more home baking in South Central); almost a third less butter; 134 fewer quarts of milk; 84 pounds fewer of potatoes; less than half as much tea but 24 pounds more coffee. The only item showing the same consumption for both is eggs.

TABLE 13: Consumption Patterns of Wage-earners, 1913

	Unit	WEIGHTS U.S.	South Central*
Sirloin steak	pound	70	63
Round steak	"	70	63
Rib roast	"	70	63
Chuck roast	"	70	63
Plate beef	"	70	63
Pork chops	"	114	128
Bacon	"	55	124
Ham	"	55	124
Lard	"	84	143
Hens	"	68	53
Bread	"	253[a] 225[b]	200 178
Flour	"	454	653
Corn meal	"	227	327
Eggs	dozen	85	85
Butter	pound	117	89
Potatoes	"	882	798
Sugar	"	269	246
Milk	quart	355	221
Cheese	pound	16	19
Rice	"	25	47
Coffee	"	47	71
Tea	"	11	5

* Includes Dallas, Houston, New Orleans, and Little Rock.
[a] Sixteen oz. of dough.
[b] One pound baked.

Comparing prices of items in 1913 in which the weights used in the South Central area are greater than those for the nation, we are forced to conclude that there is little support for any contention that lower food prices were a basis for lower wages. In Dallas, the prices of bacon, ham, potatoes, rice, and coffee were higher than in any other city listed. Bacon was higher both in Dallas and Little Rock than in any other cities.

The Texas Survey. The decrease in the purchasing power of the dollar spent for food commonly used is shown by the estimate (p. 130) by the Texas Bureau of Labor Statistics for the quarter-century following 1890.

Using records of the state purchasing agent, the Bureau noted that the cost of necessities of life had increased within the past year from

TABLE 14: Prices (by Standard Units) in Selected Cities, 1913

	Dallas	*Minneapolis*	*New York*	*San Francisco*	*Seattle*	*Little Rock*	*New Orleans*
Round steak	$0.204	$0.198	$0.250	$0.193	$0.208	$0.200	$0.187
Pork chops	.214	.185	.215	.236	.240	.210	.228
Bacon	.376	.264	.251	.337	.317	.363	.304
Ham	.311	.294	.29	.310	.302	.296	.273
Lard	.169	.154	.161	.180	.175	.159	.149
Corn meal	.029	.024	.034	.034	.031	.025	.027
Flour	.033	.029	.032	.034	.029	.036	.038
Eggs	.284	.283	.403	.373	.376	.291	.299
Potatoes	.022	.012	.025	.017	.012	.020	.021
Sugar	.058	.055	.049	.054	.061	.056	.052
Milk	.103	.074	.090	.100	.090	.100	.098
Cheese	.200	.206	.197	.200	.219	.225	.218
Rice	.093	.089		.085	.077	.083	.074
Coffee	.367	.308	.274	.320	.280	.308	.262

Source: Compiled from U.S. BLS, Bulletin No. 270, pp. 160 ff.

Average Dollar Would Buy	*1890*	*1916*
Bacon	8 pounds	3.5 pounds
Bread	10.8 pounds	5.7 pounds
Eggs	4.8 dozen	2.7 dozen
Butter	3.9 pounds	2.5 pounds
Flour	1.41 bags	.93 bags
Corn meal	52.6 pounds	29.4 pounds
Potatoes	3 pecks	2.5 pecks
Sugar	14.5 pounds	12.5 pounds

25 per cent to 100 per cent, and for some items used by the average worker's family, the cost had increased beyond 100 per cent. Groceries had increased by 25 per cent. The price of flour bought in wholesale lots of a hundred pounds or more had increased by 20 per cent but if bought in smaller quantities the percentage was even greater.[2]

According to the Bureau, minimum weekly wages of lumber workers in the Beaumont and Port Arthur area were at that time $7.50; the average was $9.50. After the close of the First World War the average was $8.08. During the war years workers in the east Texas lumber industry had lost ground economically.

War Prices. After the war began in 1914, prices rose rapidly. At Little Rock annual expenditures for food rose from $390.14 in 1913 to $711.09 in January, 1919, and had increased by $43 more at the close of the year; in New Orleans they rose from $369.29 in January, 1913, to $694.24 in December, 1919. By December, 1919, the total spent for twenty-two items of food in Dallas had risen to $728.11, an increase of 92 per cent over January, 1913. In Houston, for which figures were available for the first time in 1919, the amount spent was $699.70 (Table 15).

By 1921, the average annual wage in lumber manufacturing in Texas was $808, but a detailed report by the federal Bureau shows about 8,000 of almost 13,000 workers receiving from $12 to $20 per week and more than 2,000 receiving from $6.00 to $12 per week—at most, $600 for a 50-week year. The average daily wage had decreased by more than 25 per cent during the year.

[2] Texas Bureau of Labor Statistics, *Biennial Report*, pp. 21, 106 ff.

TABLE 15: Average Family Expenditures for Twenty-two Items of Food, 1913–19

City	*1913*	*1914*	*1915*	*1916*	*1917*	*1918*	*1919*
Dallas	$395.41	405.96	402.20	439.96	572.22	650.54	728.11
Houston	...	...	...	...	...	...	699.70
Little Rock	390.14	396.82	393.70	429.92	562.06	649.47	711.09
New Orleans	369.29	376.56	377.38	414.73	546.78	621.97	694.24
Seattle	265.35	265.84	263.07	278.81	358.02	420.21	474.48
San Francisco	271.48	274.39	274.99	286.39	352.03	423.36	463.05

Source: U.S. BLS, *Retail Prices, 1913 to December, 1919,* Bulletin No. 270, pp. 166 ff.

Real Earnings. Paul Brissenden, working under the auspices of the Bureau of the Census, studied the trend of real wages in the United States during the first two decades of the twentieth century. Using 1914 as 100, he found that money earnings for Texas workers were: 85 per cent in 1904; 97 per cent in 1909; 191 per cent in 1919; 175 per cent in 1921; and 205 per cent in 1923.[3] But the per capita real earnings of manual labor for Texas in 1899 were $561 and in 1923 were $648—an increase of $87, or 16 per cent. Between 1899 and 1914 they had decreased by 5 per cent, but during the following decade they had increased by 25 per cent.

After a careful weighing of all available data, Brissenden found that in the first two decades of the century Texas workers experienced a greater decline in real earnings than workers in any other state in the Southern areas. Furthermore, Texas wage-earners already had low per-capita earnings in 1899 and they had gained little by the end of the first quarter of the century. Since workers in the processing of lumber were the largest group of the industrially-employed, it must be concluded that their financial status differed little if at all from that of the body of workers.

FROM THE FIGURES given in the beginning of this chapter there seems to be no basis for assuming that low money wages were based upon a cost of consumption goods lower for the workers in Texas than

[3] *Earnings of Factory Workers*, 1929, pp. 81, 179, 209.

that in the Midwestern and Western areas. As we have seen, the first survey of the scale of living of workers, made by the U.S. Department of Labor in 1901, showed the amount spent for food by workers of the South Central area to be the lowest in the nation. Such a ranking might have, of course, resulted from lower prices of food—in which case these workers would have been as well fed for less money. But figures on prices gathered throughout the nation do not support such a conclusion. Not only were the prices of certain basic food items higher in this area but the proportion of wages spent for food was a higher percentage of the average yearly wage. That factors other than regional ones were responsible is indicated by the fact that in the nation the largest increase of real wages occurred in the South during the first quarter of the present century—in North Carolina with 77 per cent; Oklahoma with 62 per cent; South Carolina with 61 per cent; Alabama with 44 per cent. These were all above the national average of 39 per cent. The real wages of Texas lumber workers were low compared to those in other areas. And low pay means a low scale of living.

Other factors which might seem to create wages in the industry are certainly subjects for consideration. Though they are not easily determined and the data, as exact statements, are more than questionable, an effort to limn them within the framework is certainly not extraneous to a full delineation. They are the material of the next chapter.

CHAPTER EIGHT

So far as labor is a factor of production, cost depends not merely upon wages, but upon wages as compared with output. Under certain conditions there is a true economy in high wages; the more a workman is paid, the less he may cost.—EDWIN R. A. SELIGMAN

A JUDGMENT OF EFFICIENCY

THE COST OF PROCESSING LUMBER, as is true of any other product, is the sum of all costs incurred—from the purchase of the raw materials to the output of the finished product. The "value of product" is the market-price value of all articles turned out by the factory. When the cost of raw materials as they come to the mill is subtracted from the value of product, the result is the "value added by manufacture." The costs of producing this value are the wages paid to workers and salaries paid to executive, managerial, and clerical staffs, plus interest on capital invested and other capital costs such as depreciation, replacement, insurance, taxes. When the total value of product or the total value added is divided by the number of wage-earners employed in the process of manufacture, the result is the average value of product or the average value added per wage-earner. This average value would seem to be an indication of the economic efficiency of the workers, that is, of their capacity to add to the total output. Since value of product is determined at the market price, which tends to be the same for all products, a low proportion of wage costs to the total value means a large margin between wages paid and the value added by the process of manufacture.

Since the payment of wages forms so large a part of the total cost of processing lumber, there would seem to be a significant relation between the value added by manufacture per worker and the average wage. For the next few pages we shall examine some figures to see whether they support the assumption that wages are high where workers add high value through manufacture.

In 1890, wages amounted to 27.7 per cent of the cost of manufacture in lumber and planing mills in Texas.[1] Only two other states, Colorado and Maryland, showed wages as so low a part of the total cost in lumber and planing mills. Wages accounted for 40 per cent of such cost in California and Washington. At the time, the average yearly wage in Texas was $15 more than the national average. But wages in Texas could be higher than those in California and Washington and still not lessen unduly other shares of the gross income from production.

In 1921, in lumber and furniture production for plants having products of $5,000 and over, the average wage in Texas was $808, compared with $861 for the nation.[2] Average value of product per worker was $2,241—less by $237 than the average for the nation. Average value of product per worker added by manufacturing was $1,302—less by $128 than the average for the nation.

By 1925, wages in Texas had increased a little less than 2 per cent. Value of product per worker had increased by the same proportion, and value added by manufacture had risen by 3 per cent. For the nation, wages increased almost 12 per cent, while value of product and value added by manufacturing per worker had increased about 20 per cent. Of 9,207 establishments in the United States having production value of more than $5,000, Texas had 196. They employed 18,200 wage-earners. When average yearly pay in various states is

[1] *U.S. Census, 1890, Report on Manufactures*, p. 47.

[2] U.S. BLS, *Wages and Hours of Labor*, 1926, p. 8.

shown with average value of product and average value added by manufacture, it is possible to make significant observations.

	Wages	*Value of Product*	*Value Added by Manufacture*
Texas	$ 821	$2,618	$1,681
Arkansas	792	2,909	1,608
California	1,340	2,918	2,065
Connecticut	1,984	3,074	1,947
Idaho	1,281	3,498	2,421
Indiana	1,012	4,677	2,249
Massachusetts	1,042	4,280	2,029
New York	1,170	4,345	2,326
Oregon	1,359	3,862	2,217
South Carolina	657	1,887	1,153
Washington	1,406	4,237	2,207
Nation	$ 964	$2,998	$1,776

Source: U.S. BLS, Bulletin No. 497, Wages and Hours Ser., p. 25.

In Texas, as in Arkansas, value added is more than twice the average wage. In California average wages are 65 per cent of average value added, and in Washington and Oregon the ratio is about the same; all three are high-wage states. Factors other than productivity of workers, then, would seem to be the important ones in determining wages. In California, value of product is $2,918, just $300 more than in Texas. Value added in California is about $384 more than in Texas, but wages there are approximately one and two-thirds higher than in Texas.

In 1927 the average wage in Texas had increased by $56, average product by $70, and average value added by $42.[3]

	Average Wage	*Product per Wage-earner*	*Value Added by Manufacture*
Texas	$ 878	2,688	1,723
Georgia	559	1,893	1,136
Oregon	1,345	3,701	2,217
Washington	1,422	4,261	2,154
South Carolina	643	1,662	1,043
Alabama	653	1,963	1,218
Louisiana	850	2,684	1,723
Mississippi	798	2,634	1,560

[3] *Ibid., Wages and Hours of Labor*, 1932, p. 23.

Paul Douglas[4] made critical use of available information to determine the relationship between real earnings of workers and value produced per employee in the lumber industry. He found an increase of 31 per cent in real value produced from 1904 to 1925. During the same period real wages rose only 4 per cent. His study is the source of the following figures.

Relative Value of Product per Employee and Relative Real Earnings in the Lumber Industry

Year	*Relative Value of Product per Employee*	*Relative Real Earnings*
1899*	100	100
1904	101	113
1909	109	105
1914	106	106
1919	98	118
1921	113	104
1923	138	119
1925	132	117

* The year 1899 = 100.

Using 1914 as a base year, the increase in real earnings for thirty-nine manufacturing industries was 30 per cent, while the lumber industry showed a decrease in real earnings.

Regional Cost of Production. The lower wages paid in Southern industry does not necessarily mean that labor costs were cheaper. In a survey covering the years 1926–35 for 7 Pacific Coast sawmills and 9 Southern sawmills, A. J. Van Tassel found that man-hours per board feet or equivalent production ranged, over the ten-year period, from 8.34 to 7.76 in Pacific Coast mills and from 18.42 to 15.38 in Southern mills.[5] The difference in wages was such that labor costs per thousand feet was in no year as much as $1.00. An increase in wages in Southern mills would have had at that time one of several

4 *Real Wages in the United States, 1890–1926*, p. 531.

5 *Mechanization in the Lumber Industry*, Works Progress Administration, Report No. M5, 1940, p. 130.

results. Many mills might have been forced to close down, causing many workers to lose their jobs. Production would necessarily have been concentrated in the lowest-cost plants and that would have greatly restricted output. Moreover, the price of lumber would probably have risen and that would have restricted sales still more. It is true, however, that Southern mills might have increased productivity per unit of labor by increasing their use of machinery or through more efficient management. Texas mills have not always been technically backward. Around 1900, the Texas mills passed through a period of rapid mechanization, and some mills became models of the newest in machinery and methods. This progressiveness lapsed, however, and after a quarter of a century they had become technically stagnant.

In his study, Van Tassel included an excerpt from a report of the U.S. Forest Service (1938) which stated that the "difference in outputs (of labor) arises directly from differences in condition of resource (size of trees, stand density, etc.) and indirectly from greater mechanization thereby made possible for handling large Pacific Coast timber." The excerpt also said that if Pacific Coast wage rates were applied in Southern pine operations "trees under about twenty inches in diameter and forests lacking a considerable volume of larger trees could not profitably be cut for saw timber unless price levels should be greatly increased."[6]

Such a consequence probably would have had positive economic and social values. Though some laborers might have been forced into other lines of work, denudation of Southern pine forests likely would have been checked, and a higher level of living for inhabitants of the region might have emerged. The transfer of workers to other kinds of employment would probably have required positive action from outside sources, but one cannot avoid the conclusion that forces external to individual choices of the workers have operated to confine them within the area and the occupational nexus.

While the figures cited can scarcely form the basis for a judgment as to the relation between productivity and wages, taken in connec-

[6] *Ibid.*, pp. 131–132.

tion with other figures they do tend to strengthen the suggestion that workers in the Texas lumber industry were not poorly paid because they were ineffective and unproductive. They were no doubt less efficient than they would have been with better food and better living conditions.

That the amount paid out in wages was a smaller part of value added by manufacture in Texas than in Washington and Oregon questions any assumption that workers in the Southern pines did not produce as much as did those on the West coast. It also further strengthens the suggestion that low wages were not essential to the profitable operation of the industry—a suggestion which appeared as the result of continuing investigations to determine the effects of the higher wage set under the Fair Labor Standards Act. The rate was to be set "without substantially curtailing employment or earning power." Since the timber industry is one in which wages account for a large part of the cost of production, there was some concern about the effect that a higher minimum wage would have upon the number of persons employed.

The Minimum Wage. On January 1, 1950, a minimum wage of 75 cents per hour went into effect. Among Southern sawmills, less than 2 per cent of the plants contacted during a survey made between October and December of 1949 had closed before March, 1950. None of the operators of the closed plants held the new minimum wage wholly responsible. Moreover, the opening of new mills during the January–March period raised the total number in operation above that of 1949. The requirement that there must be premium pay for overtime work did have a significant effect upon the hours of work available to individuals and groups of workers, and again it was the most skilled workers who were least affected. Though logging plants with 12 or fewer workers were exempt from the requirements of the law, the lateral effects of sawmill wage increases are evident. In March, 1950, 9 per cent of sawmill workers and 12 per cent of logging workers had average subminimum wages. Three years later (April, 1953) 1 per cent of sawmill and 2 per cent of logging workers averaged subminimum wages. Between December, 1949, and March, 1950, while total employment in Southwestern sawmills fell by 5 per cent, the number of mills in Texas increased from 272 to 326 and the number of workers employed from 15,751 to 16,826.

With the setting of the $1.00 minimum per hour in 1956, the increase in straight-time average hourly earnings might be termed dramatic: from the early thirties to the mid-fifties per annum increase in earnings had been 3.6 cents; in the first quarter of 1956 it was 16 cents. In the fall of 1955, about three-fourths of nonsupervisory workers earned less than $1.00 an hour and more than a third earned 75 cents. Since sawmills with fewer than 8 employees were not covered, it is possible that competition forced many of them to close but even if that did happen, the effect of their closing upon total numbers employed would have been inconsiderable. Certainly if the low wages paid before 1937 had been essential to the operation of the industry, the effect of the minimum wages would have been notable if not spectacular.

Although many Texas workers were raised to the legal level each time a new minimum wage was set, comparative regional disadvantages continued. In January, 1958, for the South, weekly hours of 38.7 at an average of $1.23 per hour resulted in earnings of $47.60; in the West, 37.7 hours at $2.23 resulted in $84.07; in the nation 38 hours at $1.80 resulted in $68.40 per week.[7] But the wage disadvantage cannot be explained as a regional difference. Methods of transportation and marketing tend to unify wages, and where they are high in a given industry in one section they tend to be high throughout the nation. During the 1950's, for instance, for chemical and petroleum products average hourly straight-time earnings for the South were only a few cents below those of the Northeast and Middlewest and but 28 cents below those of the Far West. For lumber and furniture the difference was 53 cents below Midwest earnings and $1.16 below those of the Far West.[8] In the South 56.1 per cent of workers in lumber and furniture received less than 90 cents per hour, as contrasted with 25 per cent in the nation, while in another low-

[7] "Effects of the $1 Minimum Wage in Five Industries," *Monthly Labor Review*, Vol. 81 (May, 1958), pp. 492–501.

[8] "The Distribution of Factory Workers' Earnings," *Monthly Labor Review*, Vol. 78 (April, 1955), pp. 410–415.

paid industry—textiles—the rate was 13.9 per cent for the nation and 19.1 per cent for the South.

While there is a tendency for modern marketing to make wages uniform between areas nationally and even internationally by widening areas of competition, certain persistent factors do tend to preserve real limitations on the expansion of competitive regions. Among these are immobility of workers and differences in the quality of labor. Differences in the cost of living are not a reason for differing *real* wages, but only for *money* wages. It may be true that there is a tendency for wages to fit into the wage pattern of areas, but as pointed out above, the low-wage tendency of the South is not a prevailing force.

In summary, let us say that it is evident from figures cited in this study that there is in the production of lumber within Texas a concentration of wage-earners in groups whose wages are low in comparison with those paid for equivalent work in other areas and in other occupational groups. At the turn of the century the situation of lumber workers was no better and no worse than that of other workers in the state and no worse than that of lumber workers in other areas in the nation. That their conditions have not kept pace with the improvement of other workers in the state and lumbers workers throughout the country is due partially to the fact of their isolation, their exclusion from urban trends, and a collateral half-legendary aura accepting their "roughness," their "toughness" and their lack of interest in bettering their conditions. In prohibition campaigns, for instance, the "East Texan" became a symbol of the evils of alcohol. Of east Texas tales reported by a writer in *Southwest* in August of 1904, the following dialogue is typical:

> Mabel: Mama, do tie makers eat hay?
> Mama: Yes, dear, if you sprinkle a little whiskey on it.

Low-paid labor is not cheap labor. Efficient production is gained not by the lowest wage-bill but by the lowest labor cost per unit of output. By drawing and holding efficient labor, comparatively high absolute wages tend to give a low labor cost per unit of output—the only comparative advantage there is in the use of labor. And another facet is presented by the fact that in any area the largest numbers of consumers of goods are the wage-earners; hence they are the largest market, actual or potential, for the sale of goods. The wider the experience horizon of individuals comprising the labor force, the greater is their incentive for efficient production, an incentive generated by their high standard of living. It follows, then, that the power to consume which results from high wages tied to efficient labor is the soundest basis for industrial development for the simple reason that it furnishes a home market for goods.

CHAPTER NINE

While the earlier economists argued as though man's character and efficiency were to be regarded as a fixed quantity, modern economists keep constantly in mind the fact that it is a product of the circumstances under which he has lived. In particular they did not see that the poverty is the chief cause of that weakness and inefficiency which are the causes of their poverty.—Alfred Marshall

THE COMPANY TOWN

EARNINGS AND HOURS OF WORK are important to a man, but other features determining the conditions under which he and his family work and live are of great importance, too.

In 1880, the national census made a report on wages, cost of living, trade societies, strikes, and lockouts for each state. The report included two Texas mills. The mill of D. R. Wingate at Orange, which had been established in 1874 to manufacture yellow-pine lumber, reported that all its employees had received an increase in wages in the six years since its establishment.[1] Foremen received from $100 to $104 per month; all others were paid by the day: sawyers and filers, $4.00; teamsters, $1.50; and laborers, 75 cents. The work day

[1] *U.S. Census, 1880, Industry and Wealth,* pp. 491 ff.

was 10 hours and work was steady throughout the year. The only stoppages were due to the mill's closing down a few days for repairs. Wages were paid monthly, two-thirds in cash. Accounts at the company were deducted from wages.

The Amsler Mill at Prismoid, which had been in operation since 1866, reported that its employees had free houses, gardens, wood, and the privilege of keeping a horse and cow, increments which increased wages 15 per cent. The payment of wages was 80 per cent in cash and 20 per cent in merchandise at the company store. Store orders were never used. The work day was 10 hours and there were no deductions from wages. Records of the Gilmer Company emphasize the same features: cash wages and a close personal relation within the plant circle.

But in the closing years of the nineteenth century a change came over the industry. As the forests around towns such as Orange were cut down, the intimate relation between employees and individual operators was necessarily changed. Logging operations moved into isolated areas and the employers built their own communities. As the mills moved away from houses and stores of established community life, the employer—who had become "The Company"—must perforce furnish homes and retail outlets for consumer goods needed by the workers. When employees were family men, as the majority were, the inevitable result was the company town built upon land owned by the employer. Homeownership was impossible and a man's acceptance of a job determined his family's living quarters.

"Company towns" became an ever-present, even a dominating, feature of the eastern Texas scene. They sprang up with startling rapidity. The St. Louis *Lumberman* in April, 1910, noted that 500 men were working in a Trinity mill town where a year ago there had been nothing but pine trees. We can safely assume a village of 1,500 or more people.

This description of the town of Ragley, which appeared in *Southwest* in the early 1900's could be accepted with little or no alteration for any "lumber town":

Ten miles from Timpson in the heart of the East Texas yellow pine region, and situated on their own railway line, is the town of Ragley and the extensive mills of the Ragley Lumber Company. This company represents one of the largest and most important milling interests in the Southwest. The plant covers seventy-five acres. In addition to the mills, there are one hundred two-dwelling houses, which are picturesquely scattered about on the sloping hillsides on well laid-out streets, and shaded by groves of hardwood trees, which were wisely left standing when the pine was cut off, as they came from nature.

Messrs. Ragley have for their own use a commodious and comfortable bungalow, where the most charming hospitality is dispersed to their fortunate guests. The house is one story, built in such a manner as to catch breezes from all quarters. One hardly would look for a private billiard room in the wilds of the East Texas woods, but that is one of the luxuries to while away the hours when the day's work is done, which the hospitable Ragley "boys" provided.

The houses built for employees are comfortable and homelike. Every two houses have a well of pure freestone water. There are from 800 to 1000 people living at Ragley, all depending on the mill for support. The company has an extensive commissary store carrying a full line of supplies. There is also a drug store, barber shop, and other establishments that figure in the make-up of a well-regulated town. All this is part of the mill interest.[2]

In the first decade of the century, the town of Diboll was described as an up-to-date lumber town. It had about 1,500 inhabitants, 400 men working in town at the mill and 200 at two camps in the woods. It had a 3-teacher school with 125 pupils, a brass band, and a baseball team. A library was being constructed to house a gift of five thousand volumes donated by the president of the company. The camps were not so good, of course. At Groveton, the Trinity Lumber Company had a program of adult education for their employees and about 35 attended.[3]

Writing in 1911 of the improvements that had been made in the living conditions of the workers in the towns, a correspondent looking back fifteen years remembered not so roseate a picture. Workers then were living "in an old box house with no water and light, with

[2] *Southwest*, Vol. 13 (July, 1905), p. 14.

[3] *Ibid.*, Vol. 17 (July, 1909), p. 49; (December, 1909), p. 66.

hog wallows around the door, hogs and goats in the house, and children sticking heads through the holes."[4]

Under the conditions, homeownership was almost impossible. In 1911/12 the state Bureau reported on the number of homeowners among workers in plants of the lumber industry.[5]

County	*Persons Employed*	*Homeowners*
Angelina	499	13
Cherokee	193	0
Hardin	840	10
Jefferson	275	0
Liberty	269*	13
Nacogdoches	255	22
Orange	167	38
Tyler	331	60
Walker	197	10

* There were two firms at Liberty.

It might be noted that homeownership among workers in all other Texas industries was by no means common, either. Employers were not opposed to homeownership for workers. In fact, Mr. Kirby, owner of the Kirby Lumber Company and a man who might be considered the spokesman for employers in the lumber industry in Texas, believed in the home as "the unit of social progress." Homeownership was a constitutional right:

Our forefathers at Philadelphia, when they formulated the Declaration of Independence declared that men were "endowed with certain inalienable rights, among them the right of life, liberty and the pursuit of happiness." Pursuit of happiness would be in vain if men could not acquire homes. Whatever thought of a socialistic nature this may be to the contrary, we Americans have always believed, and we doubtless always shall believe that human happiness is the object of all human life, and it is one thing to which every man should lend his energies in its attainment, happiness not only for himself, but happiness for his fellow man. That happiness cannot be secured should we ever become a nation of tenants. It is the home where there is peace and love and contentment and sweet-

[4] *Ibid.*, Vol. 19 (August, 1911), p. 23.
[5] *Biennial Report*, pp. 48–92.

ness. It is the home that is the citadel of patriotism. It is the home that inspires men with all those lofty things that will make him want to die, if necessary, for his country, give up his life, if necessary, for the promotion of happiness of others. . . .

If you will provide the American citizen an opportunity to own his own home and induce that citizen to make the acquisition, you will have absolutely closed the door to the I.W.W. sentiment throughout this republic.[6]

The Commission on Industrial Relations that in 1912 studied the conditions of labor in the nation more thoroughly than had been done up to the time of the First World War included on-the-spot studies of the "lumber towns" of the Sabine area.[7] John R. Commons, as chief of the technical staff, headed a group whose names make a distinguished list. Investigators visited typical labor camps in New York, Michigan, North Dakota, South Dakota, Montana, Washington, and Texas, selecting the best, the average, and the worst. As representative of the eastern Texas camps, three—designated as "T. Lumber Co.," "A. G. Lumber Co.," and "K. Lumber Co."—were studied in detail.

The T. Lumber Co. employed 350 men as mill hands, a section gang, and a logging crew. All the houses, hotels, churches, schools, and the commissary were owned by the company. The store handled drugs as well as general merchandise, which was of usual quality. All the people in town had to buy at the commissary, which accepted at face value the merchandise checks with which the workers were paid. Those who wished to trade elsewhere had often to take a discount of from 5 per cent to 10 per cent. Little cash was in circulation in the town. Wages were paid on the twentieth of each month. Deductions were made for hospital fees—$1.00 a month for married men and 75 cents for single men—and a flat insurance fee of $1.25 a month for married men but $1.00 for single men who were paid less than $2.00 a day and $1.25 if paid $2.00 or more. The town had a population of about 1,500 of whom approximately 60 per cent were Negroes. All

[6] *Official Report of Fourth Annual Meeting*, Southern Pine Association, Feb. 25–26, 1919, p. 58.

[7] Unpublished records of Commission on Industrial Relations, 1912. On file on microfilm, University of Texas Library, Austin, Texas.

employees were native-born. Married men paid house rent ranging from $3.50 to $12 a month, an average of between $5.50 and $6.00. Single men paid $18 or $20 a month for room and board. The company tried to promote saving among the workers through circular letters and by paying from 4 per cent to 6 per cent interest on money deposited with it. It was the judgment of the investigators that the workers were steady and that the company tried to provide facilities for family life.

The A. G. Lumber Co. had 150 laborers engaged in sawmill, logging, and railway work, only 10 of whom were skilled. Wages differed little from those paid by the T. Lumber Co.: filers, $10 per day; sawyers, $6.00; foremen, $125 per month. Wages of unskilled labor ranged from $1.55 to $1.75 per day, and whites and Negroes received the same rate of pay. The work day was 10 hours, with an hour allowed for lunch at the job. The men left home at 6:00 o'clock in the morning and traveled from thirty minutes to an hour to the place of work. They left the woods at 5:30 P.M. Pay checks, issued daily, were cashed at face value by the company if they were presented one month after the date of issue. If cashed even one day earlier a 4-per-cent straight discount was taken. Local merchants and banks cashed them at any time, with a 4-per-cent to 5-per-cent straight discount.

The company claimed that payment in daily checks had two purposes: to encourage saving among the men and to avoid handling cash. Since the majority of the workers received less than $1.75 per day, they generally cashed their checks before the date of maturity. They lost the discount, of course, and the company thus collected interest on its monthly wage bill. Local merchants claimed they accepted the checks at par even with the discount but when they presented them to the banks they were discounted. The rent for a house—described by the workers as a pretty "sore affair"—averaged about $6.00. Single men paid about $20 a month for room and board. Hospital and insurance fees were taken out of the wages of all workers from their third day's wages each month. Consequently, any man working as much as three days for more than one employer during any given month paid the fee more than once.

K. Lumber Co. rented land from the Houston Oil Company but

K. Lumber Co. owned the houses used by its workers. Citizens not employed by the company had built privately-owned homes in the surrounding areas. The company employed about 400 men, mill hands, a section gang, and a logging crew. About a third of these, mainly the lowest paid, were a shifting group. About 70 workers were skilled, but their wages were lower than those paid in the other two companies investigated by the Commission. Payday—in cash—was supposed to come once a month but the last one, previous to the visit of the investigator, had been in July and the next was promised for December. Meanwhile the workers were paid in checks which stated that they were "good for merchandise only," that is, they were never cashed by the company. If a worker needed cash for an "emergency" —a burial, wedding, quitting the job—he might get a time certificate which the company would cash on the next payday. Two banks would cash them before that time, taking from 10 per cent to 20 per cent straight discount. A worker could get such a certificate only if he could show that he had an urgent "need for merchandise which could not be bought at the Company's store." The worker who could not get a time certificate had to cash his merchandise checks with local businessmen at a straight discount of from 10 per cent to 20 per cent, and often more.

One of the local businessmen explained how the transaction worked. He had accepted $200 in merchandise checks for which he gave $160 cash value. He sold them for $160 cash to another local businessman who wished to build a house and had to buy lumber from the company. The company accepted the checks at face value. The first man had discounted the checks 20 per cent, but sold them at their discounted value, so he neither gained nor lost. The second man actually gained 20 per cent. Only the wage-earner lost. Since businessmen accepted merchandise checks as did private individuals, there were more merchandise checks in the town than cash. But because the businessmen, like the workers, could spend the checks only with the company, it meant they were forced to buy goods at the commissary at prices higher than wholesale prices elsewhere. The company attributed its postponement of payday to hard times and the difficulty of collecting from the customers. It is true that at this particular time the mill was operating only 5 days a week, but since the use of merchandise checks and time certificates had existed for many years, the explanation was scarcely adequate for the over-all situation even if the company was justified in temporary retrenchments. The manager of the company admitted that the workers lost by the check system, but he placed the blame on the men. They were ignorant, he said, and they did not save money. They did not need to cash their checks or ask for time certificates because they could buy everything they needed from the company store, where their checks were accepted at face value.

The investigations of the Commission had covered the mining camps of the West from Lead to Ludlow, the lumber camps of the Northeast, and the textile towns of the South, but the member of the Commission who came to the K. lumber town stated:

> The time certificate and the merchandise check, especially the latter, are the most reprehensible thing your investigator has discovered in his work of investigation in this country; the merchandise check controls the town, it compels all the townspeople to buy the necessities of life in the commissary store of the Company at whatever price the Company chooses to make.

R. G. Lillard quotes memoranda sent to headquarters by two labor organizers:

> Southern Pine at Diboll: Wages $3.00 to $3.54 a day; Board $1.00 and conditions are rotten. The place is policed for agitators by the servile slaves. This is a very pleasant habit they have in Texas.

> Kirby Lumber Company at Browndell: Rotten shacks; rotten commissaries; rotten doctors; rotten insurance and always from fifty cents to $1.00 a day under the other mills.[8]

Labor organizers can seldom be accused of looking through rose-colored glasses, but wages of $3.00 and over were not those of the lowest-paid workers, we may be sure.

In 1922, the Texas Bureau of Labor Statistics found that it was "the prevailing custom for the lumber companies to furnish living

[8] *The Great Forest*, p. 300.

TABLE 16: Housing in Thirty-two Counties, 1950

		NOT DILAPIDATED				DILAPIDATED	
	All Dwelling Units	*Hot Running Water; Private Bath, Toilet*	*Cold Running Water; Private Bath, Toilet*	*Running Water; No Private Toilet, Bath*	*No Running Water*	*Hot Running Water; Private Bath, Toilet*	*No Hot Water or Private Bath, Toilet*
Anderson	10,385	3,837	433	1,019	2,041	78	2,561
Angelina	11,376	3,865	246	1,809	2,947	157	2,095
Bowie	19,364	8,290	459	2,017	4,127	185	3,784
Camp	2,812	709	57	414	934	10	566
Cass	8,227	2,039	109	817	3,093	20	1,991
Cherokee	11,282	3,005	250	1,261	2,934	107	2,982
Gregg	19,932	11,119	318	2,227	2,468	283	2,837
Grimes	4,883	1,027	146	486	1,382	28	1,321
Hardin	5,900	1,700	211	897	1,378	90	1,453
Harrison	14,304	4,769	239	1,943	3,037	125	3,693
Henderson	7,688	1,983	255	1,101	2,218	71	1,625
Houston	7,448	1,657	149	743	2,260	78	2,222
Jasper	5,803	1,591	106	940	1,585	26	1,446

Liberty	8,077	3,005	300	1,047	1,612	64	1,806
Marion	3,090	671	34	341	968	7	1,017
Montgomery	7,927	2,421	193	781	1,731	55	2,118
Morris	3,029	833	66	375	1,016	24	635
Nacogdoches	9,226	2,568	253	1,223	2,391	178	2,257
Newton	3,066	378	39	429	1,200	13	952
Panola	5,720	1,610	57	528	1,800	97	1,449
Polk	4,966	1,223	140	642	1,316	44	1,320
Rush	13,224	5,267	240	1,366	3,141	163	2,573
Sabine	2,569	385	89	301	1,158	6	572
San Augustine	2,742	475	41	223	1,066	2	872
San Jacinto	2,145	175	37	114	759	13	949
Shelby	7,615	1,788	117	822	2,442	45	2,245
Smith	23,031	11,152	624	2,894	4,236	261	3,180
Titus	5,638	1,861	84	642	1,812	67	962
Trinity	3,437	624	85	393	1,153	24	972
Tyler	3,491	818	127	444	1,212	20	767
Upshur	6,603	1,809	131	904	2,120	67	1,319
Walker	5,531	1,621	99	644	1,579	49	1,359

Source: Compiled from preliminary report of *U.S. Census, 1950; Report on Housing*, Texas, based on a 20-per-cent sample.

quarters for employees, the companies usually owning all real estate adjacent to the mills." By the mid-twenties another survey by the Bureau disclosed that "in the milling districts inadequate housing conditions, poor sanitation, and lack of social diversions are the rule, though many exceptions were found where companies operating the mills had apparently made every effort to provide the most modern facilities."[9] Practically every sawmill in the east Texas milling districts was visited and reports were secured from 87 mills. In these districts 228 homes were visited, and

> while a number of noteworthy exceptions were encountered it was found that the homes or living quarters provided by the mill for their employees were inadequate to the needs of a normal family. As a rule very poor provisions are made for sanitation; the houses are built close together, and little yard or garden space is provided.

Four years later, the Bureau inspected 16 lumber camps in east Texas, employing more than 4,000 workers.[10] The investigators visited 825 homes. Of 781 families living in rented houses, 669 rented from the companies. Fewer than half the houses had electric lights and 510 had running water; "no adequate sewer facilities were found in any of the camps."

From the U.S. Census report on housing made in 1950, a picture of present-day housing conditions appears (Tables 16 and 17). In Sabine County somewhat less than one-sixth of the homes reported upon were "not dilapidated" and had a private toilet and bath with hot running water; in San Jacinto County this was true of less than one-tenth.

A report to the Congressional committee which reported on the Economic Report of the President in 1951 describes a company house during the last decade:

> The Littles live in a three-room "company" house which consists of a living room-bedroom combination, a kitchen and bedroom. There is an outdoor toilet. There are no bathing facilities, nor do they have electricity. Although they have an ice box, they get ice for it when they go to town

[9] *Biennial Report* (1923/24), pp. 612 ff.
[10] *Biennial Report* (1927/28), p. 45.

for groceries. Their household furnishings are scant, consisting of one table, four straight chairs, one armchair, an ice box, a double bed, and pallets on the floor upon which the children sleep.[11]

The descriptions given above outline only the physical aspects of the village and may omit some of those. But the heart of the company town was not the physical surroundings furnished—it was the company control over any and all activities of workers living in it. A writer in the St. Louis *Lumberman* at the time of the First World War put the matter simply:

He [the owner] hired married men by preference and let them all keep their families in camp. Had schools and churches. No Sunday work. No cursing, or drink. Get rid of trouble breeders as quickly as possible. . . . "I try to keep out disorganizers on my timber cutting operations. Sometime ago I found that one of the men was complaining about the price. Finally located him and invited him to leave. Had no further trouble."[12]

From 1894, when the revolt of the workers in Pullman's ideal village shocked the nation into an awareness of the power and control implicit in the company-owned town, until the same abuses in the villages of the textile and mining industries disappeared from the old South, the company town was the object of Congressional committee attention, of investigation by students of social conditions, and of protests from workers. After the First World War, the company town was under continuous, vigorous, and at times violent, attack by workers, by unions, by investigators of social conditions, and by public-spirited citizens. The company town did not cease to exist, but it did become somewhat isolated and sporadic in the growth of American production. Texas "lumber towns" were not greatly different from those in other sections of the country, but by the third decade of the twentieth century those still in existence were living on borrowed time.

[11] Joint Committee Print, *Making Ends Meet on Less Than $2,000 a Year: Case Studies of 1,000 Low-Income Families*, 82d Cong., 1st Sess., 1951, pp. 50–51.

[12] Vol. 60 (Nov. 1, 1917), p. 42.

TABLE 17: Number of Homes in Thirty-two Counties by Year of Construction

	Number Reporting	YEAR BUILT 1919 or Earlier	1920–1929	1930–1939	1940–1944	1945
Anderson	10,095	2,795	1,995	2,635	870	1,800
Angelina	11,060	1,855	2,325	2,950	1,295	2,635
Bowie	18,735	2,940	3,970	4,050	4,450	3,325
Camp	2,745	775	470	850	220	430
Cass	8,035	1,505	1,600	2,715	780	1,435
Cherokee	10,515	2,790	2,205	2,655	1,005	1,860
Gregg	19,465	1,465	2,070	10,575	1,640	3,715
Grimes	4,530	1,605	900	960	330	735
Hardin	5,590	1,235	1,085	1,250	635	1,385
Harrison	13,810	3,450	3,205	3,340	1,340	2,475
Henderson	7,315	1,520	1,435	1,915	730	1,715
Houston	7,200	1,980	1,710	1,655	635	1,220
Jasper	5,660	1,165	885	1,215	770	1,625
Liberty	7,790	935	1,645	2,610	755	1,845
Marion	3,010	770	350	1,010	270	610
Montgomery	7,265	925	1,095	2,245	815	2,185
Morris	2,945	875	450	620	300	700
Nacogdoches	8,755	1,630	2,055	2,665	735	1,670
Newton	3,045	605	560	740	280	860
Panola	5,615	1,345	945	1,370	440	1,515
Polk	4,690	1,155	930	1,305	405	895
Rush	12,790	1,775	1,770	6,020	900	2,325
Sabine	2,425	905	455	465	190	410
San Augustine	2,640	595	380	860	300	505
San Jacinto	2,040	365	375	550	225	525
Shelby	7,415	1,705	1,665	1,990	703	1,350
Smith	22,260	3,920	3,580	8,055	1,780	4,925
Titus	5,390	1,015	850	1,715	560	1,250
Trinity	3,160	1,255	625	610	160	510
Tyler	3,355	860	830	835	365	865
Upshur	6,410	1,085	990	2,185	705	1,445
Walker	4,990	1,005	915	1,450	450	1,170

Source: Compiled from preliminary report of *U.S. Census, 1950; Report on Housing,* Texas, based on a 20-per-cent sample.

After the Commission on Industrial Relations had visited Dallas in 1912, a writer observed:

Similar conditions in the lumber industry, however, are only now being brought to light. Investigators of the Commission on Industrial Relations, exploring in Texas, have discovered that the sawmill is as much a "baron's stronghold" as the coal or gold mine. The lumber communities of the Lone Star State are as far removed from freedom and democracy as though time had rolled back to the days of Ivanhoe.[13]

Not long after the description of the town of Ragley was written, another observer, paraphrasing the famous description of a more noted company town Pullman, written twenty years earlier, characterized the life of a millworker in east Texas:

He is born in a Company house; wrapped in Company swaddling clothes, rocked in a Company cradle. At two years of age he toddles out on the Company street and takes his first infantile look at the Company mill. At five years of age he goes to the Company school. At eleven he graduates and goes to the Company woods. At sixteen he goes to work in the Company mill. At twenty-one he gets married in a Company church. She is not a company girl, but when she stands at the chancel rail with her groom, it is noticed that her veil has been bought in the Company store. At forty, he sickens with Company malaria, lies down on a Company bed, is attended by a Company doctor who doses him with Company drugs, and then he draws his last Company breath, while the undertaker is paid by the widow in Company scrip for the Company coffin in which he is buried on Company ground.[14]

The writer of those lines and Mr. Kirby looked upon the same scene, but their interest and the context of their comprehension were worlds apart.

At about the same time, the head of a mill in Kirbyville reported a walkout of members of the Brotherhood of Timber Workers on the first day of the Graybeaux trial (discussed at some length in the following chapter). "We paid every man in full and demanded our houses. . . . We are not in sympathy with the Brotherhood of Timber Workers and have no employment for them."[15]

After spending much time in Texas, the Commission on Industrial Relations made the judgment:

[13] George Creel, "The Feudal Towns of Texas," *Harper's Weekly*, Vol. IX (January, 1915), pp. 447 ff.

[14] *The Rebel* (Hallettsville), Feb. 17, 1912.

[15] *Southwest*, Vol. 19 (October, 1912), p. 27.

We find that many entire communities exist under the arbitrary economic control of corporation officials charged with the management of an industry or group of industries and we find that in such communities, political liberty does not exist and its forms are hollow mockery. . . . Free speech, free assembly, and a free press may be denied as they have been denied time and again, and the employer's agent may be placed in public office to do his bidding.[16]

A few years later a suit brought against the Kirby Lumber Company in the courts of Louisiana set forth the many possibilities that the company town has for control.[17] The Kirby Lumber Company operated a large sawmill plant and general merchandise store at Merryville, Beauregard Parish, Louisiana. O. E. Johnson, manager of the store and sawmill, had the power to employ and discharge employees and to direct all activities of any nature whatsoever connected with, or incidental to, the operation of the company. A man named Deon bought a lot near the sawmill, built a store, stocked it with merchandise, and "opened it as a general mercantile store for business with the public." A few days before the store opened, the company, acting through Johnson and foremen in charge of various departments, called a mass meeting and publicly notified all employees of the company that they were "prohibited from purchasing any goods or wares at petitioner's [Deon's] store and further warned said employees that any of them who dealt or traded with petitioner or who visited his store or family would be immediately discharged." The company did discharge some workers and threatened to discharge others for trading with and visiting the Deon family, and it reduced the wages of some employees for this offense. It was inevitable that this infringement on the personal liberty of the workers should also restrain their political protest. Roscoe Martin, in his study of the People's Party in Texas, reported that the vote in eastern Texas was a controlled vote.[18]

[16] Unpublished records of Commission on Industrial Relations, 1912.

[17] *Deon* v. *Kirby Lumber Co.*, Supreme Court of Louisiana, 162 La. 671, 111 So. 55, 1927.

[18] *The People's Party in Texas*, University of Texas Bulletin 3308, 1933, p. 68.

Nor was control limited to the workers; even an adjacent town could be brought under the domination of the company. The town of privately-owned homes and businesses which grew up around the Kirby Lumber Company tried to incorporate to secure better sanitary conditions, better street cleaning, and police and fire protection.[19] The real basis of the movement, it was reported, was "to get rid of the Company's grip on the town." The company successfully opposed the attempt, ostensibly because it would mean higher taxes. It threatened to close the mill and stop its business.

There were certain factors implicit in the lumber situation that made opposition to the company almost impossible. The company town was a "lumber town"—the only jobs available were those in the mills and the logging camps. In the area of the Sabine pineries there was no other industry which workers might turn to during lay-off periods in the lumber plants, and there was no opportunity which they might venture into. Since even the "service" industries, including retailing, were in the hands of the company, no independent middle group developed. Lumber towns were made up solely of the executives, the skilled craftsmen—few in number—and the great majority, the low-waged laborers.

Since a large percentage of the cost of producing lumber goes to wages and since the level of wages was low, it follows that most of the money paid out in wages was spent in the immediate area, for foodstuffs and other supplies furnished by the immediate region. The development of industries was greatly restricted by the company monopoly. Wage work for women, for instance, which has as a matter of necessity so often served to raise the incomes of low-earning groups, was nonexistent. One can only wonder—almost marvel—that no "women's industries" were organized to use this pool of labor. An area dominated by a man's industry, abutting on one dominated by a woman's industry, is a familiar pattern of industrial life.

Connected with the company village was the inevitable commissary. As noted above, expansion took the industry farther and farther away from the centers of population. Sometimes other stores were

[19] Unpublished records of Commission on Industrial Relations, 1912.

allowed to do business, but the general rule was that the operating company owned the mercantile establishment. In the nineteenth century, Alexander Gilmer, owner of the Gilmer mills, refused to operate a commissary. In 1895 he wrote that he paid his hands cash each Monday night and "avoided curses I would get if I had a commissary."[20] In his opinion he saved the expense of a commissary and also enabled the workers to buy cheaper. The Gilmer mills had an arrangement with L. Miller, who ran a general store, to pay off hands and sell them goods.

By 1906, the Gilmer interests had become a corporation. A reporter for *Southwest* described the new town and railroad station at Brookeland (now known as Weed).[21] One hundred houses for employees and families had been built and as many more were under construction. Houses were all rented on the basis of 5 cents a room per day—$4.50 per month—for a three-room house. The dynamos, with seven arcs and the twenty-two-candlepower incandescent lamps, would be sufficient to light mill yards and the better houses perfectly. For workers who did not have families, the mill had contracted with a New Orleans firm to furnish a boardinghouse, to be operated by the manager of the hotel at Brookeland. Gilmer's opposition to operating a commissary was no longer tenable, and the new town had a store 100 feet by 40 feet, with a fully-stocked upper deck around three sides. At about the same time, Gilmer wrote to the manager of the commissary at another of his towns, Remlig (the town, the name of which was the reverse spelling of Gilmer's name, no longer exists), about two miles from Brookeland:

> I hear you have increased prices on some goods in the store making dissatisfaction. I hear your new manager does not know business. We must sell goods like they do in Brookeland. You had better sell at the old price. We expect to get customers from the country folks as well as our own hands. We must meet competition. You will have them delivering goods from Brookeland if they are not already doing so.[22]

[20] Letter Press, No. 12, p. 50; No. 31, p. 412; No. 53, p. 317.

[21] *Southwest*, Vol. 13 (May, 1906), p. 34; Letter Press, No. 75, pp. 354–359, 379–385.

[22] Letter Press, No. 77, p. 279.

For the mid-twenties the Texas Bureau found that "most concerns maintain commissaries. The prices charged at these commissaries were approximately the same as those charged at the retail stores in the vicinity of the mills."[23] But investigators for the Commission on Industrial Relations also made some comparisons between prices charged at a commissary and those at private stores.[24] The brand of lard known as Silverleaf sold for $1.65 for 10 pounds at the commissary, $1.50 at private stores; a sack of cottonseed meal, $1.75 as against $1.60; 100 pounds of chopped corn, $2.00 and $1.85; 35 pounds of corn meal, $1.00 and $.90. Commissary prices were, the Commission concluded, from 5 per cent to 10 per cent higher than in other stores. The greatest differences would probably be found only in isolated or closely controlled situations. And the more trade a commissary could draw from a potential market among nonemployees of the company, the more profitable were its operations, of course. In preparing this study I searched all available newspaper files for prices listed in advertisements of groceries. It is an interesting commentary that no such advertisements appeared in the Silsbee *Bee*, the Jasper *Newsboy*, or any other papers whose principal circulation was in the lumber-producing areas.

A correspondent writing in *Southwest* in 1915 remembered commissaries of years before as having "limited stocks of such things as the sawmill laborers had to have in order to get along: meat, flour, molasses, sugar, coffee, shoes, tobacco, and clothes."[25] But by 1915 commissaries were serving the general trade, not just employees of the mills. Accounts of the stores operated by the Kirby company indicate that a well-managed store could be highly profitable, and the Gilmer commissary at Remlig was reported in 1906 to have shown a net gain of $960.93 in a month.[26] Furthermore, during periods of unemployment and of shutdowns, workers still had to eat, and the commissary and the rental of houses furnished a more or less steady income to the operators in an unstable industry. A story was cited by

[23] *Biennial Report* (1923/24), p. 15.

[24] Unpublished records of Commission on Industrial Relations, 1912.

[25] Vol. 22 (February), p. 26.

[26] Letter Press, No. 77, June 4, 1906.

Southwest as a favorite of Ben Woodhead, a lumber operator, about the "old days." In answer to the usual question, an old lumberman said that everything was getting along fine except the commissary. He had had several good men in charge, but the commissary was still a failure. "I simply can't understand what's the matter. . . . We have never succeeded in making more than eighty per cent on that end of the business."[27]

But the Sabine pine forests grow in two states—divided but not separated by the river. Just after the First World War, when troubles with the Brotherhood of Timber Workers and the Industrial Workers of the World had emphasized the resentment of the workers, the Louisiana Department of Labor made a report on the "company store" as operated in the pineries:

> We have made a study of "the company store" and commissary problem, and [feel] free to admit it is a perplexing one in so far as related to a satisfactory solution. However, we feel justified in offering comment, and shall confine same to conditions as we actually found them. We admit there are two sides to this question, but investigations have thoroughly convinced us that some law should be passed regulating the operation of company stores or leased commissaries since conditions show conclusively the real sufferer in the final analysis is the laborer. Similar laws have been passed by sister states and proven a blessing and saving to those who ordinarily receive a low rate of wages. Statistics show that leased commissaries are even worse than those operated by employers themselves.
>
> On account of many industries, particularly among the lumber operators and sugar manufacturers, being located at outlying or isolated points where there are no other stores, it might become necessary to operate either a company store or a commissary, at the same time it does not follow such operations should be necessarily an evil. If such places were properly conducted, that is, sell laborers such goods and wares as were necessary and furnish same at cost of maintenance or even at a small margin of profit, no adverse comment would come from this office, but ordinarily these conditions do not exist. It is true that some of the more humane employers are doing this, while a few claim to be operating stores

[27] Vol. 16 (July, 1909), p. 30.

at a slight loss, but the average company store or leased commissary is operated as a money-making proposition and prices are fabulously high, and as proof this statement will say that during the month of last July, while flour was selling throughout the state at about $11.50 per barrel, some commissaries were charging their employes as much as $19.00 for same, and at the same time were charging laborers 42 cents per pound for salt meat and 10 cents per pound for second grade rice, while the public market prices were about 28 and 6 cents respectively for these commodities.

While similar conditions existed at many commissaries, though possibly not so bad in most of those operated by the employers themselves, we are convinced the greatest evils exist in commissaries leased by the employer to outside parties, for the reason that the employer gets a part of the profits, and as the operators must live, the laborers are penalized, to use the slang phrase, "both going and coming."

Inquiries developed the fact that there are chains of commissaries operating within the state that are domiciled elsewhere, and are paying a tribute to employers to furnish supplies to their laborers. We learned from both parties to this policy that often the operators paid as much as ten per cent of the gross sales to the commissary for this privilege. One particular manager of a lumbermill admitted his company did not have one penny invested in the commissary, was at no expense, assumed no responsibility for losses in any way, yet ten per cent of the gross sales was paid for the privilege of operation. The manager of this same store stated that of necessity he had to make a profit of from twenty-five to thirty-five per cent to pay for the privilege of operation and make a fair profit for himself on his investments. Commissaries operated under these or similar conditions are not only a menace to the community in which located, but the state at large and a curse to humanity. It is no hard task to solve who are the real sufferers under such conditions as these. What profit is derived by the laborer even though wages are increased ten, twenty, or even thirty per cent if there are no restrictions thrown around such conditions as these and unscrupulous employers and their allies are permitted to literally rob them by charging exorbitantly high prices?

We wish to make it very plain that even though experience is a dear teacher, the laborers are beginning to look with distrust upon all such employers and the time is fast coming when all such conditions must be changed or employers of this class will not only be complaining of labor shortage, but will be unable to secure help at any price.[28]

In 1922, the state Bureau reported that of 77 mills employing 12,675 persons, 62 operated commissaries. A year later, of 87 mills employing more than 14,000 persons, most of them operated commissaries.[29]

Not until 1937 was a state law passed that corporations paying their employees in "coupons, scrip, punchout store orders or other evidence of indebtedness" be required to guarantee such payment to be redeemable in "good and lawful money of the United States." Redemption must be at face value, meaning that the employee would receive in cash exactly the same amount as called for in the scrip or coupon. Such payment was redeemable only on a regular payday.

Peonage. The company town was always identified with the existence or nonexistence of peonage. But national interest in peonage was largely concerned with its relation to immigrant labor, and immigrant labor, as has been said already, was insignificant in Texas. The Congressional Immigration Commission investigating the conditions of immigrants found that in the South peonage occurred in almost every industry—farming, lumber, logging, railroading, mining, factories, and construction work. The chief bases for peonage listed by the Commission were advances to laborers for transportation which the laborers must agree to work out, operations under convict-labor laws, and misrepresentations. It stated as a finding:

So far as the Immigration Commission has been able to discern, there has never been any attempt to prosecute for peonage in any states and territories west of the Mississippi River except in the Southern states of Missouri, Arkansas, Louisiana and Texas, and one case at Omaha.[30]

In 1906 a writer in the *Nation*[31] attributed peonage to the benev-

[28] *Ninth Biennial Report of the Department of Commissioner of Labor and Industrial Statistics*, Louisiana, 1915/16.

[29] *Biennial Report*, pp. 13–15.

[30] U.S. Immigration Committee, *Reports*, Senate Doc. 747, 61st Cong., 3d Sess., Abstract Vol. II, 1911, pp. 444–445, 447, cited hereinafter as Immigration Committee Abstracts, 1911.

[31] Anonymous, Vol. 82 (May 10, 1906), p. 379.

olent practice whereby white men volunteered to pay the fines of Negroes convicted of minor crimes, and thus got them out of jail. The next step was to assure, by physical restraint, that the Negroes worked out the debt thus incurred. Last came the co-operation of justices, constables, and other officials in providing a supply of this forced labor. Some of the whites, he said, had not outgrown "the idea that in some way they were entitled to the labor of the Negro, and were justified in getting it at as small an outlay as possible."

Investigating the widespread rumors and charges of peonage, the Commission reported that in every state except Oklahoma and Connecticut it found evidence of practices between employers and employees which, if substantiated by legal evidence, would constitute peonage as defined in the Clyatt decision.[32] It defined peonage as a situation in which a laborer secures advances either in money or the payment of transportation expense and agrees to work it out. If he leaves before the debt is fully paid, the employer has him arrested for obtaining money under false pretenses or under laws controlling vagrancy. The employer then makes a new agreement for the man to work if criminal proceedings are dropped. Peonage was legally defined as "a status or condition of compulsory service based upon the indebtedness of the peon to the master. The basic fact is indebtedness."

In 1913 three federal cases in the West Texas District were dismissed.[33] Two years later two cases were tried in the East Texas District. In one the defendant was convicted; in the other a plea of guilty was entered. Fines amounting to $5,200 were assessed. Twelve cases in Louisiana were carried without action—for three years. In 1917, two cases in the North Texas District were dismissed; of two in the East Texas District, one defendant was acquitted and one was found guilty; three in the West Texas District were dismissed. Charges of peonage in the lumber camps along the Sabine persisted. In 1921 the U.S. Attorney General reported that "complaints of peonage increased during the year and peonage was found to exist to a shocking extent in Georgia, Alabama and some parts of Texas."

[32] *U.S.* v. *Clyatt* 197, U.S. 207, 1905.

[33] Reports of U.S. Attorney General from 1896 to 1921.

Vernon Jensen in his study of labor conditions in the Southern lumber industry states that reports of peonage have trickled out at various times and that individuals accused of establishing peonage have been prosecuted and convicted when proved guilty. Strictly speaking, however, he concludes, a system of peonage has never existed on any real scale in Southern lumbering.[34] In the sense of an organized national system, Jensen was probably correct. Though New Orleans was one of the centers of the padrone system for furnishing immigrant workers, the lumber industry of the Texas Sabine area did not use foreign labor. The labor pattern was home-built and was woven closely into a scheme of personal-official relations.

IT SEEMS, then, that a dominant and persistent strain in the heritage of east Texas has been the company-owned town, with all its ramifications of control and limitation on individual freedom. Furthermore, the "cash nexus"—the basis of economic freedom for the wage-earner and for the consumer—has not been a part of the job and the environment of the workers of the area.

[34] *Lumber and Labor*, p. 84.

CHAPTER TEN

In contest of endurance between buyer and seller (of labor) nothing but a close combination among the employed can give them even a chance of successfully competing against the employers.—J. S. MILL

LABOR UNREST IN THE PINERIES

INDUSTRIAL RELATIONS in the lumber industry of Texas have never been marked by peace. The workers in the pineries of the Sabine area have made sporadic but continuous attempts, both organized and unorganized, to protest. One district assembly of the Knights of Labor covered the area, but so far as can be discovered, its locals were among workers in towns.

Reverberations from the national labor unrest of the 1870's, which culminated in 1877 in the great railroad strike and the "Molly Maguires" of the coal-mining areas of the Monongahela Valley, were felt in Texas. In August of that year the Galveston *Daily News* reported that 250 Negro mill workers at Harrisburg (Texas) were armed and were threatening to burn the town.[1] Militia were sent from Houston. It is difficult in this instance to distinguish between troubles arising from race tension and those rooted in what are commonly accepted as "labor questions." And distinction may not be significant,

[1] August 2, pp. 1, 2; August 7, p. 4.

for there was between Negroes and whites very little difference in the competitive disadvantages as to jobs and working conditions in a situation where all held low-wage jobs. Certainly newspapers reporting the trouble considered the situation as just "Another Strike in Texas."

It is also important to remember throughout this discussion of labor unrest that the nature of the market for its product made the lumber industry vulnerable to work stoppages in other industries, especially the railroads. A railroad strike deprived the lumber mills of their principal means of transportation, forcing them either to close or greatly to limit production. The strike on the Gould lines in the mid-eighties, for instance, is reported to have deprived 90,000 lumber workers of their jobs.[2]

Unorganized Revolt. Each decade since 1870 has seen conflicts in Texas over the pay and working conditions of those employed —with or without any connection to an official organization. In May, 1886, the entire force of 70 workers at the Eylan sawmill struck without having the support of any organized movement.[3] They demanded a reduction in hours from 66 to 60, with no change in the daily wage —reported as $1.71 a day. After 7 days they won on both counts. In 1890 there was a walkout in all the mills in Orange.[4] The strikers demanded a reduction in hours from 11 to 10 per day with no decrease in pay. Again, no organization seems to have ordered the walkout, but it threatened to spread through the entire area. After about a month the workers returned to the mills with no change in conditions. Three years later the Orange mills had more serious trouble. All were completely shut down. Mr. Gilmer wrote in September, 1893, "No mills running, the laborers are intimidated and are afraid to work at the wages they have been getting."[5] A month later he wrote, ". . . anarchy prevailing in town." There were some changes in the

[2] Ruth Allen, *The Great Southwest Strike,* University of Texas Bulletin No. 4214, 1942, p. 68.

[3] Third Annual Report, U.S. Commissioner of Labor, *Strikes and Lockouts,* 1888, p. 579.

[4] Gilmer Letter Press, No. 16; *Daily News* (Galveston), Dec. 14, 16, 1890.

[5] Letter Press, No. 24, September 5.

situation, but about a year later there was another "general strike" which lasted 3 months.

After 1900, official records of the U.S. Bureau of Labor Statistics note a strike in 1902 which closed one establishment for 23 days, but finally failed.[6] No labor organization was involved. In the same year a strike ordered by a labor organization closed 3 establishments for 42 days. The two strikes involved more than 250 workers. In the following year, a "quickie" strike closed one establishment for a day.[7] On Saturday, October 9, 1903, payrolls failed to arrive at the Kirby mills in Beaumont. The men refused to work on the following Monday and seem to have stayed out several days. Temporary arrangements were made for workers to get money and supplies from local merchants and by the end of the week all except 2 mills had reopened.

Opposition of the Operators. But the operators had decided to take action. Members of the Texas Lumbermen's Association were called to a meeting in Houston "to discuss the question of unionism in sawmills," though the avowed purpose was to consider "the proposed change in the freight rates system." As to its interest in unionism the meeting was "one of secrecy." The communication from the secretary of the Lumbermen's Association of Texas, dated October 17, 1903, was marked "Strictly Confidential":

GENTLEMEN:

A meeting is desired in Houston on Friday the 23rd of this month to discuss the question of unionism at the sawmills. This is a most important matter and your interest in it is great. Please don't fail to have one of your officers present who will have the power to act in the premises. The meeting is one of secrecy as to this particular object.

Its calling will be based on the proposed change in the freight rates system which will be thoroughly discussed and action taken on the argument to be presented to the Commission at its meeting in Houston on November 10th.[8]

[6] Twenty-first Annual Report, U.S. Commissioner of Labor, *Strikes and Lockouts*, 1906, pp. 635–637, cited hereinafter as *Strikes and Lockouts*, 1906.

[7] *Leader* (Orange), October 16, 1903.

[8] Documents included in files of the Gilmer company.

In the 1900's there was much unrest in the Sabine lumber camps and in industries allied with them.[9] The record indicates considerable resentment among sawmill workers, at least, though no items found suggest that the "men in the woods" were infected by the unrest. A major strike involving 750 men closed 2 establishments, one of them for 10 days.[10] On the other hand, in 1901 an employer let out 75 workers in one establishment for 28 days and brought in 40 men from other Texas mills. Workers seem never to have been brought in from other states to replace strikers. But during the same year a strike at Groveton protested some abuses of the lumber camps, and the Groveton Federal Labor Union No. 11444 sent a Negro delegate to the meeting of the State Federation of Labor.[11] He described the "virtual chattel slavery conditions which today affect labor in the piney woods of Texas." He reported that wages averaged from 80 cents to 90 cents a day but that since the visit of Organizer C. W. Woodman, the bosses had given up the metal-check system and were issuing a paper check for wages which "is discounted ten per cent for merchandise and twelve and one half per cent for cash." The one labor organization mentioned in official records as ordering a strike was probably connected with the American Labor Union.

Another letter,[12] written under the letterhead of the Southern Lumber Manufacturers' Association and carrying its Executive Board, was sent to the lumber operators, apprising them of certain activities among the workers:

Nov. 28, 1904
St. Louis, Mo.

SUBJECT—*LABOR CONDITIONS*

TO ALL MEMBERS:

The enclosures handed you herewith speak for themselves. A report

[9] *Strikes and Lockouts*, 1906, pp. 384–387, 658.

[10] Sixteenth Annual Report, U.S. Commissioner of Labor, *Strikes and Lockouts*, 1904, pp. 635–637.

[11] *Proceedings*, Seventh Annual Convention, Texas State Federation of Labor, Galveston, 1904, p. 32.

[12] From files of the Gilmer Company.

from you of any attempt at organization in your locality will be appreciated.

Yours truly,

ENCLS. GEO. K. SMITH, *Secretary*

DEAR SIR:

I think it would be well to advise all members in regard to the action of Jn. W. Davis & J. H. Craighead, Jr. Both of these men have been in our employ this season and will, no doubt, be looking for employment among the other mills within a very short time. Davis is at present organizing Labor Unions among the manufacturers. Craighead is at present looking for a position as Superintendent of a mill, but is now working up and down the Ark. Sou. Ry. with Davis agitating the Labor question. These men have already organized three or four lodges upon the Ark. Sou., and we understand that the intentions of Davis is to organize this territory. We enclose you one of their circulars.

Yours truly,
WINN PARISH LUMBER COMPANY
LEWIS FREDERICK, *Mgr.*

There can be no doubt that Davis was indeed active in attempts to organize the lumber workers of the Sabine area. Even as the warning was issued, a handbill[13] was being circulated throughout the area:

TO THE LOGGERS, SAWMILL WORKERS, AND LUMBERMEN OF THE SOUTH:—

Nov. 30, 1904

You, workingmen, with your labor, have changed the lumbering districts of the South from a wild wilderness into busy thriving cities and towns.

It is your combined labor that makes the rugged forests into the finest and most expensive wooden materials.

It is you alone who have made it possible for the merchants, the bankers, the professional men and the railroad companies to become rich and powerful.

You have created the great wealth that is now enjoyed by the millionaire mill owners, who seldom even see their property to say nothing of doing any useful work connected with it.

[13] Gilmer papers.

And yet you are the poorest paid lumbermen in America.

You work more hours each day for less wages than any other lumbermen in the country.

In Montana the lowest wages paid to the commonest laborer in the lumber districts is $2.50 a day for nine hours of work, and from that up to $4 and $5 for more skilled labor.

In Idaho, Washington and certain parts of Northern California, where the American Labor Union is organized, the same wages are paid.

Why do the Western lumbermen get better wages, work less hours than you, and why are they treated more like human beings?

Simply because the Western lumbermen realize that one working man alone is weak, and that many are strong and powerful.

So they long ago organized lumbermen's unions in every lumber district, and through these unions presented a united front to the mill owners. United the Western lumbermen are strong, divided the Southern lumbermen are weak.

The Western Lumbermen are not only supported by their own lumbermen's unions, but they have back of them the strength of hundreds of thousands of other union men of every trade and calling, who are their brothers in the American Labor Union; and in time of strike or lock-out, entered upon according to the laws of the A.L.U., they are sure of cash weekly benefits from the Central Defense Fund, to keep them and their families from starvation.

Another period of hard times is breaking upon the country. Your employers will try to continue their enormous profits and dividends by reducing your pay even lower than the present miserable wages you receive. You may not be able to force your employers to pay the same that Western lumbermen receive, but you can at least make your conditions a little better by forcing the mill owners to stand their share of the hard times that are coming, instead of placing the whole burden upon you.

GET TOGETHER ALL OF YOU, UNITED IN LUMBERMEN'S UNIONS. BE PEACEFUL. ACT QUIETLY. USE GOOD JUDGEMENT. BUT BE FIRM AND DETERMINED IN PROTECTING YOUR OWN MANHOOD AND SELF RESPECT, AND INSIST UPON A MORE HUMANE EXISTENCE FOR YOURSELVES AND YOUR FAMILIES.

ALL LOGGERS, SAWMILL MEN AND LUMBERMEN MEET AT —— for the purpose of organizing a union.

JOHN W. DAVIS, *Organizer*,
AMERICAN LABOR UNION.

Three years later, operators in eastern Texas and western Louisiana, faced with a very low price for lumber, began a general retrenchment by restricting output and reducing wages. In November, 1907, the New Orleans *Times Democrat* reported cuts between 25 per cent and 35 per cent in Texas mills.[14] The Kirby mills announced a 4-day run and shortly thereafter closed 5 of its most important plants. Other mills followed Kirby's example. *Southwest* reported that so many mills were shut down that "a vast army of men are already out of employment and have no immediate hope of resumption." In protest against the wage reductions the workers in Texas and Louisiana pineries walked out in a spontaneous general strike. Under the conditions the strike was short and unsuccessful.

In the following year numerous difficulties culminated in more decisive action. When the Lufkin Land and Lumber Company lengthened the workday from 10 to 11 hours, its employees refused to work and remained out for about a month.[15] They finally went back with the same 11-hour day, but with the promise of a 10-hour day later. About the same time and for the same reason workers at Southern Pine Lumber Company walked out and remained out for a week. Somewhat later the Orange Sawmill Company closed down because of the demand for a weekly payday in place of the monthly one in force; the management hired an entirely new crew and continued to operate. On the same issue of a shorter workday there were strikes against Central Coal and Coke Mill at Kinnard and against mills at Westlake.

R. M. Simmons, a member of a small firm operating a plant at Kirbyville, described their method of dealing with discontent among their workers:

> We had no strike but we did deem it necessary, that we might conduct our business in a satisfactory manner to ourselves, to discharge some 30 to 40 men, and we did it. We employ about 100 men in our plant, and about one third proved they were union men.
>
> You doubtless will remember that some two months ago we found it

[14] See also the files of *Southwest.*

[15] *Ibid.*, Vol. 16 (July, 1908), pp. 29, 42, 44, 57.

necessary to discharge these men, and as a consequence the men, or a portion of them, made demands upon us to have them reinstated. We refused to comply with the demands and after the mills had been shut down for two days a committee from those who had made the demands came to us and requested that the men be permitted to go back to work, with the exception of three men whom we had discharged. Things moved along nicely until a proclamation was issued by the headquarters of the Brotherhood of Timber Workers telling the men not to work on Oct. 7, but to celebrate on account of it being the first day of the trial of A. L. Emerson, president of their union, who stands indicted at Lake Charles, La., charged with first-degree murder, as a consequence of the trouble which occurred at Grabow, La., several weeks ago.

Some 30 or more failed to show up at their work on last Monday, October 7, and my brother, Mr. E. C. Simmons, who is manager of the mill, with my hearty approval, issued instructions to the superintendent not to let any man who failed to show up for duty on that day go back to work, who could not give other than a union reason for his absence, but to give each a discharge. The mill ran Monday, the day of the celebration, and five of the men who belonged to the union worked, but they called for a settlement that they might go out with the others. We gladly gave them their time.

We paid every man in full and demanded our houses. Some have moved and others have not, but we do not anticipate any inconvenience in getting possession of our own.

We have a full crew of non-union men ready to go to work as soon as we can make some necessary repairs of the boilers. We will doubtless be running in full blast by Saturday morning. Only the mill proper was affected by the incident, as the planers, sawyers, log teams, lumber teams and construction crews have made full time.

We are grateful to some of the staunch farmers who proffered assistance until we could get a new crew, some of them going so far as to say that they would [illegible] their crops until we could get things shaped up.

We regret that the occasion arose to demand upon our part the steps we took, but we did it, and would act in a like manner upon any other similar occasion. We are not in sympathy with the Brotherhood of Timber Workers and never have been, and we have no employment for them. We are willing for them to conduct their affairs as suits them best, but we are not willing for them or any one else to conduct our business for us. The plant belongs to us and we propose to direct its affairs. We owe a duty to God, our homes, our country and to society, and we are going to continue to perform it as we have in the past as becomes honorable, just and fairminded men.[16]

Organized Revolt: Brotherhood of Timber Workers. In the period 1910–14, it seems fair to say, there was turmoil among the lumber workers throughout the nation, and the Sabine area did not escape. The I.W.W. had made a drive there in the early 1900's and according to its reports had had some success. In 1910 the Brotherhood of Timber Workers was organized independently in eastern Texas and spread to western Louisiana, with headquarters established in Alexandria. Two years later it affiliated with the I.W.W.

The Brotherhood had as its expressed purpose "to improve the conditions of those who are engaged in labor connected with the timber and lumber industry."[17] As set forth in the Preamble to its constitution, membership was open to "all persons, regardless of vocation, who may be in sympathy with the labor movement, and who comply with the constitution, rules, and bylaws of the organizations, excepting only, officers and employers in the above industries [timber and lumber] and those whose livelihood is obtained by questionable means."

The very name "Brotherhood" suggested that its ideological roots were deep in the Lassallean socialism of the Knights of Labor, and the constitution provided for a permanent chaplain who was to open and close all meetings with prayer. The basic concept of the organization required that membership be open to Negroes as well as to white, but the Southern tradition of segregation was respected by providing for "colored lodges," which were forbidden to retain their initiation fees and dues. Seldom, if ever, has a labor organization expressed so clear a recognition of the position of the employer and so optimistic a rejection of the use of violence:

While demanding our rights, we, at the same time, concede that the

[16] *Ibid.*, Vol. 25 (October, 1912), p. 27.

[17] Preamble to the constitution of the Brotherhood of Timber Workers. The best study of this organization is an unpublished Master's thesis (1958) by Charles McCord, on file in the library of the University of Texas.

employer is entitled to, and we promise him, an absolutely square deal in every sense which this implies. We ask for nothing which we are not willing to grant. To secure justice we must do justice. Violence, in all its forms, shall be discouraged. Property rights shall be respected. . . .

But shortly after its organization the Brotherhood was denounced by Mr. Kirby to the association of operators as having as its purpose to affiliate with the I.W.W., "a socialist organization composed largely of foreign-born citizens . . . which would plunge all the states into anarchy and bring disorder and the rule of brute force into every community in America."

For a period the eastern Texas and western Louisiana district was filled with struggle, culminating in the "Grabow riot." A group of workers marched to the town of Graybeaux (there are various spellings of the name) in western Louisiana to support an organizer for the Brotherhood of Timber Workers who was to make a speech.[18] Guns were fired. Five persons were killed, among them a bystander named Roy Martin, and 47 were wounded. The operators of the mill at Graybeaux—two brothers named Galloway—and about 60 workers were arrested. The Galloways were not indicted but 59 workers were and were later tried at Lake Charles. The trial, which was dramatic and long, resulted in the acquittal of the first 9 defendants; consequently the court ordered charges against the other 50 dismissed.

To workers in the Southwest and to militant Western workers their personal symbol was A. L. Emerson, president of the Brotherhood of Timber Workers. The task of raising funds to defend the workers centered around him. Under the heading "Shall Emerson Die?" the Timber Workers Union circulated the following appeal throughout the district:

BROTHERS, COMRADES, FELLOW-WORKERS: On Sunday evening, July 7, 1912, while the Brotherhood of Timber Workers were holding a mass

[18] Material relating to the Graybeaux riot can be found in the files of the daily newspapers, the *Lumberman*, and *Southwest*. It was the "news of the day" at the time of the riot and later during the trial. Records of the trial are available in the Courthouse at Lake Charles, La., and on microfilm in the library of the University of Texas. See also the Charles McCord thesis, cited in preceding note.

meeting on the public road at Grabow, La., thugs concealed in the office of the Galloway Lumber Company fired upon our people with rifles and pumpguns loaded with buckshot. When the firing ceased three men were found to have been killed outright, several mortally and seriously wounded, and 30-odd others injured. The great majority being union men. Immediately following the "riot" as it is called by the capitalist class, President A. L. Emerson, who was our chief speaker on the occasion and other members of the brotherhood, were arrested, denied bail, and placed in the county jail at Lake Charles, La., which prison is totally inadequate to accommodate the number of men now confined there, and is in a deplorably unsanitary condition, besides. Despite the conditions of this prison, sick and wounded men are confined there, the authorities giving the excuse that there is no room in the hospital for them and our boys are still being arrested.

This, so far, is the outcome of the "riot" at Grabow. Such trouble is borne witness to by the fact that many of them had taken along their women and children, and that none of the last were killed by the trust's gunmen is a miracle.

All the news and evidence so far reported shows that our men were not only ambushed, but that the "riot" had been carefully planned by the Lumber Trust, and we have every reason to believe that, hidden in the office of the Galloway Lumber Company, were gunmen who had been sent over from other places by the Southern Lumber Operators' Assn. The "riot" was but the culmination of a long series of outrages against the Brotherhood and all other union labor, and was staged by the Operators Assn. for the purpose of crushing out the union in the Southern timber district and terrorizing its workers back into meek submission to peonage. This had been the boasted purpose of the Operators' Association: "To crush all union labor out of their mills and camps, drive all socialist speakers out of their towns, and run things as they damned please." For 20 long months we have fought this might and merciless combination of capital, this vicious combination of grafters and gunmen, and because they have not been able to whip us back into their mills and slave pens they have planned the massacre of Grabow, and failing there to kill our President Emerson and his bravest associates, they have taken him and them to jail and are preparing to stage another legal murder. And so, brothers, all, we appeal to you to come to our aid in this, our time of great trial, with the funds necessary to defend our President and fellow workers, to help us save their lives and freedom, to tear from their throats the blood-stained hands of the Southern Lumber Operators' Assn., as we appeal to you to help us while we have a splendid chance to succeed to break up forever the infamous labor conditions existing in the South.

Brothers, fellow-workers, comrades, all, we appeal to you. Send all funds to J. Smith, Secretary of the Brotherhood of Timber Workers, P. O. Box 78, Alexandria, La.

Yours for a united working class, and life and freedom for all workers.

(*Signed*: JAY SMITH, *Gen. Sec'y.*)[19]

During the trial, *Southwest* "respectfully" suggested that "the Southwestern daily papers carefully censor the reports from Lake Charles of this case. No right-minded man wants to accuse his neighbor of hiring murder done and the so-called lumber barons are the leading citizens of every community in this part of the world."[20]

The "Grabow riot" and the acquittal of the 59 workers indicted was a part of a more spectacular and more successful movement among workers in the forests of the Northwest, and the east Texas operators felt reverberations from activities in the Pacific Coast areas. In July, 1911, the Houston *Chronicle*[21] noted that the "fight is on" between operators of the lumber mills and the Brotherhood of Timber Workers, and that the Southern Sawmill Operators' Association, which had been organized to fight unionism in 1906 but had been inactive, would be revived. A month later the same paper listed 21 mills which had closed down.

At a meeting in Leesville in April, 1911, attended, according to reports, by 700 or 800 workers, the union members insisted upon their constitutional right to organize to "benefit themselves morally, mentally, socially and financially," but the leaders advised the members "to exercise prudence, moderation, firmness and obedience to laws."[22] To counteract the organizational work of the Brotherhood, however, vigorous antiunion activities developed among other work-

[19] *Southwest*, Vol. 20 (August, 1912), p. 27.

[20] *Ibid.*, Vol. 20 (October, 1912), p. 89.

[21] July 23, 1912, p. 14; Aug. 12, 1912, p. 11.

[22] *Newsboy* (Jasper), Nov. 6, 1911; July 27, 1912.

ers. At meetings throughout the Sabine area they passed resolutions denouncing the Brotherhood and all its works. A cursory check finds accounts of a meeting at Call, Evadale, Buna, Bessmay, and Silsbee. At Pineland employees of Temple Lumber Company set up a committee of 13 to report at the regular meeting anything that might interest the club. At Bessmay workers for Kirby Lumber Company organized a "mutual protective association" and appointed a committee to thoroughly investigate anyone who came to town and to report to the organization. At Call, whites and Negroes met separately, "to demonstrate that employees have no grievance, at least none susceptible to correction through means of a labor union."

To prevent the spread of unionization, the mill men used the "yellow-dog contract"—a card which they required all employees to sign declaring that they would not join the Brotherhood.[23] Every man who applied to a lumber company for work was given the following application form and ordered to fill it out in its entirety:

DEAR SIR: Please furnish —— my complete record while in the service of your company. Address to ——.
Employed as: —— From Date: —— To Date: —— Title: —— Address: ——.

Please also state why I left your employ, and whether my conduct and services were satisfactory or not; also give any other information, including your opinion, concerning my personal character, conduct, and qualifications for the position of ——.

I now represent and declare to —— in whose service I now seek employment as —— that I am physically and mentally competent to perform all duties connected with the said position, being fully experienced therein and thoroughly familiar with the duties thereof.

I hereby release —— and you from all liability for any injury or damage whatever on account of furnishing the above information requested by me.
Witnesses:[24]

The statement, it may be noted, includes a voluntary release from all liability for damages for slander or false information. The inclu-

[23] *Southwest*, Vol. 19 (August, 1911), p. 22.
[24] Unpublished files of the Commission on Industrial Relations, 1912.

sion of the applicant's assurance that he is sound in mind and limb, as well as fully experienced, is explained in the following letter:

Please find herewith enclosed a revised form of Application Blanks; the only change in this form over that now in use by our members is that the applicant states that he is physically and mentally competent to perform the duties connected with the position he seeks, and states that he is fully experienced and thoroughly familiar with the duties thereof. This clause was suggested by our local attorneys, Messrs. Blackman and Overton; they state in their practice defending personal injury suits, that in nearly every instance the plaintiff alleges that the result of his injury was caused by a work or machine with which he was not familiar and they advise us by all means to insert this clause, and we have complied with their wishes. This office is prepared to furnish these blanks without charge and wishes to urge upon every member the necessity of using these forms in every case. (The entire objection of this Association will be defeated if members employ labor without first getting clearance from their former employers.)

Yours truly,
Executive Committee
by (*signed*) S. J. Carpenter

Association members were required to keep a list of their employees at the central office, supplementing it daily by reports on men discharged and new men employed. A principal query on each report was, "Have you any reason to believe that he sympathizes with or is a member of the order of Timber Workers of the World?"

The lumber operators used other methods to control unionization also. One of the witnesses for the state at the Lake Charles trial, L. T. Mabry, testified that as an operative for the McCain Detective Agency of Dallas, he had joined the Brotherhood in the summer of 1911.[25] He had worked his way up to the position of state organizer, in which post he had aided in the establishing of 12 locals of the Union.

Protest expressed itself also through the ballot box. In 1912, the Social Democratic Party displaced the Republican Party as the second in the state. *The Rebel*, a Socialist paper at Hallettsville, pro-

[25] Records of trial at Lake Charles; see notes 17, 18 above.

vided a forum for the workers, and much information about the conditions in the forests along the Sabine is contained in its pages. Some of the Party's strongest voting precincts were in the "fringe areas" of the lumber industry. In Kirbyville, 26 Socialist and 26 Republican votes were cast. A Socialist convention was held at Jasper, and William Haywood addressed a mass meeting there when he came south at the time of the Graybeaux trial. But during the war period, the arrest of subversives by state and federal officers gave the party a stigma of disloyalty, and *The Rebel*, which had been the vigorous voice of Socialist activity, was denied the use of the mails. Though on the national scene the Socialist vote following the war revived and reached its greatest strength, in Texas it continued to decrease. In spite of the decline, the Socialist Presidential vote in 1916 in many counties had increased surprisingly.[26] In Van Zandt County, 648 Socialist votes were cast; in Wood County, 416; in Harris County, 433. Angelina, Comanche, and Henderson Counties each cast more than 300 Socialist votes, and Bowie, Burleson, Cherokee, Hopkins, Rains, and Parker Counties more than 200.

The demands of the Brotherhood, which remained unchanged for the two years of its existence, were stated by their most vocal spokesman as:

1. A minimum wage of $2.00 per day.
2. A workday not to exceed ten hours.
3. Pay every two weeks in United States and not commissary money.
4. The right to free trade; workers not to be forced to buy from company stores where prices are 33⅓ per cent to 50 per cent higher than in nearby "free towns."
5. Discontinuance of the practice of discounting wages.
6. Reasonable rents.
7. A revision of insurance, hospital and doctor fees; the men to have the right to elect their doctors, to see the insurance policy and to have representatives on a committee which would control these funds.
8. A general improvement of living and sanitary conditions in the lumber towns and camps.
9. Disarming and discharge of all gun-men.

[26] *World Almanac*, 1917, pp. 813 ff.

10. The right to free speech, press and assembly.[27]

The St. Louis *Lumberman* considered the demands such that "no yellow pine manufacturer could do business under them," and rather than submit, "wholesale shutdowns of plants will be ordered."

The first Texas strike led by the Brotherhood was in 1910, against the Sabine Tram Company at Deweyville for shorter hours of work. The mill closed down for 2 months and reopened with no Brotherhood men on its payroll. Other mills used the same strategy. The organizers of the Brotherhood had been at work among the employees of the Nona Mills Company and "as a result about fifty of the order were discharged yesterday." When the Southern Lumber Operators' Association met in New Orleans that year they "decided to stomp out the Brotherhood" and ordered six additional mills to close down. The Texas and western Louisiana operators "decided to work with the Southern Lumber Operators' Association in fighting the Brotherhood."

J. H. Kirby. A writer in *Southwest* stated that "the Kirby Mills are being given special attention on account of the fact that Mr. Kirby has taken the lead in opposition to the Brotherhood."[28]

By the second decade of the twentieth century, J. H. Kirby dominated not only the Texas lumber industry but the entire Southern industry as well. John Moody in his study of the trusts listed the Kirby Lumber Company as "a lesser industrial trust. Incorporated in 1901 in Texas, it controlled about 25 plants and had a total capitalization in stocks and bonds outstanding of $21 million dollars."[29] In 1906 *Southwest* reported that "the Kirby Lumber Company is not only the largest enterprise of its kind in the State, but also in the South and possibly in the U.S."[30] In addition to several million acres of splendid pine lands in the various counties of east Texas, the company owned and operated the following mills:

	Daily Capacity (in Board Feet)		*Daily Capacity (in Board Feet)*
Mill A, Beaumont	100,000	Mill O, Fuqua	110,000
Mill G, Call	180,000	Mill P, Bronson	70,000

[27] *The Rebel*, Feb. 8, 1913, p. 3.

[28] Vol. 19 (August, 1911), p. 23–24.

[29] *The Truth About the Trusts*, p. 462.

[30] Vol. 14 (Sept., 1906), p. 28.

Mill J, Roganville	70,000	Mill R, Bessmay	200,000
Mill L, Village Mills	100,000	Mill S, Browndell	220,000
Mill M, Woodville	70,000	Mill T, Kirbyville	180,000
Mill N, Mobile	75,000	Mill U, Evadale	70,000

Mr. Kirby's position among lumber interests is suggested by the many offices to which he was elected. At different periods he was president of the National Lumber Manufacturer's Association, president of Southern Pine Operators' Association, vice-chairman of the Manufacturers' Section of the Standing Committee of the American Lumber Congress, and representative of the American Lumber Congress at the International Congress at Paris in 1920. He was president of the Southern Tariff Association; timber administrator for the South for the U.S. Emergency-Fleet Corporation in 1914; and in 1921 was a member of President Harding's Conference on Unemployment. He was twice a member of the House of Representatives of the Texas Legislature and a member of the Board of Regents of the University of Texas.

He had, furthermore, become almost a legend—lumberman, lawyer, oil operator, and business executive. A brief biography stated that Kirby was the "outstanding industrialist in the South if not the nation. He literally changed the geography as well as the history of East Texas. . . . There is no way of estimating the number of millions of dollars earned by him during a busy lifetime, but his life and all of his earnings were given to his friends."[31]

One of his first acts as head of the Kirby mills was to give a shorter workday to employees in all the mills with no decrease in pay. This action gained him the reputation of being a friend of the worker. He accepted the title and increasingly spoke to the workers and for the lumber producers in regard to labor policy. His statements, which received wide publicity, speak for themselves. No industrialist of that time stated more explicitly the policy of paternalism, as it has come to be called, with all its ramifications and implications. *The Rebel* seldom mentioned him except as "the Peon's Pal."

[31] *The Life and Times of J. H. Kirby*, Tyler County Dogwood Festival, 1950, p. 9.

In 1901, when the Kirby Lumber Company operated 40 sawmills with planers, railroads, and logging equipment, it held barbecues each July Fourth, and had Christmas trees each Christmas. Mr. Kirby made sure that Santa Claus visited every child of every employee. He held that the laborer is worthy of his hire and that no nation ever became great where the rank and file were underpaid. At the time, the average wage of laborers in the Texas lumber industry was 26 cents an hour. With a working week of 60.3 hours, the weekly full-time wage was $15.62.

He was sent to the state Legislature and while there introduced a bill which bespoke his concern for the welfare of the workers. The bill, which passed the House but was killed in the Senate, provided that an employee could not make assignment of wages, earned or unearned, to any other person without the employer's consent.[32]

Mr. Kirby was an able and effective representative of the interests and attitudes of employers everywhere, not only those in the lumber industry. When the lumber industry was faced with widespread protests from employees and the threat of unionization, he was called upon to use his influence. J. H. Kirby was not only the "plough boy with the million dollar smile" and "premier orator," but he was also the largest employer of lumber workers in the area.[33] In 1914 he had 7,000 workers employed in 17 big sawmills which did $40 million worth of business. In addition, the company operated 15 commissaries which did a $1.5 million business in a year, serving mill people and the general market. As the largest employer of labor and the most important operator, he used all of the considerable means at his command to dissuade the workers from any ill-considered action.

The Brotherhood continued to increase its membership until it reached numbers estimated variously between 18,000 and 35,000. But the trial at Lake Charles left it financially exhausted. Fees for the panel of distinguished lawyers and costs of investigation were high for a young organization, and there was no national parent body from whom it might expect aid. As noted above, the Brotherhood was organized by, for, and among the Southern lumber workers.

[32] *Southwest*, Vol. 37 (April 8, 1930), pp. 18–19.
[33] *Lumber*, Vol. 64 (May 3, 1920), p. 16.

Now when it needed help the Industrial Workers of the World stood ready to greet it with open arms and financial support. An ex post facto judgment is that the merger was a mistake. The antireligious attitude, the addiction to violence, and the uncompromising antisegregationism of the I.W.W. probably alienated it from the loyalty of most Texas workers.

In 1914, reports that the I.W.W. was coming into the Sabine lumber area led *Southwest*—after suggesting the probability that the mills would be closed down as they had been in 1912—to add the comment that a closing down at that particular time would help the industry because of light demand and unfavorable prices.[34] It may need to be emphasized that most of the action taking place was the lockouts by employers, not strikes by the workers.

While there were many strikes in Texas during the war years, detailed information about them is lacking. There were also many strikes among lumber workers throughout the nation, but whether any of the strikes in Texas were in the lumber industry is not a matter of official record.

During the early twenties, the Texas lumber industry faced the first real threat of unionization, and even then it was largely reverberations from the Northwest. By 1920, the national magazine of the lumber industry was proclaiming the excellence of the Beaumont Plan as a way of dealing with unions.[35] The lumber and oil operators claimed major credit for the plan. According to Ben S. Woodhead, of the Beaumont Lumber Company, "So far as is known Beaumont is the first city previously working under closed shop conditions which has had the red blooded Americanism to stand upon its hindlegs and shake itself free from the tentacles and shackles of the closed shop."[36]

At the time, Beaumont was threatened with "a general strike by the craft unions of the town." Employers in the neighboring city of Port Arthur did not sign the open-shop agreement, and granted a raise. One of the features which gave the Beaumont Plan unique

[34] Vol. 22 (November, 1914), p. 32.

[35] *Lumber Manufacturer*, Vol. 64 (Oct. 27, 1919), p. 64; (Nov. 3, 1919), p. 15.

[36] "The Doctrine of the Open Shop," *Lumberman*, Vol. 64 (March, 1920), pp. 39–40.

effectiveness was that it secured from the state a charter which made its "activities legal and amenable to the laws of the State." The state Attorney-General examined the charter to see that it did not conflict with the antitrust laws, and as required by law, the Secretary of State approved it. Furthermore, it was not an organization for employers only; membership was open to all citizens. The Beaumont organization claimed 100 workingmen among its 1,400 members. In March, 1920, six local organizations existed in Texas, six in Oklahoma, two in Arkansas, and four in Louisiana. Under the leadership of the Beaumont group the Southwestern Open Shop Association was organized to cover the foregoing states plus New Mexico. Mr. Woodhead, it might be noted, was president of the American Wholesale Lumber Association.

The Southwestern Open Shop Association was succeeded by the Texas Employers' Association. That the Beaumont Plan was a successful repellent of unionism seems clear—or it may merely have operated in an environment where unionism died a-borning for other reasons. It is true, however, that across the Sabine in Louisiana, employers in the lumber industry continued to be troubled by "outside agitators" as well as local unrest. It is probably also true that prompt and effective action saved the Southern operators from having to accept the participation of the federal government in establishing peace as did the operators of the Northwest.

In Texas from 1933 to 1936, three strikes among the workers in lumber and allied products are listed by the U.S. Bureau of Labor Statistics.[37] They involved more than 600 workers, and approximately 14,000 days of work were lost.

At present, workers in the basic lumber industry in the Far West are extensively organized.[38] The two principal unions are the International Woodworkers of America and the United Brotherhood of Carpenters and Joiners. Chartered under the United Brotherhood are loggers, lumber and sawmill workers, plywood and veneer workers,

[37] U.S. BLS, *Strikes in the United States, 1880–1936*, Bulletin No. 651, 1938, p. 118.

[38] *Ibid., Wages in the Basic Lumber Industry in the Far West*, Bulletin No. 840, 1945, p. 9.

lumber builders, and shingle weavers, among others. Roughly one-half of the logging camps and sawmills and all plywood mills have collective agreements with labor unions. More than 80 per cent of all workers were in unionized operations at the time of the survey in August, 1944. In Texas, only 5 of 43 establishments studied were unionized; in Louisiana, 6; in Arkansas, 10; in Mississippi, 5. As of January, 1956, no major union-management agreements existed in the West South Central area, though there were 9 agreements covering 21.8 per cent of workers in the Pacific area.[39]

Failure of Unionization in Texas. Until quite recently, very few locals have been organized in the east Texas lumber area though, as pointed out, persistent attempts to organize date back to the days of the Knights of Labor. The reasons for the failure can only be suggested, but they do not seem to be based upon the happy satisfaction of the workers.

One characteristic of the industry has made a successful strike difficult. If there is an increase in wages, the high ratio of wages-paid to value-of-product causes the "zone of indifference" for producers to be very narrow. An increase in wages raises total costs by a comparatively large proportion. When a plant closes down, its loss of revenue is offset by approximately one-third because of the fact that it has not been paying wages—an item taking a very large percentage of total production cost. When the saving from other going costs of production are added to the wages saving, it becomes clear that a strike of workers in the lumber industry means a comparatively small loss to employers. Even a small increase in wages means, therefore, a considerable increase in cost of production.

In contrast, wages-paid in petroleum refining, for instance, represent approximately 5 per cent of the value-of-product, as shown by the following figures:[40]

Year	*Wages*	*Value-of-Product*	*Value Added by Manufacture*
1925	$15,933,452	$448,181,732	$113,095,438
1935	23,512,282	437,790,250	78,576,696
1939	32,515,958	698,850,077	122,469,388

[39] *Ibid.*, p. 8; *Monthly Labor Review*, Vol. 79 (July, 1956), pp. 805 ff.

[40] *Census of Manufactures*, 1925, p. 824; 1935, p. 750; 1939, Vol. III, p. 991.

Closing down a refinery over a wage demand would represent a loss to employers so much greater than any probable increase in the wages bill that comparatively high wages are to be expected in the refining of oil products. The national average weekly wage in petroleum refining in 1952 was $88.42; in 1953, $94.19. In the lumber industry in logging camps in 1952, the national average weekly wage was $77.68; in 1953, $79.00. In sawmills and planing mills it was in 1952, $63.24; in 1953, $65.37. In the South in sawmills and planing mills the average weekly wage in 1952 was $43.03; in 1953, $43.78.[41]

A second possible reason for the failure of unionization was a lack of unity among the workers themselves. While the industry in eastern Texas was not numerically dominated by Negroes as was the industry in some other areas of the Southern pine region, the feeling between the two races was not only a continuous harassment to employers but it made unified organization impossible. An inspection of the files of *Southwest* reveals mention of many difficulties. Not only did fellow-workers sometimes resent the presence of Negroes, but sometimes farmers who leased stumpage would refuse to allow Negro workers to come on their land. Though one of the important and effective leaders of the People's Party in Texas was a Negro, pronouncements by local party groups had strong undertones of racism. It was the "white farmers" whose wrongs must be righted. Employers might accept good workmen whether white or black. As mentioned previously, Mr. Gilmer, desperate for a sawyer, wrote an employment agency, "Send Negro sawyer." When organized groups of workers demanded that jobs be given to white men the employer insisted upon his right to select his own workers without dictation from a union.

In 1908 *Southwest* stated that there had been war at Press, Texas.[42] Bad feeling against foreign and Negro labor at the Attayac Lumber Company in the first week in June broke out "something serious." The company had leased land from farmers but the farmers refused to allow the Negro employees to work in the woods on the land. Considerable trouble resulted. White residents, in trying to prevent

[41] *Monthly Labor Review*, Vol. 77 (November, 1954), pp. 1280 ff.

[42] Vol. 16 (August, 1908), p. 35.

the company from using foreign and Negro labor, had used "high-handed piracy." The company attempted to enforce its right to use the men that it found best for its own interest. Results were in favor of the company. Rangers arrested more than a score "and broke up the War." Both sides were "in arms and waiting to do battle when the Rangers arrived." The I.W.W. insisted upon nondiscrimination and their meetings followed that pattern. But racial division was a two-edged sword that could cut for workers and employers alike. Furthermore, Negroes were always available and were often used as "scabs" to displace white workers.

H. T. Warshaw in his study of the lumber industry states that one important reason for the failure of any organization of workers to develop in the Southern area was the lack of immigration from either foreign countries or other sections of this country.[43] In April, 1910, a writer in *Southwest* agreed and saw the meaning of this for the future: "The South has fewer foreigners than any other section of the country and it is freer from strikes, riots, and like disturbances. . . . If the area can be kept free from labor troubles for the next few years, its development industrially will exceed all other sections." He would not rank among the major prophets.

The nature of the workers themselves was a serious drawback to effective organized activity. They were native sons who married native daughters. They were family men. In the Western and Lakes states single men made up about two-thirds of the labor force in the lumber industry; in the South, about two-fifths. That dependent families were a deterrent to active protest was recognized by many employers. When Mr. Kirby used this tack in pleading with the workers along the Sabine to cease their troubling, he was at his eloquent best:

> I am talking for the man who has a wife and babies at home, the man who, perhaps, has been visited by misfortune, the man who may not be a good manager, the man whose meal barrel is not full and who could not stand a shutdown. It is in his behalf that I would ask his fellow laborers not to push upon him conditions that will destroy him and bring tears to

[43] H. T. Warshaw (ed.), *Representative Industries in the United States*, p. 481.

the cheek of his good wife, anxiety into both their hearts and distress and hunger to the little ones who toddle about their homes.[44]

But he said later in the same speech that he would not hesitate to close down the mills if the Brotherhood of Timber Workers were to make demands upon the operators.

A fourth reason for the failure to achieve organization was undoubtedly the overt hostility of the operators toward any unionization. The paternalistic attitude of employers in the industry toward their workers precluded any recognition of an official group of workers speaking through a representative. That the workers were ignorant and dependent made paternalism seem to be the easiest if not the only method of dealing with them. The situation was self-perpetuating:

> The lumber manufacturer . . . in the South knows that his workmen are dependent entirely upon the continued operation of the mills for food and shelter. They are "his people." He is usually mayor of the mill town, and arbiter of the differences that arise between the men. The relationship between management and plant employees is entirely different from that found in industry generally.[45]

Among their duties the operators included protection of the workers, shielding them from advances and activities of those who might suggest organization. A Socialist speaker in 1912 reported through the pages of *The Rebel* that he had registered in the hotel of the company town of Ratliff. Later the superintendent of the mills ordered that he be put out of the hotel. The reporter may be considered biased, but other evidence indicates that his was not an isolated experience.

Carl F. Drake, secretary of the Texas Lumber Manufacturers' Association for many years, dealt with the question of labor organization in an article in a trade paper. He stated as his considered judgment that where associations among skilled labor and capital did not

[44] *Southwest*, Vol. 19 (August, 1911), p. 31.

[45] "Economic Conditions in the Southern Pine Industry," Southern Pine Association, quoted by Vernon Jensen, *Lumber and Labor*, p. 78.

violate legal restrictions, they should be fostered, subject to restraining clauses which would prevent their being oppressive.

I do not believe in the organization of labor that is not skilled. The man who has served his apprenticeship at the bench, at the forge, or at the case, and who by years of effort has acquired a trade, by the time he has perfected himself, will be capable of self-government. And when he has reached this stage of mentality, then he is in a condition to organize, but the man who has reached the middle stage of life and is still a street sweeper, or shovels, or waits upon the table, I do not believe has sufficient reasoning power to be capable of governing himself, much less a mass of minds that are on an equally low plane. Therefore, I believe that such organizations should be scrutinized very carefully. If the brute strength far exceeds the mental development, then he becomes, when organized, a dangerous factor in the government, and in addition to this, as a rule, he is not willing to submit to arbitration, but generally resorts to brute force, which means anarchy. Then the unprincipled politician steps in and cleverly directs this class of men who are ready to follow an apostle who seems so much their superior, with the result that honest government is almost in danger.

In conclusion, as I stated at the outset, I believe that the true spirit of associate work should be that which educates and does not coerce.[46]

As suggested by the numerous associations in which lumber executives, owners, and managers were interested, it seems evident that they did not object to organized activities to better their own economic situation.

J. C. Dione, secretary-treasurer of the Southern Logging Association, argued the merits of organization in 1912:

Jesus Christ himself set the seal of approval, legality and rectitude upon Association (which means organized effort) nearly twenty centuries ago. . . . The organized effort of honest men is just as legal, just as sacred and just as useful today as it was when the Saviour decided twenty centuries ago that the work of saving the world could best be accomplished by uniformity of action.

. . . .

[46] *Ibid.*, Vol. 11 (January, 1904), p. 33.

The history of association work is the history of civilization. When man lived apart, each fighting his own battle against the world and against his fellow men, the world was a state of savagery. When they began grouping, exchanging ideas, securing uniformity of action, leaning on each other for support, and contributing toward the maintenance of law that applied to all—that is, when they began doing association work—civilization appeared.[47]

Finally, the attitude of employers and the community tended to erect a barrier between the mass of workers and the skilled craftsmen. In a society in which wage differentiation carries strong implications of status and privilege, the hierarchical structure strengthened the demarcation. It is probable that the attempt to organize the "laborers" in an industry without the support of the more highly-paid and skilled workers is a cause defeated before its birth.

While there were many strikes by workers in the lumber industry, they never enlisted large numbers of persons. "Lockouts" by operators were the significant and unique activities in the period from 1912 to 1918. Such action constituted a categorical refusal on the part of employers to talk with representatives of the workers and consider their grievances. If the aftermath had been an improvement in conditions it would have meant that employers actually did accept the responsibility for the lives of their workers upon which they insisted. However questionable one-sided action may be as a democratic process, it might be defended as a consistent expression. But the test of time has destroyed the defense. The 1950's compared to the 1920's speak in language universally understood.

[47] *Ibid.*, Vol. 20 (October, 1912), p. 30.

CHAPTER ELEVEN

For now that we are aware of past mistakes, it is not necessary that we continue to make them in the future. If we do continue to make them, no doubt we shall have to pay the price. The choice is ours.—LYLE W. SHANNON

DECISION FOR FUTURE GENERATIONS

AN IMPORTANT ASPECT that any investigation of low levels of living must consider is the history of the situation. Is the condition one of long persistence or is it temporary, a frictional crisis in the process of adjustment? The present study has been concerned with the chronicle of one group that forms an island of poverty in the midst of plenty. While it is not in all senses typical of similar populations, it is enough so that its features should make more understandable the process by which such variants emerge.

Figures cited in this account on the incomes of workers in the lumber industry of the western Sabine pineries should aid in understanding the concentration of low incomes everywhere and should serve as a basis for formulating a policy to raise the economic level of not only this region but all regions in similar economic situations. Any section of population, however small, is of interest, but these people are not an inconsiderable segment in the economy of the state. For decades they were the largest group of industrially-occupied workers in Texas, and in the sixth decade of the twentieth century they still form one of the largest. Their activities and environment have dominated a large area.

The lumber industry has been concentrated in the northeastern corner of the state. For three generations the people who have lived here are those who have lived in close connection with lumber production, its organization, its wage system, its methods of work, and the surroundings engendered by it. Since in the processing of lumber, wages account for a larger part of the cost of production than in the average industry, the failure of industry and the state to develop economic and social vision holds implications for human beings beyond those implicit in general policy.

The workers and families in Texas lumber camps have been born and reared among the Southern pines. They have been little infiltrated by newcomers, especially by non-Southern groups. In family backgrounds, in work experience, in social and economic environment, they have had and have a uniquely homogeneous experience.

The processing of lumber and timber with their various products was in the early twentieth century increasingly organized under a pattern which might be described as a plantation system molded to fit a wage-labor situation. Its central feature was the "lumber town," where workers lived in houses owned by their employer and spent wages paid in noncurrency media at a company-operated store. Many of these villages grew, thrived, and disappeared—even their names barely remembered today. Many are ghost towns. But the lumber town with its pattern of living and of control is probably the strongest legacy of the east Texas pineries.

The counties of the area are now, as they have always been, deeply rural. In 1950 the state had a population of 29.3 persons per square mile. Montgomery County had 22.5 persons per square mile; Jasper, 20.7; Newton, 11.5; Polk, 14.8. In 1950 Newton was 100 per cent rural, Montgomery 70 per cent, and Polk 82 per cent.

The educational level of the inhabitants has been lower and is still lower than that of the state and the nation and increasingly below that required for acceptance in any jobs but those at the lowest level of training and competence. For the armed forces, 16 per cent of men from the Southwest were rejected through tests "consisting of an elementary knowledge of the English language, arithmetic and the ability to solve simple problems." One reason given was the poor schooling in rural areas. "A large proportion of the young men accepted are judged so poorly educated that it does not appear feasible for the armed forces to train them in any particular skill other than basic soldiering."

The loggers and sawmill workers of east Texas have had little contact with big organizations. In 1947 only 76 of a total of 915 establishments employed more than 100 workers; more than half of them employed fewer than 19 workers. In addition, the industrial experience of these workers is far removed from a world of collective agreements, annual increments in pay, and fringe benefits. Large numbers of the plants are removed from legal regulation, some because of the law exempting mills employing fewer than 8 employees, and many others serve only a local market.

In the nineteenth century Texas lumber workers were in general as well paid as wage-earners in the same industry in other sections of the country and as those in other industries in the state. But since around 1910 they have gone steadily downward in the economic scale. In a period of rising wages and a rising standard of life for the state, their economic position has progressively grown worse. In the expanding forties the area in which they live was spotlighted as a section of low incomes. Though tied to a report on agriculture, the conclusion of the students of changes in methods used in processing timber and lumber seems pertinent: "Superficially the relief problem in such areas appears to be an agricultural one, but closer study reveals that it is frequently traceable in large measure to loss of income from the lumber industry."[1]

Elaborate theoretical foundations are scarcely necessary to support the conclusion that incomes are low because there is generally, considering the wages offered, a more-than-sufficient supply of labor. Periods of "tight labor" are not unusual, but the emergency is not

[1] A. J. Van Tassel, *Mechanization in the Lumber Industry*, pp. 1, 123–124.

met by higher wages. Striplings might be hired to replace men. During wartimes, positive steps were taken to prevent the men's responding to the economic pull of higher pay elsewhere.

We need not picture the human being as "economic man, a globule of unalloyed desire" to suggest that with few exceptions workers prefer more wages to less wages. Given a choice they will choose the work from which the greatest return may be expected, and an increase in wages—unless earned under worsened conditions—almost always increases the physical and mental strength and personal well-being of the workers themselves, of their children, and of their children's children. We may accept as true also that wages will be highest in those areas where employers are willing to pay premium rates for the labor they need. It seems clear that *low wages are accepted by laborers because they are immobile.* The causes of this immobility are generally to be found in ignorance of economic possibilities—which is tied to illiteracy and fear of the unknown. A recent study[2] of occupational mobility finds restrictions upon mobility inherent in unequal educational and vocational training opportunities and limited occupational ambitions.

Without any undue rejection of realism, it may be assumed that any and every economic system, however organized and controlled, is interested in the efficient use of available resources and it is also concerned with redefining those resources, insofar as is possible, with changing economic conditions. Labor mobility is essential to the proper functioning of the labor market and has social values both in times of prosperity and in times of depression. It is a prerequisite for industrial expansion and for a fuller use of productive resources.

A basic assumption of an economic system based upon freedom of choice is that productive agents are free to move and do move in response to the possibility of greater return. Per-capita income can be increased if individuals are willing to move from places where they can produce and earn less to places where they can produce and earn more. Furthermore, *the decision to use each item of productive power at the position in which the total output is greatest is a judg-*

[2] Natalie Rogoff, *Recent Trends in Occupational Mobility.*

ment of efficiency in the use of resources. Again, the hypothesis is that units of producing power are infinitely mobile and shift easily from less fruitful to more fruitful locations in the organization of factors.

A complex division of labor requires a great deal of flexibility and mobility within single careers and between generations. When free movement of labor is at the core of a system—both economic and political—the coming of industry, with its inherent implications of rapidity of change and fluidity of producing agents, suggests that it is necessary to scrutinize closely those areas where mobility of any factor—be it capital, labor, or managerial capacity—seems hampered or limited.

Because of the greater possibilities of human tragedy from dislocation, conditions of the labor supply have a pertinence implicit in no other of the factors. Problems relating to these conditions have an immediacy when the controlling movement of economic organization is toward rapid technical change, with its consequent uprooting of individuals and groups of workers. Reservoirs of passive labor in the midst of a highly dynamic economic situation are certainly among the most baffling of economic phenomena. They may be overlooked or ignored because the nimbus of excitement and drama attendant upon the increasingly-high standard of living for the many obscures the predicament of the few. But when these pools are located and a careful analysis is made of the environmental features which have produced them, it should be possible to suggest policies which would not only increase efficient use of these human resources but also lessen individual tragedy.

One pool of labor that seems to have been little affected by traditional incentives to seek more remunerative jobs and whose use in a machine set-up will be restricted are the wage-earners in the lumber industry of the southern United States, some of whom are dealt with in this study. On the American scene, they have characteristics which, to most of their fellow-citizens, are strange and inexplicable. They have accepted almost without protest wages far below those of other workers and probably far below those which might have been available to them as individuals. In Texas they have tolerated a scale of life far below that of other citizens of the state.

When even the pressure of a low standard of living cannot impel laborers to move from one area to another even though there is no legal restriction against their migration (as might occur during wartimes), it means they are governed by barriers which prevent them from developing their economic capacities to the fullest. They are unwilling, for instance, to tackle a new type of job, for change represents the unknown and therefore carries risk. Their chain of cultural characteristics, developed through social situations similar to, but not synonymous with, those in the industrial life of a community, has been so strongly forged that it withstands the assault of economic pressure.

The nature of the lumber industry forces it to locate in situations more rural than farm areas, and one result of this isolation is the absence of variety in occupations. For young people growing up in lumber camps, there is little to suggest the possibility of their entering other lines of work. That the counties in which lumber is the controlling industry offer little to suggest the desirability of change is indicated by the fact that 82 per cent of persons over one year of age in Newton County had not moved during 1950; 75.5 per cent in Montgomery County had not; and 83.3 per cent in San Augustine County had not. For the state as a whole, only 73.6 per cent of Texans had not moved during the year.

Even the folk drama of "oil" left this segment of the population largely untouched. In some of the lumber counties young men went to the east Texas oil fields, but by 1940, reported the House Committee to Investigate Interstate Migration, "there was almost no traffic between the oilfields of Texas and the farms of East Texas. . . . This country is peopled by stranded sawmill workers turned farmer on a small scale." A social worker reported to the committee that "there is comparatively little migration either into or out of the area with the exception of Gregg County (and, to a lesser extent, Rusk County)."[3]

[3] *Hearings*, House Special Committee, Interstate Migration Hearings, 76th Cong., 3d Sess., 1941, Pts. 5–6, pp. 1911–1912.

Movement has not within itself social and economic advantage. Change is not per se necessarily good. Immobility is passive resistance to change, and a person brought up in an immobile environment usually accepts change only if forced to do so by hunger and the breakdown of the economic structure. Migration in response to better opportunity is a gain; migration compelled by the disappearance of opportunity is a loss.

For a person to be able to appraise the advantages of a change in occupation depends in some degree upon literacy, economic understanding, and—probably most important—confidence that a new job is not simply another means of exploitation. Mobility requires that he be informed about alternative possibilities and that he have training—or is capable of being trained—for transfer to changed employment and environment. He must be willing to move occupationally and, if desirable, geographically without being forced to by unemployment, poverty, or displacement.

A person attains rational approach to mobility, occupational as well as geographical, by education, by being at liberty to move, and by having enough economic understanding to instill confidence in new ways. But the kind of education needed must go beyond attempts to increase the degree of literacy. Literacy is merely a prerequisite to acquiring knowledge of processes, care of machines, and instructions for group collaboration, qualities which make for effective labor on farms but which in machine production are essential. The general object of education must be to spread the idea of acceptance of change throughout society.

The refusal to be bound by tradition and custom is the basis of economic innovation. It is also the dearest right of free men. Conformity must not be the aim of social policy, but nonconformity must be based upon freedom. Economic pressure through poverty and ignorance forces nonconformity.

Texas needs skilled labor. Figures cited previously in this study on the wages of skilled workers in the lumber industry indicate her lack. But in the United States skilled workers (craftsmen) have 9.31 median years of school. In the airplane and radio industry the median is a little more than 12 years. No group of skilled workers averages less than 8.1 years. The chances, therefore, for workers in the Texas lumber industry to transfer to other occupational areas except at the lowest level would seem to be very small. If abundance of education is an important factor in the economic welfare of the United States, these people have little to offer to an efficient productive system.

If, as contended by Adam Smith and many others, development tends to become cumulative, why does it pass by, not individuals or small isolated groups, but large segments? Or, rejecting automatic forces, why has Texas allowed a continuous deterioration in the life of a large group of her citizens?

It may be suggested that an agrarian romanticism, which has centered interest on cotton, tied to a Western romanticism, which moved the cowboy and the ranch from the fringe to the very "heart of Texas," has nurtured an escape from problems connected with wage employment. It has further welded social and legal tools ready to the hands of those desiring to use unrealistic attitudes for realistic purposes of power and profit.

Even the Congressional Industrial Commission that held executive hearings on industrial unrest in 1912 came to Texas expressly to investigate the land problem and the widespread protests among farm tenants and sharecroppers, though at the time the lumber workers were attempting to organize under the Brotherhood of Timber Workers. The Commission made reports on life in the timber areas, but its published volumes contain only the records relating to the life of workers on the large plantation-farms.

The community decadence associated with cutover areas is familiar. Abandoned towns, mills, and railroads are the more dramatic aspects of this phenomenon. These features, however, tend to divert attention from the fact that there exists a considerable residual population that has attempted to make a transition from lumbering to some other means of livelihood and has failed. When a particular community is struck by the closing of a large mill, the rise of new employment opportunities in sufficient number and in time to avoid the ill effects of economic dislocation is largely a matter of chance.

The conclusion seems inescapable that Texas is and has been denying herself the use of capacities already existent; that she is not making it possible for latent productive capacities to emerge. Since the efficient use of the potentialities of every individual is basic to a prosperous and efficient economic organization, careful thought should be given to this situation.

Attempts to sketch with clearer outline the half-lit world of the future must draw heavily upon the more fully limmed outlines of the past and the emerging pattern of the present. A highly fluid now can be projected into tomorrow only with many reservations and qualifications. But since the present is pregnant with the future, it is necessary to make some judgment, at least tentatively, of the course of that projection.

Beyond doubt the situation described in this study represents a "backward area." The problem of measuring the extent of this backwardness is complicated by neither political boundaries nor language barriers. Industrialization of the area carries no threat to existing institutional arrangements. Nor are there any large skilled groups that would have to be dislocated. The workers of the area have lived in a putative money-and-wage economy; their family system is the semipatriarchal monogamy of Western society; their religion is Protestant Christianity; the virtues proclaimed for Western capitalism —saving, hard work, getting ahead—are their virtues; prestige patterns based upon income and type of work are the accepted patterns of their world.

These people are "deprived children of a difficult history," a history which includes not only defeat in a war but a period of reconstruction which neither reconstructed the old nor laid the basis for the new, an experience common to all Southern areas. It embraces also a complex population pattern; a spoilation, with little advantage to the workers, of rich timber lands; company towns persisting well into the second quarter of the twentieth century; wages paid in kind or in nonmoney symbols; denial of a right to organize for presentation of their interests by subtle methods when possible, by overt ones when necessary. Their history may be characterized as the story of a plot, and "the plotter's names were inertia, ignorance, and [must one add the third?] tyranny."

Though the delineation of the situation described here is largely in terms of figures, behind and beneath the figures lies a complex and difficult pattern of institutions and attitudes. If society can talk much about these intangibles and ease its conscience with such spurious conclusions as that people are happiest when they are poor and ignorant, then it becomes possible for it to evade what are, after all, clear-cut suggestions as to policies that might increase mobility and at the same time protect the free movement of labor, so essential a foundation stone for our kind of society.

In the industrializing areas of the South, there are many workers —industrial wage-earners in a nonindustrial environment—whose experience gives them little preparation for transferring to industrial jobs in an industrial pattern. Their past cannot be rewritten, but their future can be prepared for. Unless it is, they can only be displaced by other workers and become the unskilled and probably the unemployable in a factory system.

BIBLIOGRAPHY

BOOKS

Ahearn, Daniel, Jr. *The Wages of Farm and Factory Laborers, 1914–1944.* New York: Columbia University Press; London: King & Staples, Ltd., 1945.

Allen, Ruth A. *The Great Southwest Strike.* Austin: University of Texas, Bulletin No. 4214, 1942.

American Lumberman. The Personal History and Public Achievements of 100 Eminent Lumbermen of the U. S. 3 vols. Chicago, 1905.

Anderson, Dewey, and Percy E. Davidson. *Recent Occupational Trends.* Stanford: Stanford University Press, 1945.

Bakke, E. W., *et al. Labor Mobility and Economic Opportunity.* Massachusetts Institute of Technology, Cambridge, 1954.

Beney, M. Ada. *Wages, Hours, and Employment in the United States, 1914–1936.* New York: National Industrial Conference Board, 1936.

Bing, Alexander M. *Wartime Strikes and Their Adjustments.* New York: E. P. Dutton & Co., 1921.

Bolton, Herbert Eugene. *Texas in the Middle of the 18th Century.* Berkeley: University of California Press, 1915.

Brawley, Benjamin G. *A Social History of the American Negro.* New York: The Macmillan Company, 1921.

Brissenden, P. F. *The I.W.W.—A Study of American Syndicalism.* New York: Columbia University, 1919.

Brown, Nelson C. *The American Lumber Industry.* New York: John Wiley & Sons, 1923.

———. *Lumber Manufacturing, Conditioning, Distribution and Use.* New York: John Wiley & Sons, 1948.

Bryant, R. C. *Logging: The Principles and General Methods of Operation in the United States.* New York: John Wiley & Sons, 1913.

———. *Lumber: Its Manufacture and Distribution.* New York: John Wiley & Sons, 1922.

Chapman, Herman. *Forest Valuation.* New York: John Wiley & Sons; London: Chapman & Hall, Ltd., 1914.

Clark, Colin. *Conditions of Economic Progress.* London: Macmillan & Co., Ltd., 1940.

Clark, V. S. *History of Manufactures in the United States.* 2 vols. New York: Published for the Carnegie Institution of Washington by McGraw-Hill Book Company, 1929.

Coombs, Whitney. *Wages of Unskilled Labor in Manufacturing Industries in the United States, 1890–1924.* New York: Columbia University Press, 1926.

Cowan, Edwin T., and Helen M. Gibbs. *Time, Tide and Timber: A Century of Pope and Talbot.* Stanford: Stanford University Press, 1949.

Dalton, Hugh. *Some Aspects of the Inequality of Incomes in Modern Communities.* New York: E. P. Dutton & Co., 1920.

Defebaugh, James E. *History of the Lumber Industry of America.* 2 vols. Chicago: *American Lumberman,* 1906–1907.

Douglas, Paul H. *Real Wages in the United States, 1890–1926.* Boston: Houghton Mifflin Company, 1930.

Duerr, William A. *The Economic Problems of Forestry in the Appalachian Region.* Cambridge: Harvard University Press, 1949.

Elchibegoff, Ivan M. *United States International Timber Trade in the Pacific Area.* Stanford: Stanford University Press, 1932.

Fries, Robert. *Empire in Pine.* Madison: State Historical Society of Wisconsin, 1951.

Gagliardo, Domenio. *The Kansas Labor Market.* Lawrence: University of Kansas, Department of Journalism Press, 1937.

Green, L. J., and C. G. Woodson. *The Negro Wage Earner.* Washington, D.C.: Association for the Study of Negro Life and History, 1930.

Griffen, Robert. *The Progress of the Working Classes in the Last Half Century.* New York: Society for Political Education, 1885.

Grossman, Charles J. *The Economic Importance of Manufacture and Its Leading Lines in Texas.* Austin: University of Texas, Bureau of Business Research, 1931.

Guthrie, John A. *The Newsprint Paper Industry.* Cambridge: Harvard University Press, 1941.

Herberle, Rudolf. *The Labor Force in Louisiana.* Baton Rouge: Louisiana State University Press, 1948.

Herring, Harriet. *Passing of the Mill Village: Revolution in a Southern Institution.* Chapel Hill: University of North Carolina Press, 1949.

Holbrook, Steward. *Holy Old Mackinaw: A Natural History of the American Lumber Jack.* New York: The Macmillan Company, 1951.

Hoover, Calvin B., and U. Ratchford. *Economic Resources and Policies of the South.* New York: The Macmillan Company, 1951.

Industrial Workers of the World. *The Lumber Industry and Its Workers.* Chicago: 1922.

Jaffe, A. J., and Charles D. Stewart. *Manpower Resources and Utilization.* New York: John Wiley & Sons, *c.* 1951.

Jenks, Cameron. *Development of Governmental Forest Control in the United States.* Washington: Institute for Government Research, Brookings Institution, Studies in Administration, No. 19, 1928.

Jensen, Vernon H. *Lumber and Labor.* New York: Farrar & Rinehart, 1945.

Johnson, Charles S. *The Economic Status of Negroes.* Nashville: Fisk University Press, 1933.

Labor Research Association. *Labor Fact Book.* New York: International Publishers, 1931.

Lang, Aldon S. *Financial History of the Public Lands in Texas.* Waco, Texas: Baylor Bulletin, Vol. XXXV, 1932.

Larson, Agnes M. *History of the White Pine Industry in Minnesota.* Minneapolis: University of Minnesota Press, 1949.

Lauck, W. Jett. *The New Industrial Revolution and Wages.* New York and London: Funk & Wagnalls Company, 1929.

Lillard, R. G. *The Great Forest.* New York: Alfred Knopf, 1947.

McKittrick, Reuben. *The Public Land System of Texas, 1823–1920.* Madison: University of Wisconsin Bulletin No. 905, 1918.

McWilliams, Carey. *Ill Fares the Land: Migrants and Migratory Labor in the United States.* Boston: Little, Brown & Company, 1942.

Martin, Roscoe C. *The People's Party in Texas: A Study in Third Party Politics.* Bulletin No. 3308, University of Texas, Bureau of Research in the Social Sciences, Study No. 4, 1933.

Matthews, Donald M. *Cost Control in the Logging Industry.* New York: McGraw-Hill Book Company, 1942.

Meier, Gerald M., and Robert E. Baldwin. *Economic Development: Theory, History and Policy*. New York: John Wiley & Sons, 1957.

Miller, Edmund T. *A Financial History of Texas*. Bulletin No. 37. Austin: University of Texas Press, 1916.

Miller, Herman P. *Income of the People of the U. S. Census Monograph.* New York: John Wiley & Sons, 1955.

Miller, J. *Trade Organizations in Politics*. New York: Oxford Publishing Company, 1887.

Moody, John. *The Truth about the Trusts*. New York: Moody Publishing Company, 1904.

Moore, Wilbert E. *Industrialization and Labor: Social Aspects of Economic Development*. Ithaca: Cornell University Press, 1951.

National Industrial Conference Board. *Differentials in Industrial Wages, Hours, and Employment in the United States, 1849–1936*, Study No. 229. New York, 1936.

———. *A Graphic Analysis of the Census of Manufactures of the United States, 1849–1919*. New York, 1923.

———. *Wages, Hours, and Employment, American Manufacturing Industry, July, 1914–January, 1924*, Research Report No. 69. New York, 1924.

———. *Workmen's Compensation Acts in the United States: The Legal Phase*, Research Report No. 1, Boston, April, 1917; rev. August, 1919.

Naylor, Emmet Hay. *Trade Associations: Their Organization and Management*. New York: The Ronald Press Company, 1921.

Neal, R. M. *High Green and Bark Peelers*. New York: Duell, Sloan & Pearce, *c.* 1950.

Neff, Phillip. *Production Cost Trends in Selected Industrial Areas*. Berkeley: University of California Press, 1948.

Nordhoff, Charles. *Cotton States in Spring and Summer, 1875*. New York: D. Appleton & Company, 1876.

Petrini, S. *Elements of Forest Economics*. London: Oliver & Boyd, Ltd., 1953.

Pierson, Frank Cook. *Community Wage Patterns*. Berkeley: University of California Press, 1953.

Pope, Liston. *Millhands and Preachers*. New Haven: Yale University Press, 1942.

Reynolds, Lloyd. *The Structure of Labor Markets*. New York: Harper & Brothers, *c.* 1951.

Robinson, W. W. *Land in California.* Berkeley: University of California Press, 1948.

Rogoff, Natalie. *Recent Trends in Occupational Mobility.* Glencoe, Ill.: Free Press, 1933.

Schwartz, Harry. *Seasonal Farm Labor in the United States.* New York: Columbia University Press, 1945.

Scott, Emmett Jay. *Negro Migration During the War.* New York: Oxford University Press, 1920.

Todes, Charlotte. *Labor and Lumber.* New York: International Publishers, 1931.

Vance, Rupert B., and Nicholas J. Demerath. *The Urban South.* Chapel Hill: University of North Carolina Press, 1954.

———. *Human Geography of the South.* Chapel Hill: University of North Carolina Press, 1932.

Warner, W. L., and J. C. Abegglen. *Occupational Mobility in American Business and Industry, 1928–1952.* Minneapolis: University of Minnesota Press, 1955.

Warshaw, H. T. (ed.). *Representative Industries in the United States.* Chap. XIV. New York: Henry Holt and Company, 1928.

Webb, John N. *The Migratory Casual Worker.* Washington: WPA Administration, Division of Social Research, 1937.

Wesley, Charles. *Negro Labor in the United States, 1850–1925.* New York: Vanguard Press, 1937.

Wilson, Walter. *Forced Labor in the United States.* London: M. Lawrence, Ltd., 1933.

Woodson, Carter G. *A Century of Negro Migration.* Washington, D.C.: Association for the Study of Negro Life and History, 1918.

———. *The Negro in Our History.* Washington, D.C.: Associated Publishers, *c.* 1922.

Woofter, Thomas J. *Southern Race Progress—The Wavering Color Line.* Washington, D.C.: Public Affairs Press, 1957.

PUBLICATIONS OF THE STATE OF TEXAS

Board of Pardons and Paroles, Report, 1919.

Bureau of Labor Statistics, Biennial Reports file, 1910–1956.

Commissioner of General Land Office, Report, 1928–30.

PUBLICATIONS OF THE UNITED STATES GOVERNMENT

Department of Agriculture

Forestry Service

Benson, H. K., *By-Products of the Lumber Industry,* Special Agents Series No. 110, 1916.

Bray, W. L., *Forest Resources of Texas,* Bulletin No. 47, 1904.

Hough, Franklin, *Report on Forestry.* 3 vols. Vol. I, 1878; Vol. II, 1880; Vol. III, 1882.

Mattoon, W. R., *The Southern Cypress,* Bulletin No. 272, 1915.

Mohr, Charles, *The Timber Pines of the Southern United States,* Bulletin No. 15, 1897.

Pierson, A. H., *Exports and Imports of Forest Products: 1907,* Circular No. 153, 1908.

Growing Pine Lumber in the South, Publication No. 24, 1928.

Lumber Used in Manufacture, 1933, 1933.

National Forest Areas, 1933, 1935, 1936, 1937.

Report by Forest Service, submitted June 1, 1920.

Statistics of Cross Ties Production, 1915.

Studies of the Lumber Industry: Part I, Wm. B. Greeley, *Some Public and Economic Aspects.* Part II, Rolf Thelen, *The Substitution of Other Material for Wood,* Reports 114–117, 1917.

Timber Depletion and the Answer, Circular No. 112, 1920.

Miscellaneous Publications

Crafts, Edward C., and Martha A. Dietz, "Forest Resources and the Nation's Economy," *Yearbook of Agriculture,* 1949.

Ducoff, Louis, Jr., *Wages of Agricultural Labor in the United States,* Technical Bulletin No. 895, 1945.

Fox, William F., *History of the Lumber Industry in New York,* 1902.

Sierey, Daniel, *Small Sawmills,* Bulletin No. 718, 1918.

Steer, Henry B., *Lumber Production in the United States, 1799–1946,* Publication No. 664, 1948.

American Forests and Forest Products, Statistical Bulletin No. 21, 1928.

Production of Lumber, Lath and Shingles, Bulletin No. 768, 1917.

Use of Wood for Fuel, Bulletin No. 753, 1919.

Bibliography

Department of Commerce

BUREAU OF THE CENSUS

Brissenden, P. F., *Earnings of Factory Workers,* Monograph No. X, 1929.

10th Census Report, Vol. I, *Population and Social Statistics,* 1870.

11th Census Report, *Manufacturing Industry of the United States,* Pt. I, 1880.

12th Census Report, 1900.

12th Census Report, *Child Labor,* Bulletin No. 69, 1900.

13th Census Report, *Supplement for Texas,* 1910.

14th Census, Vol. III, *Composition and Character of Population by States,* 1920.

15th Census, Vol. 14, 1930.

16th Census, 1940, Vol. III, *Manufactures: Reports for States and Outlying Areas.*

17th Census, 1950, preliminary report, *Population—General Characteristics,* Texas.

Census of Manufacturees, 1947.

Turpentine and Rosin, Bulletin No. 126, 1902.

Census of Manufactures: 1905, Bulletin No. 48, 1906.

Census of Manufactures: 1905, "Lumber and Timber Products," Bulletin No. 77, 1907.

Census of Manufactures: 1905, Bulletin No. 85, 1907.

Lumber Industry of the United States:

Lumber Cut of the U.S., 1907–1911, 1912.

Lumber, Lath and Shingles, 1909.

Lumber, Lath and Shingles, 1911.

Lumber, Lath and Shingles, 1912.

Lumber, Lath and Shingles, 1913.

Lumber, Lath and Shingles, 1924.

Lumber, Lath and Shingles, 1926.

BUREAU OF CORPORATIONS

The Lumber Industry: Pt. I, *Standing Timbers,* 1913; Pt. II, *Concentration of Timber Ownership in Important Selected Regions,* 1913; Pt. III, *Land Holding of Large Timber Owners,* 1914; Pt. IV, *Conditions in Production and Wholesale Distribution Including Wholesale Prices,* 1914.

Bureau of Foreign and Domestic Commerce

Directory of American Sawmills, Misc. Ser. No. 27, 1915.

Federal Trade Commission

"Wartime Costs and Profits of Southern Pine Lumber Companies," Senate Document No. 85, 68th Cong., 1st Sess., 1922.
Lumber, Document No. 226.
Report on Lumber Manufacturers' Trade Association, 1922.

Department of Justice

Report of the Attorney General of the United States on Peonage, 1921.
Appendix to Annual Report of Attorney General, 1922.

Department of Labor

Bureau of Labor Statistics

Bureau of Labor Bulletin No. 29, *Trusts and Industrial Combinations,* 1900.
Bureau of Labor Bulletin No. 52, *Child Labor in the United States,* 1904.
Bulletin No. 78, *Industrial Accident Statistics,* 1908.
Bulletin No. 265, *Industrial Survey in Selected Industries in the United States, 1919,* 1920.
Bulletin No. 263, Misc. Ser., *Housing by Employers in the United States, 1920,* 1921.
Bulletin No. 490, *Statistics of Industrial Accidents in the United States to the End of 1927,* 1928.
Bulletin No. 541, *Handbook of Labor Statistics,* 1931.
Bulletin No. 651, *Strikes in the United States, 1880–1936,* 1938.
Bulletin No. 667, *Manual on Industrial-Injury Statistics,* 1940.
Bulletin No. 1035, *Analysis of Work Stoppages During 1950,* 1951.
Bulletin No. 1136, *Analysis of Work Stoppages During 1952,* 1953.
Bulletin No. 1163, *Analysis of Work Stoppages During 1953: Major Developments and Annual Statistics,* 1954.

Wages and Hours of Labor Series

Bulletin No. 59, *Wages and Hours of Labor in Manufacturing Industries, 1890–1904,* 1905.

Bulletin No. 77, *Wages and Hours of Labor in Manufacturing Industries, 1890–1907*, 1908.
Bulletin No. 113, *Lumber: Wages and Hours of Labor in 1890–1912*, 1913.
Bulletin No. 129, *Wages and Hours of Labor in the Lumber, Mill Work and Furniture Industries, 1890–1912*, 1913.
Bulletin No. 153, *Wages and Hours of Labor in the Lumber, Mill Work and Furniture Industries, 1907–1913*, 1914.
Bulletin No. 225, *Wages and Hours of Labor in the Lumber, Mill Work and Furniture Industries, 1915*, 1916.
Bulletin No. 265, *Industrial Survey in Selected Industries in the United States, 1919*, 1920.
Bulletin No. 317, *Wages and Hours of Labor in Lumber Manufacturing, 1921*, 1923.
Bulletin No. 363, *Wages and Hours of Labor in the Lumber Industry, 1924*, 1925.
Bulletin No. 413, *Wages and Hours of Labor in the Lumber Industry, 1925*, 1926.
Bulletin No. 484, *Wages and Hours of Common Street Laborers, 1928*, 1929.
Bulletin No. 497, *Wages and Hours of Labor in Lumber Manufacturing, 1929*, 1929.
Bulletin No. 560, *Wages and Hours of Labor in the Lumber Industry in the United States, 1930*, 1932.
Bulletin No. 586, *Wages and Hours of Labor in the Lumber Industry in the United States, 1932*, 1933.
Bulletin No. 604, *History of Wages in the United States from Colonial Times to 1928* (a revision of Bulletin No. 499), 1934.
Bulletin No. 697, *Hours and Earnings in the United States, 1932–40*, 1942.
Bulletin No. 840, *Wages in the Basic Lumber Industry in the Far West, 1944*, 1945.
Bulletin No. 854, *Wages in the Basic Lumber Industry, 1944*, 1945.
Report No. 45, *Wage Structure: The Southern Lumber Industry*, 1953.
Report No. 76, *Wage Structure: Lumber in the South, 1949 and 1950*, 1950.

Retail Prices and Cost of Living Series

Bulletin No. 5, *Retail Prices, 1890 to Dec., 1912*, 1913.

Bulletin No. 10, *Retail Prices, 1890–1913,* 1914.
Bulletin No. 18, *Retail Prices, 1907 to Dec., 1916,* 1917.
Bulletin No. 156, *Retail Prices, 1890 to Dec., 1914,* 1915.
Bulletin No. 270, *Retail Prices, 1913 to Dec., 1919,* 1921.
Bulletin No. 300, *Retail Prices, 1913 to Dec., 1920,* 1922.
Bulletin No. 357, *Cost of Living in the United States,* 1924.
Bulletin No. 369, *The Use of Cost of Living Figures in Wage Adjustments,* 1925.
Bulletin No. 445, *Retail Prices and Cost of Living, 1890–1926,* 1927.
Bulletin No. 838, *Wartime Food Purchases,* 1945.

CHILDREN'S BUREAU

Bulletin No. 276, *Occupational Hazards for Young Workers,* Report No. 4, Logging and Sawmilling Industries Series, 1942.

MONTHLY LABOR REVIEW

Vol. 50 (June, 1940), "Trends of Manufacturing Employment," pp. 1308–1339.
Vol. 52 (January, 1941), "Entrance Wage Rates of Common Labor, July, 1940," pp. 1–23.
Vol. 57 (October, 1943), "Level of Factory Wage Rates in Wartime," pp. 637–641.
Vol. 63 (October, 1946), "Labor in the South," No. 4.
Vol. 66 (February, 1948), "Family Budgets," pp. 131–185.
Vol. 67 (August, 1948), "Occupational Wage Differentials, 1907–1947," pp. 127–134.
Vol. 71 (September, 1950), "Effects of the Minimum Wage in Southern Sawmills," pp. 313–317.
Vol. 78 (March, 1955), "Economic Effects of the Minimum Wage," pp. 307–311.
Vol. 78 (April, 1955), "The Distribution of Factory Workers' Earnings—April, 1954," pp. 410–416.
Vol. 79 (March, 1956), "A Program for Raising Substandard Levels of Living," pp. 313–316.
Vol. 79 (July, 1956), "Wage Dispersion in Manufacturing Industries, 1950–1955," pp. 780–786.
Vol. 80 (March, 1957), "Effects of the $1 Minimum Wage in Seven Industries, Part I," pp. 373–428.

Vol. 80 (April, 1957), "Effects of the $1 Minimum Wage in Seven Industries, Part II," pp. 441–446.

Vol. 81 (May, 1958), "Effects of the $1 Minimum Wage in Five Industries," pp. 492–501.

MISCELLANEOUS PUBLICATIONS

Bulletin 78, *Bulletin of the Bureau of Labor*, 1908.

Bulletin 109, *3rd Annual Report, Secretary of Labor*, 1915.

Bulletin 630, *Negro Migration*, Division of Negro Economics, 1919.

Bulletin 7, *For the Fiscal Year Ended June 30, 1931*, 1932.

Economic Factors Bearing on the Establishment of Minimum Wages in the Logging, Lumber, and Timber and Related Products Industries, 1943.

Results of the Minimum Wage Increase of 1950: Economic Effects in Selected Low-Wage Industries and Establishments, 1954.

Annual Report of the Administrator, 1939.

Annual Report of the Administrator, 1953.

Congressional Documents

House Document 822, 59th Cong., 2d Sess., 1906, *Strikes and Lockouts*.

Senate Document 645, 61st Cong., 2d Sess., 1910–12, *Condition of Women and Child Wage Earners in the United States*. 19 vols. Vols. 5, 9, 18.

Senate Document 747, 61st Cong., 3d Sess., U.S. Immigration Commission *Reports*, Abstract Vol. II, 1911.

U.S. Commission on Industrial Relations, 64th Cong., 1915–16, Vols. 19, 27, 28. On file on microfilm, University of Texas Library, Austin, Texas.

Senate Document 126, 69th Cong., 1st Sess., *National Wealth and Income*, 1925.

U.S. Congressional Record, Feb. 27, 1930.

Hearings, House Special Committee, Interstate Migration Hearings, 76th Cong., 3d Sess., 1941.

Senate Document, 77th Cong., 2d Sess., Commission on Military Affairs, *Hearings, October and November, 1942*.

Senate Report No. 1012, Pt. II, 79th Cong., 2d Sess., *Supplemental Report of Committee on Education and Labor, Amendments to the Fair Labor Standards Act of 1938*, 1946.

Senate Document No. 146, 81st Cong., 2d Sess., 1950, *Low-Income Families and Economic Stability.*

Temporary National Economic Committee,

"Investigation of Concentration of Economic Power"

Monograph No. 14, *Hourly Earnings of Employees in Large and Small Enterprises,* 76th Cong., 3d Sess., 1941.

Monograph No. 15, *Financial Characteristics of American Manufacturing Corporations,* 76th Cong., 3d Sess., 1941.

Monograph No. 17, *Problems of Small Business,* 76th Cong., 3d Sess., 1941.

Monograph No. 18, *Trade Association Survey,* 76th Cong., 3d Sess., 1941.

Monograph No. 21, *Competition and Monopoly in American Industry,* 76th Cong., 3d Sess., 1941.

Monograph No. 26, *Economic Power and Political Pressures,* 76th Cong., 3d Sess., 1941.

Monograph No. 27, *The Structure of Industry,* 76th Cong., 3d Sess., 1941.

Joint Committee Prints on the Economic Report of the President, 1951.

Making Ends Meet on Less than $2,000 a Year, 82d Cong., 1st Sess., 1951.

Low-Income Families and Economic Stability: Materials on the Problem of Low-Income Families, 81st Cong., 1st Sess., 1949.

Selected Government Programs Which Aid the Unemployed and Low-Income Families, 81st Cong., 1st Sess., 1949.

Characteristics of Low-Income Population and Related Federal Programs, 84th Cong., 1st Sess., 1955.

A Program for the Low-Income Population at Substandard Levels of Living, Report No. 1311, 84th Cong., 2d Sess., 1956.

Hearings before the Joint Economic Committee, Congress of the United States, on the Economic Report of the President, 85th Cong., 1st Sess., 1957.

NEWSPAPERS, FILES

Enterprise (Beaumont)

Chronicle (Houston)

Leader (Orange)

Newsboy (Jasper)

The Rebel (Hallettsville)

Bibliography

PAMPHLETS

Barton, Sam B., *How Texas Cares for Her Injured Workers,* Denton, Texas, North Texas State College, 1956.

Cruickshank, James Walker, *Forest Resources of Northeast Texas,* Southern Forest Experiment Station, Release No. 40, New Orleans, 1938.

O'Daniel, W. Lee, *Suggestions for the Industrial Development of Texas,* Austin, Texas State Manufacturers' Association, 1940.

Van Tassel, A. J., *Mechanization in the Lumber Industry,* Works Progress Administration, Report No. M5, Philadelphia, 1940.

California Department of Industrial Relations, Division of Labor Statistics and Research, *Earnings and Hours, Selected Industries,* San Francisco, 1951.

"It's Dogwood Time in Tyler County," in *The Life and Times of J. H. Kirby,* pub. by Tyler County Dogwood Festival, 1950.

National Child Labor Commission, "Child Workers of the Nation," *Proceedings* of the Fifth Annual Conference, New York, 1909.

National Manpower Council, "Improving the Work Skills of the Nation," in *Proceedings* of Conference on Skilled Manpower, April 27–May 1, 1955.

Proceedings, Texas State Federation of Labor, files.

Southern Pine and Reconstruction, official report of the Southern Pine Association, New Orleans, Feb. 25–26, 1919.

Southern Pine Association official reports, 1918–1923.

Yearbook of Texas, 1901.

PERIODICALS

Bagnall, Robert W., "The Labor Problem and Negro Migration," *Southern Workman,* XLIX (November, 1920), 518–523.

Clark, H. L., "Growth of Negro Population in the United States and Trend of Migration from the South Since 1860," *Manufacturers Record,* LXXXIII (January 25, 1923), 61–63.

Creel, George, "The Feudal Towns of Texas," *Harper's Weekly,* LX (January 23, 1915), 76–78.

Donald, H. H., "Negro Migration of 1917–18," *Journal of Negro History,* VI (October, 1921), 383–498.

Emerson, F. V., "The Southern Long-Leaf Pine Belt," *Geographical Review,* VII (1919), 81–90.

Holmes, G. K., "The Peons of the South," *Annals* of the American Academy, Vol. IV, No. 2 (1894), 265–274.

Hood, R., "Some Basic Factors Affecting Southern Labor Standards," *Southern Economic Journal*, II (April, 1936), 45–60.

Munns, E. N., "Women in Southern Lumbering Operations," *Journal of Forestry*, XVII (February, 1919), 144–149.

Teeple, John E., "Waste Pine Wood Utilization," *Scientific American*, supplement, 81 (January 8, 1916), 27.

Lumberman (St. Louis), files.

Southwest: Southern Industrial and Lumber Review, incomplete files.

UNPUBLISHED MATERIAL

Corry, Ormond Charles, "Workmen's Compensation in Texas," Master's thesis, University of Texas, 1922.

Gilmer papers, 1870–1927 (business records, letters).

Harris, Townes Malcolm, "The Labor Supply of Texas," Master's thesis, University of Texas, 1922.

Easton, Hamilton Pratt, "History of the Texas Lumbering Industry," Ph.D. dissertation, University of Texas, 1947.

McCord, Charles R., "A Brief History of the Brotherhood of Timber Workers," Master's thesis, University of Texas, 1958.

INDEX